Promoting Peace

Promoting Peace

Via Legal and International Policy

Stuart S. Nagel

LEXINGTON BOOKS
Lanham • Boulder • New York • Oxford

LEXINGTON BOOKS

Published in the United States of America
by Lexington Books
4720 Boston Way, Lanham, Maryland 20706

12 Hid's Copse Road
Cumnor Hill, Oxford OX2 9JJ, England

British Library Cataloguing in Publication Information Available

Library of Congress Cataloging-in-Publication Data

Nagel, Stuart S., 1934–
    Promoting peace : via legal and international policy / Stuart S. Nagel.
        p. cm.
    Includes index.
    ISBN 0-7391-0164-1 (cloth : alk. paper)
        1. Criminal justice, Administration of. 2. Law enforcement. 3. Civil rights. 4. Peace.
    5. Security, International.

K3240 .N34 2001
345.73—dc21

                                                                    00-034801
Printed in the United States of America

⊖™ The paper used in this publication meets the minimum requirements of American
National Standard for Information Sciences—Permanence of Paper for Printed Library
Materials, ANSI/NISO Z39.48–1992.

Dedicated to Mikhail Gorbachev and Ronald Reagan,
who were the two people most important in ending the Cold War
and thereby bringing peace to the world for the indefinite future.

Also dedicated to Earl Warren and Warren Burger,
for the great work they did in advancing peace
through law and justice on the domestic front.

Contents

Tables

Introduction

This volume is part of a three-volume set on peace, prosperity, and democracy. Each volume is self-sufficient, although there may be reciprocal causation among peace, prosperity, and democracy.

All three volumes approach peace, prosperity, and democracy from both a domestic and an international perspective. The domestic perspective may appear to emphasize the United States, but it is generally applicable to almost any country because of the broad nature of the issues.

For the peace volume, the domestic material deals with the reduction of violence and crime within society. That material is divided into two sections. The first section deals with procedures and personnel for processing alleged criminals or other wrongdoers. The procedures include (1) arrest and search, (2) pretrial procedures, (3) the trial process, and (4) criminal sentences and civil damages. The personnel issues include (1) right to counsel, (2) society-attorney-client relations, (3) judges, and (4) juries.

The second section of the peace volume dealing with domestic peace relates to law compliance and constitutional rights. The material on law compliance deals with (1) traditional criminal behavior, (2) business wrongdoing, and (3) government wrongdoing. The material on constitutional rights deals with (1) free speech, (2) freedom of religion, and (3) equal treatment under law.

In the international section, all three volumes emphasize the role of multiple nations in promoting peace, prosperity, and democracy. The multiple nations could take the form of a world organization, such as the United Nations or the World Health Organization. The multiplicity might occur by way of a regional organization, such as the European Union (which is mainly economic), the North Atlantic Treaty Organization (which is mainly peace-promoting), or the Helsinki Watch (which is mainly democratic), along with counterparts from other regions. Sometimes the multiplicity may consist of just a couple of neighboring countries trying successfully or unsuccessfully to promote peace, prosperity, or democracy, such as the current neighbors of the Congo.

As applied to peace policy, we are especially talking about international dispute resolution, but also intra-national disputes that have international implications. These include:

1. Disputes between sovereign nations such as the United States and the Soviet Union.
2. Disputes between controlling countries and colonies or quasi-colonies, such as the United States and the Philippines.
3. Disputes between central governments and secessionist provinces, such as the provinces that have tried to secede from Russia.
4. Disputes between conflicting nations within a country, such as the conflicts within former Yugoslavia.
5. Disputes between conflicting economic classes with international implications, such as land reform in the Philippines or Central America.

Most or many of these disputes have now been resolved one way or another. All these disputes, however, have important contemporary or historical interests. Their importance stems partly from the number of actual or potential conflict-fatalities, but their importance especially stems from the fact that each of these disputes is illustrative of a type in a typology of international disputes. Each is an important learning experience for the present and the future.

Win-Win Analysis

This book contains many win-win or super-optimizing tables. A typical win-win table shows the goals to be achieved on the columns, the alternatives for achieving them on the rows, and relations between the alternatives and the goals in the cells. There are generally two sets of goals consisting of conservative goals and liberal goals. There are generally two sets of alternatives consisting of conservative alternatives and liberal alternatives.

Conservative goals tend to emphasize what is good for business, national security, and dominant ethnic groups. Liberal goals tend to emphasize what is good for labor, consumers, the environment, civil liberties, and minority ethnic groups. Conservative alternatives tend to emphasize relying on the marketplace. Liberal alternatives tend to emphasize relying on government regulation.

There is generally little controversy over what the conservative and liberal goals roughly are and what the conservative and liberal alternatives roughly are. There is much controversy over which goals are more important and which alternatives should be adopted. Solutions that are win-win are those that are capable of achieving the conservative goals even more than the conservative alternatives and simultaneously capable of achieving the liberal goals even more than the liberal alternatives. The object of the tables and the analysis is to suggest one or more win-win solutions for each policy controversy.

The phrase "win-win solution" is adopted in much of this book to refer to solutions or proposals that are exceeding the best expectations of liberals, conservatives, and other major groups in a controversy. The wording comes from the idea that both sides win beyond their best expectations, not just beyond their worst expectations which is what happens in typical compromises. Some-times the phrase "super-optimum solution" (SOS) is used to get at the idea that the proposal or solution is above the optimum of liberals and above the optimum of conservatives. Win-win is shorter and more catchy than super-optimum but has the disadvantage of being frequently used to refer to any kind of a good outcome even if it does not meet the criterion of exceeding the best expectations of the major viewpoints, parties, sides, litigants, or disputants.

One can determine the conservative and liberal goals and alternatives for each policy controversy by reading newspapers like the *New York Times*, news magazines like *Time*, and textbooks that deal with public policy controversies. Determining a win-win solution may involve some creativity, but more important is a knowledge of other solutions that have been adopted in public policy controversies so that one can reason by analogy to the controversy under discussion.

There may be controversy over how strong the relations are between the alternatives and the goals, especially if one attempts to measure them on 0 to 100 scales. There is much greater agreement if one is only interested in whether the direction of the relation is positive (+), negative (-), or neither (0). That is sufficient for clarifying that conservative alternatives do relatively well on conservative goals more so than liberal alternatives, and that liberal alternatives do relatively well on liberal goals more so than conservatives. For an alternative to be a win-win alternative, it has to do especially well on both conservative and liberal goals.

For greater detail on the relations between alternatives and goals, one can have a five-point scale rather than a three-point scale. The numbers, words, and symbols corresponding to those five points might be:

5 or ++ means the alternative is highly conducive to the goal
4 or + means mildly conducive to the goal
3 or 0 means neither conducive or adverse to the goal
2 or - means mildly adverse to the goal
1 or -- means highly adverse

Conservatives and liberals tend to perceive that conservative alternatives receive a relations score of 4 with conservative goals, and liberal alternatives receive a relation score of 4 with liberal goals. Conservative alternatives receive a relations score of only 2 with liberal goals, and liberal alternatives receive a relations score of only 2 with conservative goals. These are default scores subject to appropriate adjustments where conservatives and liberals might be closer together or further apart, but preserving 5 or ++ for a maximum positive relation and 1 or -- for a maximum negative relation.

Likewise, there may be controversy over the quantitative

importance of the goals to conservatives, liberals, and others. There is much greater agreement if one simply recognizes that conservatives by definition value conservative goals more so than liberals do, and liberals value liberal goals more so than conservatives do. Neutrals value both sets of goals approximately equally. Win-win solutions are capable of achieving a higher score than conservative alternatives using conservative weights and a higher score than liberal alternatives using liberal weights.

For greater detail on the relative weights or measures of importance of the goals, one can have a three point scale. The numbers, words, and symbols corresponding to those three points might be:

3 or +++ means highly important
2 or ++ means middling importance
1 or + means relatively less important, but still having positive value

Conservatives give a weight of 3 on conservative goals and a weight of 1 to liberal goals. Liberals give a weight of 3 to liberal goals and a weight of 1 to conservative goals. Neutrals give a middling weight of 2 to both sets of goals. These are default scores subject to appropriate adjustments where conservatives and liberals might be closer together or further apart, but preserving 3 for a maximum and a 0 for a minimum.

In light of these definitions and the way in which win-win tables are organized, these tables should be considered as mainly serving the purpose of clarifying the nature of each of the controversies discussed in this book. They are thus mainly for pedagogical or teaching purposes rather than data-based tables showing correlation coefficients, percentages, or other quantitative data.

They are based on empirical observation of the nature of the political world and political controversies, but they do not come from questionnaire surveys or from quantitative content analysis, or from other quantitative data-gathering techniques. They are not only helpful in clarifying the policy controversies, but also in showing how a proposed win-win solution relates to the goals and alternatives which are the components of the policy controversies.

It is important to note that the tables are suggestive and not conclusions. They suggest possible win-win solutions, but any win-win solution may be subject to improvement by offering new ideas that can do even better than the win-win solutions suggested here. In that sense, win-win solutions may only be temporary answers to policy controversies or only good for a certain place under certain conditions. They are thus stimulators of ideas for answering policy questions rather than answers that are good for all times and all places.

In order for a proposal to truly be a win-win solution, the proposal must not only be capable of exceeding the best expectations of conservatives, liberals, and other major viewpoints simultaneously, the proposal must also be capable of being implemented. That means it must have economic, technological, social, political, international, and legal feasibility. The text accompanying the tables in this book frequently talks about the need to overcome these feasibility hurdles. A win-win solution must also exceed the conservative, liberal, or other alternatives by a substantial enough margin so that it is not easily shot down if the relations or other aspects of the analysis are misperceived.

These generic aspects of win-win analysis are discussed in other books such as Nagel, *Super-Optimum Solutions and Win-Win Policy: Basic Concepts and Principles* (Quorum Books, 1997), and Nagel, *Public Policy Evaluation: Making Super-Optimum Decisions* (Ashgate, 1998). The purpose of these three volumes on promoting peace, prosperity, and democracy, is to go beyond those generic books and get into numerous specific policy controversies that relate to legal, international, economic, technology, social, and political controversies.

The combination of the cross-cutting methodology books and these more focused substance books adds up to a kind of win-win combination for understanding and applying win-win analysis. The editors of these books from the Dirksen-Stevenson Policy Institute, the MKM Research Center, and the Policy Studies Organization look forward to seeing these books and applications improved upon in the future, across countries, and especially across a variety of aspects of promoting peace, prosperity, and democracy.

Acknowledgments

In this book, the word "we" is frequently used rather than "I." That is not the royal we, or the *New York Times* we. It reflects the fact that this book was written in collaboration with the associate editors of the Everett Dirksen-Adlai Stevenson Institute of Interna-tional Policy Studies, the Miriam K. Mills Research Center for Super-Optimizing Analysis and Developing Nations, and the Policy Studies Organization.

Those people especially include Julian Nam, Diem-My Bui, Yuki Llewellyn, Sara Eckart, and Carol Burger who worked on the camera-ready copy. Those people also include the collaborative drafting people, such as Deni Hoffman, Connie Schradt, Julie Glassman, Paula Erwin, and Carolyn Tryon.

Other highly helpful people include Matthew Beth and Jane Young. They especially include Joyce Nagel, who is the administrator and business manager for all three of the above-mentioned organizations.

PART ONE

PEACE IN GENERAL

Chapter 1

Domestic Peace

Pretrial Release

Liberal and Conservative Positions

Pretrial release is one of the most controversial legal issues today. The key goal of conservatives in the context of pretrial release is to see that people who are released commit no crimes while on bail and show up for their trials. The conservative alternative for achieving that goal is to hold a high percentage of the people in jail–more than half. They feel that when in doubt one should hold rather than release. The key liberal goal is to reduce the anger that comes from being held simply because one cannot make bail. This can be especially important in cases in which the defendant senses that his not being able to afford the bond money is correlated with his race. These situations, which are common today, are often perceived as a form of institutional racism, and cause bitterness among minority Americans.

Liberals also have as a goal increasing the productivity of arrested individuals. If they are held in jail prior to trial they can lose their jobs, and even if they do not, they cannot be very productive while in jail. Another liberal concern is reducing jail costs. While it is usually conservatives who are more concerned about taxpayer expense, liberals find that a reduction in costs goes along with greater numbers of pretrial releases. Because it is possible that a person may be kept in jail pending trial for a longer period of time than the maximum sentence if convicted, liberals believe the release system is more cost effective. The liberal alternative for achieving these goals is to hold

Table 1.1   Pretrial Release

	GOALS	
ALTERNATIVES	Conservative 1. High show-up rate. 2. No crime committing.	Liberal 1. Decrease lost of productivity. 2. Decrease bitterness.
Conservative High holding rate.	+	−
Liberal Low holding rate.	−	+
Neutral Middling holding rate.	0	0
SOS or Win-Win 1. Low holding. 2. High appearance with- out crimes.	++	++

relatively few people–less than 25 percent.

The object is to come up with a win-win solution that at first glance looks as if it requires holding more than 50 percent and simultaneously holding less than 25 percent, which would take into account both positions. It would be impossible to do that, as the positions are mutually exclusive, but it is not difficult to come up with a win-win solution if one concentrates on the goals, not the alternatives. Such a solution would provide for a high proportion of defendants to stay crime-free while released and to show up for trial, and at the same time create a low level of bitterness, prevent job loss and maintain workplace productivity, and reduce jail costs.

Win-Win Solutions

The way to simultaneously achieve these goals is through a comprehensive, multi-step program. Similar programs have been adopted throughout the country, proving to be a win-win solution. With such a program one can get more than 90 percent of the people to make it to trial without committing crimes while on release, which represents a number higher than the best expectations of the conservatives, while at the same time holding less than 25 percent of the arrested people. In some areas it might even work to hold less than 20 percent of the people and still get the same 90 percent safe-return rate.

The first step is to devise a meaningful way of screening people to determine who is to be held versus who is going to be released. The screening process would include such factors as how long the arrestee has lived in the community and how long he/she has held his/her last couple of jobs. If the person has lived in the community for a long period of time and has held jobs for appreciable lengths of time, then they are reasonably good risks to be released, whereas individuals with a more transient past are greater risks. There are other criteria that could be used, such as age, whether or not the individual is married and has children, and the level of money at the arrestee's disposal. The best criteria are those that have high predictive value and are easy to determine without an extensive investigation.

Another step would be to have people out on bail report in once or twice a week to the courthouse to prove they are still in the community and conscious of their impending trial date. Making them appear at the courthouse can be very effective in sensitizing them to their predicament, which can help dissuade them from committing more crimes.

A third step, which would be extremely easy to adopt, is to notify defendants just before their court date, as many fail to show up simply because they have no secretarial service to remind them. Notifying them may include phoning them, sending them a postcard, or knocking on their door. Many taxpayers get upset at the idea of providing a secretarial service to arrestees, but by the numbers, it is much cheaper for everyone if defendants show up the first time.

The fourth step is to prosecute the people who fail to show up. While it seems like something that obviously should be done, it generally is not. The logic is, "Why bother to prosecute people for failing to show up when if we wait they will get arrested again, we will have two more important crimes to prosecute them for." A tangible penalty for missing a court date, however, would provide deterrent value.

The most important element in this package, though, is to reduce the delay between the time people are arrested and the time of their trial. People are generally on very good behavior following an arrest, and if released they are afraid to commit crimes for fear of worsening their situation. However, they return to their old lifestyle once they feel they have been forgotten. If the time period were shortened between arrest and trial, they would not have such an opportunity, and they would be more likely to show up for court.

Delay reduction, unfortunately, is a big problem in itself. A major reason for the delay in the courts is that the huge number of drug-related crimes and personal injury liability cases is clogging up the system.

Feasibility Hurdles

The feasibility problems of this plan are basically administrative because in theory, it should work. It is important to determine why it has become administratively difficult to screen people, have them report in, notify them, prosecute the ones who skip out, and reduce the wait. The answer is again drug-related crimes and personal injury liability cases. The criminal process, and the judicial process in general, has become so clogged up with drug-related crimes that it interferes with having adequate personnel for screening, monitoring, notifying, or prosecuting. And the clog-up of cases is greatly adding to the delay of people who are arrested for all types of crimes. If they are released and do not come up for trial for six months or a year, they have plenty of time to skip out, forget, or just return to their old ways.

Personal Injury Liability

Conservative and Liberal Positions

Personal injury liability lawsuits have also been extremely controversial of late. Congress has been a hotbed of debate, with many senators favoring limits on punitive damage awards. Conservatives are very sensitive to the fact that plaintiffs almost always receive money in personal injury liability cases, and are upset because many of these cases are strictly profit-making efforts. Conservatives feel that these cases have become a deterrent against business innovation, medical progress, etc., because these professionals are not willing to take chances due to the fear of lawsuits.

A good example of the cumulative effects of liability lawsuits may be found in the pharmaceutical sector with regard to the development of contraceptives. The United States is behind many countries around the world with regard to developing contraceptives that make tangible dents in teenage pregnancy rates. Part of the reason for the failure to develop easier-to-use contraceptives is the fear of liability. If a new contraceptive design somehow caused uterine cancer or some other serious ailment, it would result in millions of dollars of lawsuits directed at the company. As a result, pharmaceutical companies spend years testing and re-testing their products, but are still afraid to put them on the market because of personal injury liability lawsuits.

The conservative solution is to make it much more difficult to establish liability. That would mean in order to collect a company would have to show that it was free from any responsibility. If the injury could have in any way been avoided by the plaintiff, the plaintiff cannot collect. That makes a claim very difficult to establish, but the reasoning is the principle of contributory negligence. Conservatives are also interested in limiting damages by instituting fixed ceilings on punitive awards.

Liberals, on the other hand, like to make sure that people get compensated for their injuries. They also support high punitive settlements to act as a deterrent to businesses operating unsafely or inappropriately. This includes employers who do not have safe work-

Table 1.2   Personal Injury Liability

	GOALS	
ALTERNATIVES	**Conservative** 1. Decrease litigation costs. 2. Decrease lawyer fees. 3. Avoid liability.	**Liberal** Compensate the injured.
Conservative Difficult liability.	+	−
Liberal Easy liability.	−	+
Neutral In between.	0	0
SOS or Win-Win See text.	++	++

places, manufacturers who do not make safe products, doctors who are sloppy in their work, and others. Liberals are as tough on business wrongdoing as the conservatives are on individual wrongdoing (street crime, etc.). Liberals want to ensure compensation for injuries and deterrence of wrongdoing by making it less difficult to collect from defendant companies and individuals. Making it easier to collect would include not having any contributory negligence provision, conferring strict liability on employers and manufacturers regardless of who was at fault, and setting no limits on damages.

Win-Win Solutions

What is the win-win solution that will facilitate business development and at the same time result in both fair compensation for injured people and a deterrent to unsafe businesses? There are a number of possible remedies.

The pharmaceutical companies which fear marketing new contraceptives could have their problem solved by creating a system in which the government acts as a temporary insurer. This means the government would offer pharmaceutical companies insurance if they develop extremely important products, such as a cure for cancer or Acquired Immune Deficiency Syndrome (AIDS), or an infallible contraceptive device, once those products are approved by the Food and Drug Administration (FDA). If anyone is injured by the products within the predetermined period of time (probably one to three years), then the government would settle the case on behalf of the company. If an injury from an approved product is not likely to show up for a longer period of time, then the insurance agreement could be amended to reflect that. Other exceptions could also be provided on a case-by-case basis. Even though the government would be insuring products that private companies might be too scared to insure, it has a deep enough pocket that if something goes wrong, it could handle it. If everything works out, the returns of the innovations to society would be tremendous. The government serving as an insurer would enable business development to occur because business firms would not be afraid to try new products and processes. The deterrent effect would still exist because if injuries continue to occur, or occur after the predetermined insurance period, the company would be on its own with regard to liability. Any problems with products would have to be corrected within the first couple of years. Important to note is that the government would not serve as an insurer for all new products. New products would have to qualify via some type of screening process determining that care was taken during production before they would be insured.

Another option that could help decrease the amount of money paid out by businesses while maintaining equity for defendants is to set up a negligence insurance system in which people who are injured can be compensated quickly. Leaving compensation up to the insurance companies would help decrease the number of cases ending up in court. What would this entail? It would mean that if you are injured and your main expenses are medical expenses, then you are covered by your Health Management Organization (HMO) insurance regardless who is at fault. One would not have to sue to cover medical bills. If you lose time from your job as a result of the injury, your insurance company collects from the employer's insurance company or the manufacturer's insurance company in the same fashion that no-fault automobile insurance claims are settled (your insurance company collects for you from the other insurance company and handles all transactions between the two companies). This should please conservatives, as a transactions between insurance companies eliminates the tax burden of supporting a court system clogged with personal injury cases.

The use of mediation instead of court is another option. Mediators specialize in facilitating negotiations and reaching settlements outside of the courtroom environment. They can be effective for reaching compromise settlements between insurance companies representing defendants and plaintiffs, especially if the plaintiff's company has already paid him and is trying to get reimbursed by the other company. Mediation can be helpful in saving money for the taxpayer and for businesses, because lawyers' fees (usually one-third of the settlement) are not an issue.

A further option is to improve the accuracy of both bench trials and jury trials in assessing damages through videotaping, so that the judge or jury could review the tape to recall exactly what evidence was presented for assessing liability. All of these ideas would combine to reduce the taxpayer costs and business costs of personal injury lawsuits, while still at the same time encouraging business development, ensuring compensation to injured persons, and providing a deterrent for future negligence.

Another part of the solution would be a vigorous attempt through public policy to reduce accidents. That would serve the business point of view, in that insurance companies do not have to pay if there are no accidents. It would also serve the liberal point of view, in that nobody has to fight for compensation if they have not been injured. The chief cause of accidents in personal injury liability cases is automobile accidents. There are three steps that need to be taken in that context:

1. The first is to have cars equipped with airbags. When a car is equipped with airbags the occupants are much less likely to be severely injured in a crash. Seatbelt laws are also helpful, but many people do not wear them. Airbags inflate automatically without occupants needing to activate them.

2. Secondly, safer roads could be created by using devices such as median strips. It is hard to have a head-on collision with a median strip dividing a vehicle from the oncoming traffic.
3. The third step is to have safer drivers–and that means getting more aggressive about drunk driving. A really serious crackdown, including long license suspensions, appreciable jail terms, publicized arrests, and the possible development of safe breathalyser level-dependent ignition systems that will not start unless the driver is sober, would be extremely helpful.

To decrease medical malpractice and job-related injuries, more prevention may be the answer. At the workplace, inspections under the Occupational Safety and Health Administration (OSHA) are necessary to prevent accidents before they occur. In the realm of medical malpractice, the expansion of HMOs has helped a great deal to reduce medical malpractice. A doctor who has a bad record regarding malpractice will not be accepted into an HMO. If a doctor does not get admitted his practice will suffer as a higher percentage of people join HMOs. If a doctor is in an HMO and is successfully sued, his/her contract may not get renewed. It is essentially a form of internal policing, in which the HMO has a strong incentive to throw out the negligent doctors because they end up costing the other doctors in the HMO money. This might be a greater incentive for reducing malpractice than anything to do with lawsuits.

Feasibility Hurdles

The key reason why such a plan has not yet been adopted is because it is not in everyone's interest. The legal profession, which has a powerful political lobby, has tended to fight these measures. The legal profession does not like any system that eliminates lawyers. But whether they like it or not, lawyers do add a lot of expense to the personal injury system. They are getting one-third of all the damages, but they tend to try and seek extra compensation for their fee, leaving the plaintiff without money to which they are legitimately entitled. For instance, a plaintiff might legitimately be entitled to $1,000, but to justify their role in the case the lawyer convinces the plaintiff-client to seek $1,500 to cover the fee. There are many opportunities for lawyers to work in other fields, such as international law and technology law, and they should not have to live off this kind of system. Such a personal injury damages system operates as a lose-lose situation. Business firms are losing a lot of money and society is losing innovation that otherwise could occur, while at the same time a high proportion of injured plaintiffs are collecting nothing. A win-win system, like the one described above, would bring down the total amount paid out while seeing to it that a higher percentage of injured people actually get compensated.

Opposition to safer cars, machinery, or medical practices comes from car manufacturers, employers, and doctors. Adoption of new safety measures could be subsidized. Manufacturers might find safety increases sales. Employers could adopt more profitable labor-saving devices, with government help for displaced workers.

Attorneys for the Poor

Conservative and Liberal Positions

On the issue of providing attorneys for the poor, the conservative goal is to avoid the tax burden caused by providing the attorneys, which means ill betides anyone who cannot afford one. Another conservative goal is to avoid having crusading attorneys who are disruptive to people in public office. Such attorneys, with their crusades for the rights of the underclass, etc., are a bother to conservatives. Essentially, conservatives want to leave the task to volunteers, with no government involvement.

Liberals, on the other hand, are very concerned about everyone receiving adequate representation–meaning competent attorneys who aggressively defend their clients. Providing representation for the poor also causes poor people to develop respect for the legal system, which can make them more law-abiding than if they felt that the legal system worked against them by providing no representation. The goal of adequate representation leads to the alternative of salaried government attorneys.

Employing salaried government attorneys is the prevailing system in even the most conservative counties in the United States to provide representation to indigent defendants. In Champaign County, Illinois, the conservative county board members would never think of deliberately adopting something socialistic. Yet they prefer a salaried government attorney system to a volunteer system because enough volunteers simply are not available. The attorneys who have the time to spare are frequently too inexperienced to take criminal trial cases. But according to the U.S. Supreme Court, no conviction is legitimate without the defendant having representation, so the hands of the board members are tied.

An alternative to either volunteers or government salaried attorneys would be a judicare system, in which, like Medicare or Medicaid, lawyers get paid on a per-case basis–which could be very expensive. If lawyers charged approximately $1,000 per felony case, the total bill would run a lot higher than if the government paid salaried attorneys $30,000 or $40,000 per year.

Table 1.3   Attorneys for the Poor

	GOALS	
ALTERNATIVES	**Conservative** 1. Tax burden 2. Avoid crusading.	**Liberal** Good representation.
Conservative 1. Volunteer. 2. Salaried. 3. Compromise.	+	−
Liberal 1. Volunteer. 2. Salaried. 3. Compromise.	−	+
Neutral	0	0
SOS or Win-Win	++	++

The salaried attorney system prevails in most areas for providing representation in criminal cases, but not in civil cases. This is because there is no constitutional requirement of right to counsel in civil cases as there is in criminal cases. The controversy arises in regard to civil cases, where there is no possibility of going to prison. Civil cases can be serious, though. They can decide evictions, repossession, bankruptcy, child custody, and more. In such cases, the poor often have no representation. There is a legal services program run by the federal government (the Legal Services Corporation) which provides salaried attorneys to the poor. It is, however, understaffed, underfinanced, and constantly under attack from conservative politicians.

Win-Win Solutions

A plan needs to be devised that would cost the taxpayer very little while providing good representation. A number of possibilities exist. One possibility is combining salaried attorneys and volunteer attorneys simultaneously on the same staff. The combination system involves the Legal Services Corporation, which recently has received about $350 million a year from the federal government. A combination system would involve spending a portion of that budget on the recruitment of volunteers. Surveys would be done to find out what the available lawyers' specialties are, their availability, and their level of experience. They would work in the legal-aid offices and meet with clients as if they were legal-aid attorneys themselves. The volunteer lawyers would also be retrained, because even the top real estate lawyers, for example, may not know much about the rules governing public housing, and the top contract lawyers may not know much about how merchants or landlords operate in a low-income environment. The combination approach, with salaried attorneys who have as a main function the recruitment, organization, training, and coordination of volunteers, does cut the cost of legal-aid programs.

The second part of the package is to encourage more *pro bono*, or volunteer, work. Requiring volunteer work is opposed by conservatives who do not like being forced to represent poor people, or to represent public-interest causes. The state of Florida has developed a three-part volunteer program that gets virtually all lawyers to participate. The first step was to make it known that every lawyer in Florida is expected by the bar association, but not required, to put in twenty hours of volunteer work per year. Lawyers who put in more than twenty hours get awards and have their names publicized. But Florida authorities normally list all the lawyers and how many hours they have put in, so everyone knows what his or her colleagues are doing. The object is to reward lawyers by giving them publicity, and by making their contributions visible. It has been found that publicizing the lawyers who are putting in one hundred or more hours, encourages the average lawyer to put in a lot more than twenty hours.

The Florida system asks for a donation to the bar association's program to provide attorneys for the poor from lawyers who cannot put in the hours. In other words, one can pay to have someone take one's place. Lawyers can also assign associates in their law firms to put in the hours for them. This combination of publicity, cash donations, and proxy lawyer arrangements has resulted in plenty of available volunteers, thereby decreasing the need for salaried government attorneys and decreasing the tax burden. These volunteer lawyers also tend to be less crusade-oriented than full-time salaried lawyers who develop test cases they can bring to court. This kind of arrangement leads to good representation for poor people with less of a tax burden than currently exists, through a system that is not too radical in terms of its general philosophy.

Another device used in many areas of public-private relations is hiring outside contractors, whereby the government accepts monetary offers for a given amount of legal work and takes the lowest bidder. Conditions may be specified in advance for no acceptance of deterioration of quality of service as compared to the previous year's statistics–meaning that the percentage of defendants who are found guilty in trial cases does not increase, the number of defendants who receive trial cases does not decrease, and that average sentences do not increase. The contracting-out system can save money because frequently the lowest bid amounts to roughly 80 percent of the cost of the same services under a salaried attorney program. By specifying that the contractor cannot go below the previous government salaried attorneys criteria for quality, the public is are still getting just as good representation, but with less tax burden. Contracting out could cause the quality of service to deteriorate if the contract involves very little money per case, however. In such instances there are likely to be very inexperienced attorneys or attorneys who will not spend the necessary time per case. But if the contracting out is done on a bidding basis in which law firms bid for the contracts, they probably will not risk their reputations by providing poor service. It is more likely to result in good representation and reduced costs.

Drug-Related Crimes

Conservative and Liberal Positions

The last policy problem regards drug-related crime, which has become an increasing serious issue. It currently consumes a great deal of money in the United States, and is causing enormous losses in productivity. It is causing governments to engage in corruption and police officers to use abuse behavior due to the tremendous frustration brought on by the drug war.

The key conservative goal in this context is to eliminate or greatly reduce drug-dealing. This means reducing the buying and selling of illegal drugs, most commonly heroin, cocaine, and marijuana. Cocaine and crack represent the largest problem, as they are involved in a large percentage that occurs. Sixty to seventy percent of all people who are arrested for crimes against property or crimes against person are arrested under circumstances that indicate that they are stealing in order to get money for drugs, as indicated by the periodic statistics that come from the U.S. Department of Justice. Often, they are under the influence of drugs while committing crimes. The crimes against the persons usually involve power plays for staking out drug territory. They frequently lead to murder because under the influence of drugs people behave in a more aggressive way than they otherwise would.

Liberals are especially concerned about reducing the side-effects of the war on drugs. These side-effects refer to the police engaging in more illegal arrests, illegal searches, and illegal interrogations than

Table 1.4   Drug-Related Crimes

ALTERNATIVES	GOALS	
	Conservative Eliminate or greatly reduce drug-dealing.	**Liberal** Reduce illegal arrests, illegal searches, and illegal interrogations.
Conservative Law enforcement.	+	−
Liberal Legalization.	−	+
Neutral	0	0
SOS or Win-Win Medicalization.	++	++

before crack cocaine became very widespread in the mid 1980s. They also include the tremendous amount of money necessary for the imprisonment of over 1,000,000 people in our prisons and 500,000 people in our jails. That money could be much better spent on health care, education, or other more useful purposes.

The conservative solution has been to try to repress the sale and possession of drugs namely through law enforcement–an approach of repression and prohibition. One of the more extreme liberal approaches, although becoming somewhat more popular, is legalization. The policy of drug prohibition and repression is analogous to the policy of liquor prohibition. Back then, the United States realized that liquor prohibition didn't work, and that the policy's abolishment was better, even if it means more alcohol-related crime. Legalization is the liberal alternative to conservative police enforcement and repression.

A Win-Win Alternative

The object of the win-win solution is to come up with some kind of idea that wipes out the drug-dealers, but will not increase the use of drugs–to de-profitize "drug-dealing." In de-profitizing drug-dealing, the side effects are eliminated. The organized crime cartels would fall without drug money to support them, and crime would decrease accordingly. Another side effect that would be eliminated is the corruption of government officials due to the availability of "mutually profitable arrangements" with large dealers. An ounce of pure cocaine has a street value higher than that of an ounce of gold. This causes a lot of frustration for the police, because as soon as one drug dealer is arrested and imprisoned or killed, there's another set up to immediately take their place. The money is just to good for some people to turn down.

The way to de-profitize drug-dealing is to treat drug addicts like sick people, and to consider them criminals only if they engage in crimes other than possession and use of drugs. But a key part of the treatment is to treat drug addicts as people in need of medical treatment under our current health care programs. As health care plans move in the direction of becoming universal, the need to cover drug addiction is important. If drug addicts are considered to be sick people eligible for prescription drugs, this could entail a cocaine substitute or even actual cocaine under a cocaine maintenance program. The profits of drug-dealing would be wiped out because addicts would be able to get what they need through their subsidized HMO. These maintenance prescriptions would usually be given on a long-term, phase-out basis until the person is clean. If they never kick their drug habit, their doctors could be able to prescribe additional doses. Drug-dealers would no longer be interested in hooking ten-year-old kids with free samples; all they would be doing is creating new patients for the HMOs. The dealers would eventually be forced to look for some alternative occupation, as did the bootleg liquor dealers of the past. At the present time, anything would be better than the drug-dealing they were previously into.

The win-win solution is plagued by psychological feasibility problems. Many don't believe that such availability will have any effect other than to increase the use of drugs. The idea that people who are not drug addicts are going to go to their HMO and say "I'm a drug addict, I'm on cocaine," when they want to experiment is farfetched. Such a declaration would likely cause them to sacrifice many opportunities that they might otherwise have had: employers are not too enthusiastic about hiring drug addicts. The real drug addicts, though, would have an incentive to go to the HMOs. There they can get a maintenance prescription without having to rob or kill for it, and without having to run the risk of getting arrested or killed themselves.

This kind of approach appeals to some libertarian conservatives who think that a repression program involves more problematic government interference than interference in the economy. It should also appeal to liberals. It is better than legalization because legalization means that controls would be much less strict, and that anybody could have access to drugs, including children. Those children would likely grow up to be much less productive members of society. Legalization, in fact, would have a very bad effect on national productivity, whereas this kind of program, which is only for confirmed drug addicts, would nave few new effects. There are not going to be a whole lot of new drug addicts created because there won't be a set of drug-dealers encouraging the younger generation to become drug addicts.

As said before, the feasibility problem here is psychological. People are resistant to the idea of giving drugs to anyone, let alone those who are already addicts. That sounds somehow evil, but it is less evil than the present system might be. Because this plan is psychologically hard to accept, it is very difficult to adopt politically. Economically, this solution would cost far less than what is currently being done. Cocaine, for instance, is very cheap to produce. Its high price largely has to do with police regression, which causes the costs of drug-dealing to rise, and therefore the street price to rise also. There might also be some feasibility problems with regard to administering such a program. The drugs possessed by the HMOs and hospitals must be carefully monitored so that they don't fall into the wrong hands. This can be accomplished by authorizing only one doctor in the HMO to prescribe drug maintenance programs or drugs. This would greatly decrease the amount of people with access, and would thereby decrease the risk. Also, in order to be eligible to receive a drug maintenance prescription, a person would have to be a confirmed addict. This would require testing the levels of drugs in a person's system over time to see if they qualify. The administrative the program, and would cause the formation of a black market, which defeats the entire purpose. A similar program in England was unsuccessful for this reason. As long as these people are treated as sick people, not criminals, this type of administration would be likely to succeed.

Freedom of Religion

Conservative and Liberal Positions

In the field of constitutional law, some of the most important rights are delineated in the First Amendment, which includes the freedom of religion. Freedom of religion is a little more controversial these days than freedom of speech. The conservative goal on this issue is an increase in religiosity and morality in the United States. The key liberal goal in this context is free choice. Liberals emphasize choice as an important concept–that people should be completely free to be atheists or to be religious, to be Catholic, Protestant, Jewish, Buddhist, Hindu, Moslem, or whatever denomination they want to be without any governmental interference or favoritism.

In the contemporary arena, the freedom of religion is being debated in relation to a proposed amendment to the Constitution allowing organized prayers in public schools. Another conservative position is support for prayer and Bible reading, and specifically prayer in schools. Private schools are free to conduct whatever kind of prayers, ceremonies, or religious indoctrinations they want, whether they be Catholic, Protestant, Jewish, or other parochial schools. Liberals feel there should be no reversal of the prevailing Supreme Court decisions proscribing organized prayer in public schools. Organized prayer means the teacher or a student with the teacher's approval says "Now recite after me." The class would then pray in unison. The proposed constitutional amendment would allow that in public schools.

Win-Win Solutions

The object of the win-win alternative is to provide ideas that will simultaneously promote religiosity and morality without inhibiting free choice. Four proposed ideas are quite compatible with the interpretation by the Supreme Court of the First Amendment with regard to freedom of religion.

The first is to recognize that anybody who wants to pray during school time in the school building is free to do so–that is, the right of silent prayer. With this right, individuals who pray are required to be silent not because the content is disturbing, but because any kind of talking while other students are trying to read or write could be disturbing. Prayer does not have to be silent if done where it is not disturbing other people; only if it is in the actual classroom.

The second idea is the right to have organized religious indoctrination before or after school hours. That is a right even the American Civil Liberties Union recognizes. It would be discriminatory not to

Table 1.5   Freedom of Religion

	GOALS	
ALTERNATIVES	**Conservative** 1. Religiosity. 2. Morality.	**Liberal** Free choice.
Conservative "Pro" religion.	+	−
Liberal "Anti" religion.	−	+
Neutral	0	0

SOS or Win-Win
1. Silent prayer.
2. After hours religious
     use of public schools.
3. Silent meditation time.
4. Courses on ethics and
     civility.
	++	++

allow a religious group to use the school facilities like any other activity group. If before or after school hours, there is no favoritism shown toward a particular religion.

A third kind of right that could be exercised is for the school district to allocate a few minutes at the beginning of the day for silent meditation. That would be in line with the Constitution as it is currently interpreted, as long as students could use those minutes to think freely. Some of the students, who otherwise would not pray, might do so because they were provided with the opportunity. All of the above ideas do help to increase religiosity, yet they maintain free choice by making such actions voluntary. Any type of coercion is unconstitutional.

The fourth idea, directed specifically at morality, involves arranging for courses to be offered at the elementary and the high school level that deal with subjects like ethics and civility. An ethics course might teach how people should relate to each other and to society and vice versa. This could be made constitutional and more meaningful by teaching comparative ethics in which the students are informed about different ethical systems among different cultures and religions. Comparative ethics is called such because the emphasis is not on evaluating which system is best, but rather on looking at the similarities and differences of the systems, and leaving it to the students to decide which ones they favor. In addition to comparative ethics, there should be an objectively taught history of religion in which course materials do not make value judgments on religions or systems of morality. The course could be a description of what has gone on with regard to religion since the ancient Greeks through the present time. Older students could also be offered courses that examine the sociology or psychology of religion. The holy texts of the different religions should also be made available in school libraries so that students could explore them at their leisure. Since participation in these options is voluntary, such activity conforms with free choice. This kind of package can simultaneously promote religiosity and morality on the one hand, and free choice on the other.

Feasibility Hurdles

One might ask why have we not done this sort of thing? Well, we are doing it. The right of individual prayer has been emphasized by the Supreme Court. The constitutionality of prayer before and after school hours has been confirmed. We are now seeing prayer meetings at the school flagpole in the morning. President Clinton signed a bill while he was governor of Arkansas providing for a few minutes of silent meditation every day. Courses like those mentioned above are being increasingly offered. At the University of Illinois, there is a very elaborate program that did not exist a generation ago, including courses that deal with the social science aspects, the literary aspects, and the historical aspects of religion, and some of the same ideas are being taught in public high schools as well.

The feasibility obstacles are largely psychological, as is the case with many of these policy options. Psychological obstacles lead to political obstacles when public opinion is negative, and politicians tend to oppose to such ideas. The psychological obstacles come from some conservatives who think the approach doesn't go far enough, and from liberals who think it goes too far. It is a kind of mutual distrust, in that conservatives view any course that has to do with the history of religion, or religious literature or comparative ethics, as possibly anti-Christian, and liberals feel these courses might be too pro-Christian. What is needed is to experiment with these kinds of ideas and work out the kinks, and to have an objective group of people decide what materials to use. When these ideas are tried, they are likely to be found to be meaningful. After that, the likelihood of their being adopted will increase.

Merit Treatment

Conservative and Liberal Positions

With regard to race relations, the key conservative goal seems to be to judge people in accordance with merit. In the past, conservatives offered a variety of justifications for racism. That is no longer

Table 1.6   Merit Treatment

	GOALS	
ALTERNATIVES	**Conservative** Increase economy.	**Liberal** Diversity and equity.
Conservative Hiring and admissions based strictly on merit.	+	–
Liberal Preferential hiring.	–	+
Neutral Affirmative action with temporary preferential hiring.	0	0
SOS or Win-Win Outreach program.	++	++

the case. Merit treatment is now the rule, and in that context they talk about color-blind hiring and color-blind admissions, in which no preferences are given for being black, female, or any kind of minority.

Liberals on the other hand, talk about the need for diversity, equity, and better distribution and in order to achieve it, they feel quota systems should be abolished. A quota system implies accepting a certain number of black applicants for a job, or to a law school, regardless of qualifications. Liberals believe that there should be preferences given, but only in cases where a white person and a black person are equally qualified. More extreme liberals might even admit the black person when the white person is only slightly better qualified–an example of how the preference system can be used in order to achieve diversity.

A Win-Win Alternative

A win-win alternative would be capable of achieving high merit, high diversity, fairness, and equity simultaneously. How might that be brought about? One alternative that makes a lot of sense is outreach training. Outreach training does not involve giving any preferences to people who apply, for instance, to law school or to work in a management capacity at General Motors, but instead, if they have potential, they will be admitted into the program. In many cases they will have gone to an elementary school or high school in an area where the amount of money spent per student is below the amount spent across the country. In other words, they meet three criteria: (1) they can't qualify on the basis of their present scores, (2) they have a lot of potential, and (3) they had an economically disadvantaged elementary or high school education.

If they meet those criteria, then before entering law school they would be tutored on what is involved in doing well on the law school admission test, similar to a Kaplan or Princeton Review prep course for people that don't have the money available. They would not only be tutored for the law school admission test, but also trained toward what is involved in being a good law student. They could get college credit for passing these courses. If they failed the course, they would be dropped from the program. This is not a gift, it has to be earned. After taking the prep course, individuals who don't get a high enough grade on the LSAT, would be disqualified. They get no preferences or points, but get the credits and grades for the summer course which can help bring their grade point average up to a minimum threshold for admission. A similar outreach training program has been used for years by West Point, Annapolis, and the Air Force Academy to work with various minorities and bring them to a level where. they could be admitted without any kind of preferences at all. It does cost money, but it is worthwhile because if the military can achieve diversity among officers, it would be very helpful with regard to improving morale among the troops, many of whom come from various minorities.

Unfortunately, the current Congress has voted to almost completely wipe out the outreach training programs of the military academies. It is rather shortsighted, but if something involves spending money for human resources training, the payoff is not immediate, and Congress is more reluctant to put forth the money. Congress is very sensitive about producing results to show the American public before the next election, which is never far away.

One might say, "What can be done to provide for more foresight on the part of American politicians?" One plan that might be tried is the establishment of something similar to the Japanese Ministry of International Trade and Industry that consists of three representatives from industry, three from labor, and three from government. The government officials are not even directly elected. The president, or prime minister, appoints the government officials and they are given money to invest in various kinds of programs, such as outreach training programs, the training of displaced worker, or investing in new technologies. They can do this as they serve longer terms than members of Congress, who are only serving for two year terms. The members of Congress would have supervision over the new ministry. Such an organization, being non-governmental, could be associated with the department of education.

The feasibility problem of outreach training is an economic one. The training of minorities in a special summer program for law school may not pay off until after they graduate and become better role models and provide better legal service to people in the minority community. Unfortunately, economic feasibility may require that institutions such as Congress increase their respective time horizons.

Conclusions

The fundamental idea that we are trying to get across is not so much the substance of the pretrial release, personal injury liability, attorneys for the poor, or freedom of religion issues, but rather that with innovative thinking it is possible come up with ideas that can simultaneously exceed the best expectations of both conservatives and liberals; better in light of conservative goals, and better in light of liberal goals. That is win-win thinking, and it can be used instead of compromise thinking in which neither side gets what it wants. This kind of win-win thinking is the most valuable aspect of the policy options discussions above, and can be applied to policy problems of any nature, for any nation.

Chapter 2

International Peace

Disputes between Sovereign Nations

Bilateral arms reduction stemming from the Reagan-Gorbachev agreements exceeds the liberals' best expectations since liberals had been pushing for a freeze as a radical left-wing alternative to increased arms buildup. The idea of a drastic reduction clearly goes beyond a mere freeze. Bilateral arms reduction exceeds the conservatives' best expectations since it has been accompanied by a reduction in the security threat posed by the Soviet Union, rather than an increase. The reduced threat could mean a substantial increase in funds available for improving the American economy, which both conservatives and liberals should welcome.

A Joint Perspective

Such an analysis is shown in Table 2.1. The alternatives, as of about 1985, are:

1. A conservative alternative of a nuclear arms buildup and the Strategic Defense Initiative or "Star Wars."
2. A liberal alternative of a unilateral freeze or disarmament.
3. A neutral alternative of conventional arms development.
4. An SOS alternative of bilateral arms reduction.

The goals of both the United States and the Soviet Union are:

1. The conservative or nationalistic goal of avoiding being conquered and preferably conquering the other side.
2. The liberal or pacifist goal of avoiding nuclear war.
3. The neutral goal of reducing the burden on the economy.
4. A second neutral goal of choosing an alternative that is politically feasible.

The SOS alternative of bilateral arms reduction does so well on all four goals that it exceeds the best that the conservatives previously offered using a conservative goals and weights. It also exceeds the best that the liberals previously offered using the liberal goals and weights. Exceeding the best expectations of both conservatives and liberals is the essence of a super-optimum solution.

Table 2.1   Evaluating Policies toward Arms Control

	GOALS	
ALTERNATIVES	**Conservative** Avoid being conquered.	**Liberal** Avoid nuclear war.
Conservative Nuclear arms buildup and SDI.	+	−
Liberal Unilateral freeze or disarmament.	−	+
Neutral Conventional arms development.	0	0
SOS or Win-Win Bilateral arms reduction and conversion to civilian use.	++	++

Two Separate Perspectives

Table 2.2 shows how the U.S.-USSR arms control negotiations might be viewed as of 1990. Eight alternative positions are shown; four are alternatives of the United States, and four are alternatives of the USSR. Each side is faced with basically the same four alternatives. Those alternatives are:

1. Keep the arms situation as it is. This is the most conservative reasonable alternative as of 1990. It is no longer being actively proposed that the arms race should be increased.
2. Achieve a big reduction in arms. This is the new liberal alternative. It is interesting to note that liberals were formerly advocating a freeze, which is now in effect the conservative alternative. Here is a good example of how yesterday's liberal sometimes becomes today's conservative.
3. Achieve a little reduction between (1) keeping things as they are and (2) a big reduction. This is logically the neutral or compromise position. It typically involves no innovative ideas, but merely splitting the difference between the conservative and liberal positions.
4. A super-optimum solution, which could consist of a combination of a big reduction and various international trade agreements between the United States and the Soviet Union, or even more broadly between the United States plus Western Europe and the Soviet Union plus Eastern Europe.
5. The four alternatives which the Soviet Union is considering are virtually identical. In bilateral dispute resolution both sides often are faced with the same alternatives. They differ mainly regarding what their goals are.
6. Arms inspection is no longer such a big issue as a result of increased openness on the part of the Soviet

**Table 2.2   A Super-Optimizing Perspective on U.S.-USSR
              Negotiations as of 1990**

	GOALS	
ALTERNATIVES	**Conservative** National security.	**Liberal** GNP
Conservative As is.	+	−
Liberal Big reductions.	−	+
Neutral Little reductions.	0	0
SOS or Win-Win Big reductions and trade.	++	++

Union and improved surveillance technology. Afghanistan is no longer such a controversy in view of the Soviet withdrawal. Likewise, the United States has stopped giving military aid to the Nicaraguan rebels. And it looks as if there will be a reasonably meaningful electoral process in both Nicaragua and Afghanistan.

On the matter of goals, there are basically only two, although they could be subdivided, and other lesser goals could be added. There are two goals on the part of the United States and two goals on the part of the Soviet Union:

1. Promoting the national security of the United States. This is a relatively conservative goal. It is also endorsed by liberals, especially if the external threat is from a right-wing source, as in World War II, or even a dictatorial left-wing source, as during much of the Cold War.
2. Promoting the gross national product of the United States, including the idea of full employment and increased international competitiveness. This is a

relatively liberal goal, especially if full employment is emphasized, but also strongly endorsed by conservatives especially if the emphasis is on international competitiveness and reduced inflation.

3. Promoting the national security of the Soviet Union. This is definitely an important goal of the Soviet military and also the civilian government. Too often the American State Department takes the position that the Soviet Union has nothing to worry about from the United States. The more important position is not whether Soviet leaders have anything to worry about, but whether they perceive that they have something to worry about.

4. Promoting the gross national product of the Soviet Union. This is also definitely an important goal of the Soviet Union, especially the civilian government and the civilian population. Too often the Central Intelligence Agency (CIA) and the State Department take the position that the Soviet Union does not care about consumer goods and raising living standards. It is obvious at least since 1988 (if not before) that people in the Soviet Union and Eastern Europe do want a better quality of life in terms of both economic goods and political accountability.

Table 2.2 shows how U.S. negotiators are likely to perceive the relations between each alternative and each goal. If the first alternative is to keep things as they are, that is likely to have no change on either national security or the gross national product. If the second alternative is to have a big reduction in arms, that is likely to be perceived as causing at least a slight decrease in national security by the United States and by the USSR. The funds that might be released from such a reduction, however, are likely to be perceived as being capable of increasing the GNP of the United States and the GNP of the USSR by using those funds to develop and diffuse new technologies that will increase each country's economic capabilities.

The third alternative is a small reduction, but like a typical compromise, it achieves the worst and the best of both of the other alternatives. As a result, it generates about the same total score. All three of the traditional alternatives are all about equally undesirable or equally desirable. The compromise alternative, however, is more likely to be adopted because it scores higher on the unshown goal of political feasibility. It is more politically feasible because both conservatives and liberals will vote for it as a second choice. They will then console themselves by saying that matters could have been worse if the other side had won.

Under a super-optimum solution, both sides do win, and they can win even better than their initial best expectations. At first glance, one might question how a big reduction plus trade can result in more national security than a big reduction alone. That implies that national security is only dependent on how well each country is armed . A country that has a lower GNP than it could have may be weakening itself regarding arms capability and the ability to fight a war. More important, trade between two countries that might otherwise be hostile can create a mutually beneficial interdependence that decreases the likelihood of hostile interaction. Good examples include the unwillingness of the Reagan administration to punish the Soviet Union for its invasion of Afghanistan by prohibiting grain shipments, or the unwillingness of the Bush administration to punish China for its suppression of the pro-democracy movement by invoking trade sanctions. In both cases, the supposedly less anti-communist liberals were more likely to favor the grain embargo and trade sanctions partly because they were less sensitive to the value of international business transactions. In other words, active trading between the United States and the Soviet Union can do more to decrease the likelihood of their going to war and thus to increase their national security than either an arms increase or an arms decrease.

The SOS row of the GNP column reflects the fact that a big reduction alone generates large funds released from arms development that would be available for supply-side economics, industrial policy, and the development of new technologies. It is no coincidence that among the industrialized countries of the world, Japan and Germany now score the highest in productivity increases and the lowest in arms expenditures per capita. The United States and Russia score the highest in arms expenditures per capita, while they score the lowest in recent productivity increases. In addition to the effect of the big arms reduction on GNP, the SOS also produces a positive effect by virtue of the trade agreements between the West and the East. One might say that the United States does not need Russia as a trading partner. For that matter, one could say that the United States could survive with no outside trading partners, and maybe Russia could too. If both countries want to substantially improve their living standards, however, they should take advantage of their potential abilities to buy and sell products from each other. Russia is one of the leading grain buyers of the world and could be a leading buyer in almost any field, given the size of its population. Russia is one of the leading producers of oil and gold, and it could become a leading producer in other fields if it would concentrate its resources on what it can do relatively well, the way Japan has. The United States could sell grain and other products to Russia in return for gold, oil, and other products, thereby easing the international deficit which can be paid in gold and the U.S. energy problems.

Everything shown in Table 2.2 can be subjected to a computerized "what if" analysis. Such an analysis enables one to determine what it would take to bring any of those alternatives that are tied for second place up to first place. It also enables one to determine the effects of adding additional goals, changing the alternatives, or changing any of the inputs. That kind of "what if" capability may be the most important purpose served by working with decision-aiding computer software. Some of the benefits can also be obtained by working with a spreadsheet matrix (like that of Table 2.2 with alternatives, goals, relations, and total scores) even if the matrix is not computerized. One type of sensitivity analysis that is often especially helpful is to ask what would be the winning alternative if one just concentrated on the conservative goals or gave them extra weight, which in this case would be national security. Likewise, it might be asked what would be the winning alternative if one just concentrated on the liberal goals or gave them extra weight, which in this case would be having a higher GNP with full employment and lots of consumer good. One exciting characteristic of super-optimum solutions is that they win even when one only uses conservative weights or liberal weights. The reason here, and often in other SOS situations, is that the SOS alternative does better than the other alternatives on every individual goal–not just better on the overall total. There are ways of systematically arriving at super-optimum solutions. See S. Nagel and M. Mills, "Generating Super-Optimum Solutions" in Marc Holzer, *Public Productivity Handbook* (Marcel Dekker 1992).

Disputes between Controlling Countries and Colonies or Quasi-Colonies

The presence of American military bases in the Philippines is an especially challenging problem. In order to qualify as SOS, problems need to have the following characteristics:

1. There should be at least one conservative alternative and at least one liberal alternative. If there is only one alternative for dealing with the problem, then there is no problem since there is no choice, although one could say that there is still a go/no-go choice as to whether that one alternative should be adopted.
2. There should be at least one conservative and at least one liberal goal. If all the goals are conservative, then the conservative alternative should easily win. Likewise if all the goals are liberal, then the liberal alternative should easily win.
3. The conservative alternative should do better on the conservative goal, with the liberal alternative doing better on the liberal goal. That is the tradeoff requirement. If either alternative does better on both kinds of goals, then that alternative should easily win.
4. It should be possible to meaningfully say that conservatives give relatively more weight to the conservative goals and relatively less weight to the liberal goals, and vice versa for the assigning of weights by

liberals. If that is not so, then it is not so meaningful to talk about a conservative total with conservative weights and a liberal total with liberal weights.

5. There should be a super-optimum solution that does better than the previous conservative alternative on the conservative totals with conservative weights, and it also does better than the previous liberal alternative on the liberal totals with liberal weights. That is the most difficult of these five characteristics to achieve, but still manageable.

The problem of what to do about the American military bases in the Philippines is especially difficult because it goes beyond the usual dilemma of choosing between (1) a liberal alternative that clearly wins with liberal weights, and (2) a conservative alternative that clearly wins with conservative weights. An analysis of Table 2.3 tends to show that the liberal alternative barely squeaks by the conservative and neutral alternatives on the liberal totals, and the conservative alternative barely squeaks by the other two alternatives on the conservative totals. We thus have an even tighter than usual dilemma between the liberal and conservative alternatives.

Table 2.3   American Military Bases in the Philippines

	GOALS	
ALTERNATIVES	**Conservative** Conservative concerns.	**Liberal** 1. Liberal concerns. 2. Sovereignty.
Conservative Bases and more money.	+	−
Liberal No bases.	−	+
Neutral Phase out.	0	0
SOS or Win-Win Bases and massive credits to upgrade economy.	++	++

The Alternatives

Working backward from the totals to the alternatives, the conservative alternative is basically to allow the American bases to remain, but to ask for more money. The liberal alternative is to throw the bases out. The neutral alternative is something in between, generally a gradual phasing out of the bases. Other in-between positions might involve throwing out Clark Air Base but keeping Subic Naval Base, or vice versa. Another possibility is allow the bases to remain, but with more flying of Philippine flags at the bases and other symbols of Philippine sovereignty. A recent middling position is allow the bases to stay, but give the Philippine government more say in how the planes should be used, especially with regard to putting down an attempted *coup d'état*.

The phasing-out idea is probably the most common middling alternative. It, however, blends into both the conservative and the liberal alternatives. The conservatives are willing to tolerate the bases, but they are going to be eventually phased out to some extent anyhow as the Cold War decreases. They are also going to be phased out to some extent because they probably have already become rather obsolete in light of modern defense technology. Few if any of the planes or ships could ever get anywhere without being destroyed by modern missiles. The Russian equivalent of nuclear-armed Trident submarines in the Pacific Ocean could probably wipe out both the naval base and the air base almost before the alarm could ring. There are also bases that are possibly more welcome by their hosts in nearby Okinawa and Korea.

Likewise, the liberal alternative of throwing out the bases would have to be phased out. They cannot be removed within a matter of hours. For one thing, the liberal and conservative members of the Philippine House of Representatives would not tolerate a rushed departure without providing for substitute employment opportunities and some substitution for the large American expenditures associated with the bases. The Philippine Senate, elected at large, is not so sensitive to constituency pressures in Luzon where the bases are located.

One might therefore think there is really only one alternative here, namely phase out the bases. This problem, however, illustrates the importance of symbolism and language in political controversy. Whether the liberals really mean it or not, they talk about throwing out the bases now, not phasing them out. Whether the conservatives really mean it or not, they talk about retaining the bases indefinitely. Thus the controversy needs to be resolved in terms of what each side argues, not necessarily in terms of the realities beneath the surface. Perceptions, value judgments, and symbolism are often more important in resolving political controversies than empirical reality, especially in the short run.

The Goals

As for goals, Table 2.3 lists the first goal as "liberal concerns." That means a whole set of interests that liberals are especially sensitive to, including workers rather than employers, consumers rather than merchants, tenants rather than landlords, small farmers-businesses rather than big farmers-businesses, debtors rather than creditors, minority ethnic groups rather than dominant ethnic groups, and in general the relatively less well-off segments within society. The second goal is listed as "conservative concerns." That means a set of interests to which conservatives are especially sensitive, including employers, merchants, landlords, big farmers, big businesses, creditors, and dominant ethnic groups. One useful aspect of this problem is that it goes to the heart of liberal versus conservative interests and constituencies, as contrasted to lower impact problems.

The third goal is national sovereignty. In some contexts, that can be a conservative goal, such as where Russian nationalists once talked about restraining the Lithuanians, expelling the Jews, or otherwise discriminating against citizens of the Soviet Union who were not ethnic Russians. In other contexts, sovereignty can be a liberal left-wing goal, such as Vietnamese advocating becoming sovereign from China, France, Japan, France again, the United States, and China again during various points in Vietnamese history. Likewise it is a liberal concept in the Philippines when Filipinos talk about getting rid of the Spanish colonialists or the American imperialists, including what they consider to be military-base imperialism. That makes sovereignty in this analysis a relatively liberal goal. Obviously the goal of conservative concerns is a conservative goal, and the goal of liberal concerns is a liberal one.

Scoring the Relations

As for scoring the relations of the alternatives on the goals, both the liberal and conservative concerns are to some extent favorably benefited by the present and additional American dollars. Those dollars benefit both workers and employers, consumers and merchants, tenants and landlords, small and large farmers, small and large businesses, debtors and creditors, and both minority and dominant ethnic groups. The amount of money can be quite substantial. The Philippines is one of the top recipients of American foreign aid in the world along with Israel and Egypt, whose aid is lessening. The liberal and conservative concerns, however, do not benefit equally. The American presence has a conservative influence. The United States tends to be supportive of conservative pro-American politicians, especially in a country that has American military bases, such as Korea, Greece, Turkey, West Germany, Spain, and the Philippines.

To be more specific, the conservative alternative of retaining the bases with even more money is a bit of a wash or a 3 on a scale of 1 to 5 with regard to liberal concerns. The money is at least a 4 on liberal concerns, but the conservative influence of the United States is a 2 or lower. Those two sub-scores average 3. On the conservative concerns, the conservative alternative of the bases and more money gets at least a 4. On sovereignty, the conservative alternative is at least a 2 on a 1 to 5 scale, which is the equivalent of a -1 on a -1 to +2 scale.

The liberal alternative also produces a washed-out 3 on liberal concerns. It gets a 4 with regard to getting rid of some of the American conservative influence, but it gets a 2 on losing the American money. The liberal alternative of no bases gets a 2 or lower on conservative concerns. It does relatively well on sovereignty, as both liberals and conservatives can recognize, although they may disagree on the relative weight of sovereignty in this context.

The neutral phase-out approach does about middling on liberal concerns. It provides some money for a while, which is good, but not as good as a lot of money for a long time. It provides a diminishing of American conservative influence, but not as fast as the liberals would like, and not as slow as the conservatives might like. By allowing the Americans to retain the bases even under a phase-out arrangement, the neutral alternative does have a negative effect on Philippine sovereignty, although not as negative as the conservative alternative. We could show that difference by giving the neutral alternative a 2.5 on sovereignty or the conservative alternative a 1.5. Either way, the overall results are not affected.

A Super-Optimum Solution

Those overall results are that the liberal alternative wins on the liberal totals and the conservative alternative wins on the conservative totals, although not by much, as previously mentioned. Finding a super-optimum solution may be especially difficult where the alternatives are so nearly tied and where the problem is so filled with emotional symbolism. A possible super-optimum solution would involve two key elements. The first is a recognition (as much as possible on all sides) that the bases are probably going to be phased out in the future. This will not be due to the United States surrendering or to the Philippines overcoming the U.S. opposition. It will be more due to defense technology changes (as mentioned above) that makes these bases about as meaningful as the Maginot Line in France in 1940, Pearl Harbor in the United States in 1941, or the Singapore guns pointing to the sea in 1942. The phasing out will also be due to recent world changes that seem to greatly decrease the likelihood of a world war between the Soviet Union, Eastern Europe, and China on the one hand, and the United States and its allies on the other hand.

More important than a natural rather than a forced phase-out is a second key element of a possible super-optimum solution. This element emphasizes massive credits to upgrade the Philippine economy. It could involve no payment of cash whatsoever on the part of the United States and yet provide tremendous economic benefits to the Philippines. It involves a number of characteristics. First of all, the United States makes available an amount of credits that, when expressed in dollars, would be about twice as much money as the United States would be willing to pay as rent or a cash payment. The United States would be willing to pay more in the form of credits because:

1. It is normally easier to give credit than to pay cash. An example might be returning merchandise to a store and asking for cash. One may receive various negative reactions as to why the merchandise should be kept. If, however, one asks for a credit slip, the decision-maker is likely to be much more accommodating.
2. The American economy would substantially benefit if the credits could only be used in the United States to buy American products and services. That would benefit the United States more than paying out cash that then gets spent in Japan or elsewhere. At the same time, it does not substantially hamper the Philippines in buying products and services needed for upgrading its economy.
3. The U.S. economy would also substantially benefit indirectly from an upgrading of the Philippine economy, since that would enable the Philippines to buy even more American products and services in the future.

As for what the credits would be for, that is where the Philippines could especially benefit. The shopping list might include:

1. Credits to pay for personnel and facilities for on-the-job training and adult education to upgrade worker productivity.
2. Relevant credits for upgrading Philippine higher education, especially in fields that relate to engineering and public policy which could have high marginal

rates of return.

3. Relevant credits for upgrading elementary and secondary education as part of a large-scale investment in human resource development.
4. Relevant credits for seeds, pesticides, herbicides, and farm equipment to make the previously mentioned land reform programs more successful, including the hiring of experts for training programs.
5. Relevant credits for subsidizing suburban job opportunities, regional cities, and overseas employment opportunities.
6. Relevant credits to improve Philippine energy and electricity production, which is such an important aspect of improving the gross national product.
7. Relevant credits for buying technologies that can improve productivity along with upgraded skills, including modern assembly-line technologies.
8. Relevant credits for health care and housing that can be shown to be related to increased worker productivity.
9. Other credits for buying American products and services that relate to upgrading the Philippine economy, as contrasted to buying consumer goods or other products and services that have little increased productivity payoff.

There are additional benefits for both sides that should be mentioned. By both sides in this context is meant the Philippines and the United States. Both sides also refers to the liberals and conservatives within the Philippines. Some additional features are:

1. Providing credits rather than cash minimizes loss due to corruption. It is a lot easier to pocket money than it is to pocket a new schoolhouse or an expert consultant in on-the-job training.
2. Providing credits that are earmarked for upgrading the economy minimizes loss due to wasteful expenditures

including bureaucratic administration.

3. Waste is not going to be completely eliminated. The United States would not want a straitjacket system that discourages experimentation with innovative ideas for increasing productivity. If innovation is going to be encouraged, some waste must be expected since not all innovative ideas work out well.

4. This could set a precedent for future American aid to other countries and future aid by other developed countries to developing countries. The key aspect of the precedent is emphasizing credits for upgrading the economy, as contrasted to an emphasis on food, shelter, clothing, and other traditional charitable "do-gooderism."

5. In that regard, we are talking about teaching people how to fish, rather than giving them a fish. The fishing analogy is endorsed by liberals who founded the Peace Corps and conservatives who believe in "workfare" rather than charitable handouts. Actually we are talking about teaching people how to develop and apply new technologies for doing such things as fishing, growing crops, manufacturing products, transporting commuters, and making public policy decisions.

6. The kind of program that most wins friends and influences people in favor of the United States might be programs that involve bringing left-wing anti-Americans to the United States to receive training or having American trainers go to work with Philippine union leaders or Mindanao farmers. People acquire a much more favorable attitude toward Americans in that context than by receiving a sack of flour labeled "Made in the U.S.A."

It might be noted that if the Filipinos emphasize how obsolete the bases are becoming, they might succeed in getting rid of the bases faster. On the other hand, it might be wise to emphasize how valuable the bases are in order to get even more credits as payment for retaining them. On the third hand, the United States is not so unaware of the empirical realities, and it is not so unaware of bargaining techniques. The idea of retaining the bases along with an inevitable at least partial phase-out and massive credits for upgrading the Philippine economy should not be approached as a matter of traditional negotiation and game playing. Rather it should be approached as a matter that can be resolved to the mutual benefit of all sides in the sense of a super-optimum solution with all major viewpoints coming out ahead.

Disputes between Central Governments and Secessionist Provinces

Super-Optimizing Applied to Russian Secession

Table 2.4 shows the application of SOS analysis to the problem of the proposed secession of Chechnya from the Russian Federation. This application was developed in collaboration with Edward Ojiganoff, head of the Policy Analysis Division of the Russian Federation's Supreme Soviet. The Chechnya problem is partly analogous to the proposed secession of Croatia from Yugoslavia or the secession of any ethnic region from a larger country of which it has been a part.

The alternatives in the Russia-Chechnya situation are:

1. Deny independence to Chechnya. This can be considered the relatively conservative position because it seeks to conserve the country, state, or political unit as it is.
2. Grant independence to Chechnya. This can be considered the relatively liberal position because it is more tolerant of dissident attitudes.
3. Retain Chechnya as a sub-unit within the Russian Federation but grant Chechnya more autonomy. This

Table 2.4   Secession of Chechnya

ALTERNATIVES	GOALS	
	Conservative 1. Greater Russia. 2. High RSFSR GNP.	**Liberal** 1. Chechnya independence. 2. High Chechnya GNP.
Conservative Deny independence.	+	−
Liberal Grant independence.	−	+
Neutral More autonomy.	0	0
SOS or Win-Win Economic union.	++	++

can be considered the relatively neutral position.
The goals in the Chechnya situation are:

1. A key conservative goal is to favor greater Russia and seek a high national income for Russia.
2. A key liberal goal is to help Chechnya, including a high national income for Chechnya.
3. More goals can be added later, and possibly more alternatives. For the sake of simplicity, however, we will begin with three basic alternatives and two basic goals.

The relations between those three alternatives and those two goals can be expressed in terms of a scale from 1 to 3. In that context, a 3 means that the alternative is relatively conducive to the goal. A 2 means neither conducive nor adverse. A 1 means relatively adverse or negative to the goal. Relations can also sometimes be expressed in dollars, miles, 1-10 scales, question marks, or other units.

Denying independence to Chechnya is perceived as being at least a mildly positive 3 on the goal of favoring greater Russia. Granting independence to Chechnya is perceived as being at least a mildly negative 2 on favoring greater Russia. More autonomy lies in between, with a neutral score of 2. On the other hand, granting independence to Chechnya is scored a 3 on the goal of helping Chechnya. Denying independence is scored a 1 on helping Chechnya. More autonomy is in between on that goal, with a neutral score of 2. Those perceptions and scores are likely to be held broadly by both conservatives and liberals in this context.

Three total scores can be generated from this data. The total scores are neutral, conservative, or liberal, depending on the relative importance of the two goals. If the two goals are considered to be of equal importance, then the neutral totals are 4 for each of the alternatives. If the conservative goal is considered more important than the liberal goal, we can count the conservative column twice. That results in totals of 7 for denying independence (3 + 3 + 1), 5 for granting independence (1 + 1 + 3), and 6 for more autonomy (2 + 2 + 2). Thus with conservative weights for the goals, the conservative alternative wins on the conservative totals.

Likewise, if the liberal goal is considered more important, we can count the liberal column twice. That results in totals of 5 for denying independence (3 + 1 + 1), 7 for granting independence (1 + 3 + 3), and 6 for more autonomy (2 + 2 + 2). Thus with liberal weights for the goals, the liberal alternative wins on the liberal totals. The single star shows the winning alternative on each total column before the SOS alternative, or super-optimum solution, is taken into consideration.

Finding a Super-Optimum Solution

The object is to find a super-optimum solution which will simultaneously (1) win on the conservative totals over the conservative alternative and (2) win on the liberal totals over the liberal alternative. That means being better than both the conservative best and the liberal best using their own goals and weights to judge what is best. In terms of the simple scoring system, such a solution needs to score positively or better than a neutral 2 on a 1-3 scale on both goals. That also means going above traditional tradeoff reasoning.

The conservative alternative usually does well on the conservative goal, but not so well on the liberal goal. The liberal alternative usually does well on the liberal goal, but not so well on the conservative goal. The SOS alternative does at least mildly well on both goals.

Doing well on both goals does not require being a winner on each separate goal. It means being a winner on each of the two main totals. Those totals involve using conservative weights and liberal weights respectively. If the suggested SOS alternative receives a 2.5 on each goal, then it will receive a 7.5 on the conservative total (2.5 + 2.5 + 2.5). That is higher than the 7 received by the conservative alternative. Likewise, the suggested SOS alternative will receive at least a 7.5 on the liberal total (2.5 + 2.5 + 2.5).

Developing an SOS alternative which has those characteristics requires a knowledge of the subject matter and some imagination. Finding such an alternative can be aided by the checklists which have been developed from previous case studies that briefly describe eight useful approaches. Finding such alternatives can also be facilitated by decision-aiding computer software which makes use of multi-criteria decision analysis with a spreadsheet base. Such software is described in Nagel, *Decision-Aiding Software: Skills, Obstacles, and Applications* (Macmillan, 1991).

A proposed SOS solution to the problem of Chechnya seceding from the RSFSR is to allow Chechnya its independence, but as part of an economic union with the RSFSR and possibly other autonomous regions within the RSFSR and other neighboring political units. This is analogous to the RSFSR, the Ukraine, and Belarus withdrawing from the USSR and forming an economic union or commonwealth. Such an economic union could benefit both the RSFSR and Chechnya by facilitating a profitable interchange of goods, capital, workers, and ideas. It could later lead to developing a more meaningful division of labor than previously existed, with the possibility of well-targeted subsidies and incentives from the economic union to make the division of labor even more successful.

An alternative SOS might be to retain Chechnya within the RSFSR, but seek to achieve the benefits of an economic union through immediate subsidies. Such an alternative may not be economically feasible from the perspective of the presently hard-pressed RSFSR. It also may not be politically feasible from the perspective of the independence-seeking Chechnyas. To be a meaningful SOS requires satisfying the following five criteria:

1. The SOS must win on the conservative totals.
2. It must also win on the liberal totals.
3. It must win by a margin safe enough for the SOS to retain first place regardless of reasonable changes in scoring the relations between the alternatives and goals or in indicating the relative weights of the goals.
4. The SOS must be politically feasible so that it is capable of being adopted.
5. The SOS must be administratively feasible so that it is capable of being successfully implemented, including backed by sufficient funding.

Disputes between Conflicting Nations within a Country

Super-Optimizing Applied to Civil War in Yugoslavia

The above analysis can be applied to Yugoslavia through reasoning by analogy. Some special points worth noting:

1. Each republic and autonomous province of Yugoslavia could become a separate sovereign nation, or at least each republic could. Each would have a population and a national income that would be within a low to middle range among members of the United Nations.
2. They would be joined together in an economic union of six republics. This would be analogous to the joining of the former republics of the Soviet Union or the approximately a dozen nations in the European Union (EU). The so-called Commonwealth of Inde-

pendent States (CIS) is more applicable since the members were formerly part of one country, namely the USSR.

3. The new economic union could be referred to by such names as the Yugoslavia Economic Union, or the South Europe Economic Union. The latter would allow for other South European countries to join, such as Greece. An alternative would be to have a Yugoslavia Economic Union consisting of the six Yugoslavian republics, but having the Yugoslavia Economic Union later join in a larger economic union covering South Europe or possibly Central Europe.

4. The Yugoslavia Economic Union could add to its unity by having a constitutional monarchy as part of the union. The precedent for doing so is the former British Commonwealth. It is now known as the Commonwealth of Nations, but many of those nations still have a relation to Queen Elizabeth II which enhances unity, tradition, and stability.

5. In the case of Yugoslavia, a democratic constitutional monarchy could serve a unifying peacemaking role. Crown Prince Alexander does evoke a favorable response among many Serbs, Croats, Slovenes, and other Yugoslavian ethnic groups. He probably evokes a more favorable response than the Yugoslavian national or federal presidency or other governmental institutions.

6. There are increasing case studies and experiences regarding the benefits and processes related to forming an economic union. Such unions are becoming increasingly important in such places as Western Europe, the Soviet Union, and the trilateral pact among the United States, Canada, and Mexico.

7. Moving ahead toward establishing such a union might do more to help end the civil war in Yugoslavia than trying to achieve a lasting cease-fire or a military solution.

8. The economic union could at first emphasize the unhindered exchange of goods, people, capital, and ideas across all the boundaries of the former republics. It could also emphasize equality of opportunity for all ethnic groups in terms of equal treatment regardless of origin in matters of rights that relate to politics, criminal justice, education, employment, housing, and consumer rights.

9. The economic union could later develop appropriate divisions of labor in terms of making the best use of the land, labor, and capital of each former republic. That kind of division or specialization could be facilitated by well-targeted subsidies and incentives.

10. Such an economic union is a super-optimum solution since it enables conservative nationalists and separatists to achieve more national identity and stature than they otherwise would have. At the same time, it satisfies the liberal emphasis on quality of life in terms of jobs and consumer goods.

11. It makes more sense than each country going off on its own without the benefits of the economic interaction associated with an economic union. It likewise makes more sense than forcing nations into a regional government above the member nations, or even a world government.

12. Some of these ideas are summarized in Table 2.5. It makes use of a 1 to 5 system of scoring relations rather than 1 to 3. It also uses a 1 to 3 system for weighting goals rather than 1 to 2.

13. These general ideas hold much potential for Yugoslavia in terms of peace, prosperity, and political reform. The ideas need to be further developed in collaboration with policy-makers, political scientists, economists, and other relevant people, mainly in Yugoslavia.

Table 2.5 International Economic Communities

ALTERNATIVES	GOALS	
	Conservative National identity and stature.	**Liberal** Quality of life in terms of jobs and consumer goods.
Conservative Nationalism and separatism.	+	−
Liberal One world or world government.	−	+
Neutral Regional government.	0	0
SOS or Win-Win Economic community.	++	++

14. The most appropriate next step may be to engage quickly but meaningfully in that kind of collaboration in order to develop and implement a worthwhile plan for creating a Yugoslavia Economic Union of six sovereign states. It could possibly include a constitutional monarchy as a peacemaking unifying force. It could bring together Serbs, Croats, Slovenes, Muslims, Albanians, Macedonians, Montenegrins, and other Yugoslavians.

Disputes between Conflicting Economic Classes with International Implications: Land Reform in the Philippines

Table 2.6 provides an SOS analysis of land reform in developing countries, although it is especially based on the author's experiences in working with the Department of Agrarian Reform in the Philippines. The table is a classic SOS table in that the rank order of the alternatives on the liberal totals are SOS, liberal, neutral, and conservative. Likewise the rank order of the alternatives on the conservative totals are SOS, conservative, neutral, and liberal.

The Traditional Inputs

More specifically, in considering one hundred units of land, the typical conservative approach tends to advocate retaining most of the ownership of the land in the hands of the traditional landed aristocracy. The typical liberal approach tends to advocate turning most of the ownership of the land over to landless peasants to farm. The typical neutral or compromise approach is something in between, although not necessarily an even split of the one hundred units.

The two key goals in the controversy tend to be agricultural productivity and a more equalitarian or equitable distribution of land ownership. The conservative alternative (by allowing for economies of scale that are associated with large land holdings) is more productive, but less equitable. The liberal alternative (of widespread land distribution) is less productive, but more equitable. The neutral

Table 2.6   Land Reform

	GOALS	
ALTERNATIVES	**Conservative** Productivity.	**Liberal** Equity.
Conservative Retain land (0 units).	+	−
Liberal Divide land (100 units).	−	+
Neutral Compromise (50 units).	0	0
SOS or Win-Win 1. Buy the land 2. Lots of land. 3. Co-op action.	++	++

compromise is somewhere between those relation scores, just as it is somewhere between the conservative and liberal distribution alternatives.

With those relation scores, we logically have the result mentioned above, in which the conservative alternative wins with the conservative weights and the liberal alternative wins with the liberal weights. We are also likely to get the classic compromise, which is everybody's second best alternative or worse. The "or worse" means that sometimes liberals accept the compromise when the conservative alternative actually does better on the liberal weights, or conservatives accept the compromise when the liberal alternative actually does better on the conservative weights. Each side may accept the compromise even though it is the third best alternative to them, because they do not want to give in to the other side. That is not the case with Table 2.6, but it does sometimes occur in the psychology of public policymaking.

The Super-Optimum Alternative

The super-optimum alternative seems to involve three key elements. The first is that the land needs to be bought from the present landowners, rather than confiscated. If the owners are threatened with confiscation, one possible reaction is to establish death squads or vigilante groups, to bring in American military power, or to do other nasty things that might easily cost more than buying the land. The United States might have saved a fortune in military and other expenditures in Nicaragua, El Salvador, and Guatemala over the last ten or twenty years by using a fraction of the money spent to instead buy land from the owners to give to the peasants. The landowners probably also would have saved themselves money by paying a substantial portion of the taxes needed to buy the land. They would save money in the sense that the tax bill is likely to be less than the cost of fighting peasant guerrillas for approximately 30 years throughout Guatemala, Nicaragua, El Salvador, and elsewhere in Latin America.

The second element is that lots of land needs to be involved. It cannot be a token program. The landless peasants in developing countries are no longer as passive as they once were. They cannot be easily bought off with trinkets, pie-in-the sky religion, patronizing aristocrats, and other relatively worthless bribes or distractions. They have demonstrated a willingness to fight and die for land in pre-communist China, Central America, and other developing countries, including the Philippines.

The third element is the need for using modern technologies in a cooperative way to overcome the divisive effect of distributing the land in relatively small parcels to the landless peasants. Here is where the policymakers can learn from both capitalistic American farmers and communistic Russian farmers. American farmers are highly individualistic, but they recognize that it makes no sense for each of them to own one's own grain elevators, combines, and other big equipment which they can own collectively through producer cooperatives. In the Soviet Union, agricultural efficiency has been promoted through machine tractor stations where farmers can collectively share tractors which they cannot afford to own separately. This is the case regardless whether the individual farmers are associated with collective farms or private plots. Cooperative activities also involve the equivalent of county agents who help bring farmers together to learn about the latest seeds, herbicides, pesticides, fertilizers, and other useful knowledge. Cooperative action can also include credit unions and government subsidies to encourage the diffusion of useful innovations.

The fourth element is to train farmers for new non-farming jobs. This includes the former landless farmers who cannot be accommodated with land, or who would prefer to get out of farming. It also includes the newly landed farmers who themselves or their children might be better off in non-farming jobs. Caesar Chavez, leader of the American Farmworkers Union, advocated retraining and other job-finding facilitators as a long-term or intermediate-run solution to landless peasantry, somewhat on the model of Franklin Delano Roosevelt's Rural Rehabilitation Administration. Chavez recognized that grape-picking and other farm labor could soon be done more profitably by machines. Thus land redistribution may only be a temporary solution for most landless peasants.

The important point from the perspective of international and intra-national dispute resolution is that the severe class conflict resulting from landless or impoverished peasantry can lead to both kinds of disputes. Central America offers a good example of the United States and USSR choosing sides between the conflicting classes. Haiti, Cambodia, and the Zapatistas in Mexico are good examples of internal killings over land ownership and the inability of small low-technology peasant plots to be able to compete internationally. Related examples of urban guerrillas and death squads are found in Uruguay, Brazil, and pre-Castro Cuba.

With that combination of SOS elements, one can achieve agricultural productivity and equity simultaneously. That combination of elements becomes a strong winner on both the liberal totals and the conservative totals. Appropriate timing may also be required in the sense of moving fast to implement these kinds of ideas. The longer the delay, the more difficult such an SOS solution becomes. The reason is that the liberal left may acquire such a negative attitude toward the conservative right that the liberal left would consider buying the land to be a surrender to evil people. Likewise, the conservative right may acquire such a negative attitude toward the peasant guerrillas that they can see no respectable solution other than extermination of what they consider to be terrorists.

International Policy: The United States and the United Nations

Conservative and Liberal Positions

The key conservative goal in this context, relating to the role of the United States in helping the UN to bring peace to Bosnia, is to save U.S. dollars and save lives. The conservatives were not always so oriented toward isolation. They were very interventionist back in the days of the Cold War, especially with regards to curtailing the expansion of the Soviet Union. But at the present time, they do espouse more of an isolationist, less of an intervention policy than liberals do. The conservative alternative for saving U.S. dollars and lives is to keep U.S. troops at home. They feel it is more important to develop the United States first. The liberals, on the other hand, are more oriented toward being the policemen of the world with the goal of promoting world peace. More idealistic and maybe more naive, they believe what is sometimes referred to as "a social worker ideology." That necessitates intervention.

A Win-Win Solution

The win-win solution saves U.S. dollars, U.S. lives, and promotes world peace simultaneously. An approach recommended by some who specialize in international relations is the idea of a volunteer UN force. What this would mean is that American troops would not be sent to Bosnia, Somalia, or anywhere else. The UN would have its own volunteer force, similar to the French Foreign Legion. It would consist of people from many parts of the world who would join partly out of idealism, partly because it pays money. They would not be allowed to join unless they have had military experience and aptitude for military training. The force would provide an opportunity for Vietnam War veterans, Russian soldiers who had fought in Afghanistan, and others to participate in a force devoted to a righteous cause. The officers would be those who had served in the militaries of their various countries.

As a result there would be no active-duty American military personnel in this UN force. There might be Americans in the force, but they would be acting on their own. They would not be drafted, or as in the case of Americans currently serving in Bosnia, ordered to go because their unit was called. Those in the UN force would be pure volunteers, in the sense they would be joining with the agreement to go wherever they were sent. If they declined to go, for ideological or other reasons, then an option could be provided for resignation. In such a case it might be fair to have them pay back something in return for their training. Such an arrangement has many possibilities.

Table 2.7   U.S. and UN Peacekeeping

	GOALS	
	Conservative Save U.S. dollars and lives.	**Liberal** Promote peace, prosper- ity, and democracy.
ALTERNATIVES		
Conservative Isolationism, minimum U.S. involvement.	+	−
Liberal Interventionism, substan- tial U.S. involvement.	−	+
Neutral In between.	0	0
SOS or Win-Win Volunteer UN force.	++	++

Such a plan has been opposed in the past by the United States because it was feared that the UN could not be trusted to have its own volunteer force. Strictly by the numbers, the UN in the past has been under the control of developing nations or nations under the control of the Soviet Union. But now, with the breakup of the Soviet Union, the United States dominates the UN as the only superpower in the world. The volunteer force could not be a threat to the United States. Though a bit behind in its payments, the United States is the leading source of funds to the UN, which further adds to its influence. If the United States does not like what the volunteer force is doing, it could cut off the funding, use its veto power in the Security Council, or use its influence among countries of the world. This kind of volunteer force would mean that no American lives or American dollars would be directly used, yet it could still be very effective in promoting world peace. It is possible that the volunteer force might call upon the member countries to supply additional troops at some time, but this would be handled as the need arose. This represents another kind of win-win solution.

The feasibility problem for this issue is psychological. Such a force might be conceived as representing the muscle behind a type of world government which could partly deprive the United States of its sovereignty. Some might fear the volunteer force is going to march in and take over. As with all the other obstacles, it is necessary for this one to be overcome if this win-win solution is going to be adopted. People have to realize that the UN volunteer might not be a threat to them. In no way would the people with blue helmets serving in Bosnia invade the United States.

PART TWO

DOMESTIC PEACE

Section A

Legal System Procedures

Chapter 3

Arrest and Search

Deterring Illegal Searches

Law Evaluation: Evidence Illegally Obtained

The four alternatives are: (1) allow the evidence if the police testify they did not intend to engage in illegal behavior, (2) allow the evidence if the state adopts a system of suspensions on the first offense and dismissal on the second offense, (3) exclude illegally seized evidence from criminal proceedings, and (4) emphasize damage suits and prosecution to deter illegal searches.

Table 3.1   Evidence Illegally Obtained (A Simplified Perspective)

	GOALS	
ALTERNATIVES	**Conservative** Decrease crime occurrence.	**Liberal** Decrease illegal police searches.
Conservative Good faith exception.	+	–
Liberal 1. Suspension-dismissal. 2. Damages-prosecution.	–	+
Neutral Exclude evidence.	0	0
SOS or Win-Win See text.	++	++

The "good faith" rule allows illegal searches to be used as evidence if the search is not knowingly illegal, as in the tort distinction between intentional and negligent wrongdoing.

Automatic suspensions refer to suspending a police officer who has been found to have made an illegal search, with dismissal on the second occurrence. The suspensions would allow the police officers to have hearings to defend themselves.

Professionalism especially refers to receiving training in the rules governing illegal searches. It also includes a reward system of promotions and pay raises for such desirable activities as making searches which result in convictions.

Drug medicalization refers to attempts to reduce the drug market by treating drug addicts as medical patients with free treatment on demand. This is relevant to reducing illegal searches since so many of them are drug-related.

The other three alternatives are relatively lacking in feasibility because (1) the "good faith" exception has questionable constitutionality, since it may provide too little deterrence against illegal search and seizure; (2) a system of suspension and dismissals would require approval by state legislators or police administrative boards, which is unlikely; (3) prosecution of police officer for illegal searches without physical violence is unlikely, and the probabilities are low of an innocent or guilty person suing for damages, winning, and collecting anything substantial.

Evaluating Policies toward Illegal Search and Seizure

Table 3.2 is a simplified table showing two goals rather than five goals, and showing one composite SOS alternative rather than three.

The additional goal of feasibility is important in explaining why the Supreme Court has adopted the rule of excluding illegally seized evidence. The other alternatives are not so feasible. They include (1) relying on the prosecutor to prosecute illegal searches, but the prosecutor works too closely with the police, (2) relying on state legislatures to provide for automatic suspensions and dismissals, but the legislatures are unwilling to adopt such legislation, and (3)

Table 3.2 Evidence Illegally Obtained (A More Complete Perspective)

ALTERNATIVES	GOALS	
	Conservative 1. Decrease crime. 2. Anti-crime symbol.	**Liberal** 1. Decrease illegal searches. 2. Pro-privacy symbol.
Conservative Allow evidence (if not intent).	+	–
Liberal Exclude evidence (no exceptions).	–	+
Neutral Exclude with exceptions.	0	0
SOS or Win-Win 1. Allow, but prosecute and sue. 2. Allow, but suspend and dismiss. 3. Exclude with professionalism and drug medicalization.	++	++

illegally seized evidence if the police action was not deliberately illegal. The last alternative is not so feasible because of the difficulty in proving intent, and it may also lack constitutional feasibility because such a rule may go too far in allowing violations of the Fourth Amendment to the Constitution.

The additional liberal goal is exclusion as a pro-privacy symbol. It helps explain why liberals endorse exclusion, even though it does not greatly decrease illegal searches. The additional conservative goal is allowing the evidence as an anti-crime symbol. It helps explain why conservatives endorse allowing the evidence, even though doing so does not greatly decrease crime.

The first two SOS alternatives can be eliminated as not being sufficiently feasible. The alternative of encouraging lawsuits by people subjected to illegal searches is not so realistic because (1) those people generally do not want the publicity that they were criminal suspects if they really were innocent, (2) they do not make good plaintiffs if they really were guilty, (3) the police are given considerable discretion, (4) the monetary damages may be slight if there has been no physical abuse accompanying the illegal search, (5) a lawyer is not likely to be willing to take the case on a contingency percentage given the low probability of collecting substantial damages, and (6) if there are substantial damages, they are likely to be paid by the city rather than the police officer.

Deterring Related Police Abuse

Restraining Police without Increasing Crime

The components of the SOS package might include (1) increased police professionalism, which can both reduce crime and help separate the innocent from the guilty, (2) drug medicalization, designed to reduce drug-related crimes and abuse of those suspected of being on drugs, although drug medicalization may lack present political feasibility, and (3) rent supplements, providing rental

Table 3.3   Restraining Police

	GOALS	
ALTERNATIVES	**Conservative** Reduce crime.	**Liberal** Protect innocent and guilty from abuse.
Conservative Free hand.	+	−
Liberal Citizens review board.	−	+
Neutral Police review board.	0	0
SOS or Win-Win 1. Professionalism. 2. Drug medicalization. 3. Rent supplement.	++	++

subsidies to low-income applicants to facilitate economic and racial integration, which thereby tends to reduce economic and racial discrimination in police behavior.

Sweep Searches at Public Housing

The police have been conducting sweep searches of apartments in public housing projects in Chicago. Such searches involve searching all or random apartments for drugs, guns, and other incriminating evidence. The searches have been declared unconstitutional.

The liberal position (as endorsed by the federal courts) is that the Constitution allows police searches only when there is probable cause or a substantial probability of finding incriminating evidence in an apartment. The probable-cause standard should be applied to each individual apartment. It should also be used when a search warrant is issued.

The conservative position (as endorsed by the police and the public housing authority) is that the searches should be allowed since they do uncover drugs and guns, and they do deter drugs and guns in the apartments.

The liberal goal is privacy for apartment dwellers who do not have incriminating evidence in their apartments. The conservative goal is to reduce the presence of guns and drugs in the public housing projects.

The object of an SOS alternative is to simultaneously reduce guns and drugs more than sweep searches do, and to preserve privacy more than the probable-cause standard does. An approach to doing that might involve security guards at the entrance to each public housing project making use of metal detectors to detect guns, and dog sniffing to detect drugs.

The metal detectors might find and deter more guns than the sweep searches. It is easier to hide a gun from a hurried, occasional search than to hide a gun from a daily metal-detector. It may also be more difficult to hide drugs from daily dog-sniffing than from a hurried, occasional search.

Table 3.4   Searches at Public Housing

	GOALS	
ALTERNATIVES	**Conservative** 1. Effective. 2. Reduce drugs and guns.	**Liberal** Privacy.
Conservative All apartments.	+	−
Liberal Probable cause.	−	+
Neutral Relax standards.	0	0
SOS or Win-Win 1. Metal detectors. 2. Dog sniffing.	++	++

The approach of metal detectors and dog sniffing at the entrance also provides even more privacy than frequent probable-cause searches. The SOS proposal does not in itself involve any searches of apartments, although it could be supplemented with legal searches based on probable cause.

When the federal court declared the sweep searches unconstitutional, President Clinton announced that the Justice Department and Housing and Urban Development would develop a search policy for nationwide public housing that would be both constitutional and effective. That is a good example of super-optimum thinking, as contrasted to a compromise that might seek to relax probable-cause standards and thereby allow many apartments to be searched, but not all of them. The result would be less effectiveness than sweep searches, and more invasions of privacy than probable cause.

Relevant Criminal Behavior

An SOS Analysis of Problems Involved in Arresting and Testing Drunk Drivers

Police profiles refer to stopping people who fit certain characteristics associated with drunk driving or being under the influence of drugs. Such characteristics might relate to being black, poor, young, male, or other circumstances that have a statistical association with drinking or using drugs. This kind of emphasis may result in many stops or arrests, but a low percentage of convictions.

"Probable cause" refers to stopping motorists whose behavior indicates a substantial probability of being drunk or under the influence of drugs–such as weaving, driving unusually slow, or other erratic although not necessarily illegal behavior. This kind of emphasis may not result in many stops or arrests, and it thus may better preserve privacy of innocent people.

Roadblocks involve stopping all drivers at a certain point on a highway to check for drunkenness or the use of drugs. This emphasis may be in the middle on quantity of arrests generated and on privacy

Table 3.5 Drunk Drivers

	GOALS	
ALTERNATIVES	**Conservative** Reduce crime violations.	**Liberal** Preserve privacy.
Conservative Police profiles.	+	−
Liberal Probable cause.	−	+
Neutral Roadblocks.	0	0
SOS or Win-Win 1. Median strips. 2. Air bags. 3. License removal. 4. Squad car lights.	++	++

invaded. Stopping in this context is not an arrest in the sense of suspected wrongdoing.

The SOS alternative does not emphasize making arrests or preserving privacy. Instead it emphasizes decreasing fatalities due to drunk or drugged drivers by having median strips and airbags. Flashing squad-car lights also decrease the prevalence of drunk and drugged drivers, as does removing their licenses when they are caught. Those methods may do more for reducing both fatalities and preserving privacy than other methods.

A SOS Analysis of the Los Angeles Riots

Table 3.6 refers to the Los Angeles riots which occurred after the acquittal of the police officers who were accused of having used excessive force in dealing with Rodney King. The table can be broadened to refer to related riots in Miami, Detroit, and elsewhere where blacks or other minorities perceived that they were being abused by the police, the courts, or other governmental institutions. On March 2, 1991, Rodney King resisted arrest by four police officers after a high-speed chase on Los Angeles freeways and city streets. Some of the officers' frantic efforts to restrain King were captured on video by an amateur cameraman. The officers are white; King is black. Juries acquitted the officers of using excessive force.

The conservative alternative emphasizes more law enforcement, including stiffer penalties for rioters, and more use of firearms by police to deter theft. The liberal alternative emphasizes doing things that will generate more respect for the legal system thereby providing less justification for rioting. Increased respect includes a more effective reward and punishment system for police abuses of minority citizens.

The conservative goal is to achieve greater compliance with the law on the part of the minority community. Doing so might lessen abusive law enforcement. The liberal goal is to achieve greater compliance with the law on the part of the police. Doing so might

Table 3.6   Los Angeles Riots

ALTERNATIVES	GOALS	
	Conservative Compliance with law or street crime.	Liberal Compliance with law or police behavior.
Conservative More law enforcement.	+	−
Liberal Better quality law enforcement.	−	+
Neutral Somewhat more and somewhat better.	0	0
SOS or Win-Win Upgrade skills and job opportunities.	++	++

lessen the likelihood of revenge-oriented rioting.

The compromise or liberal position is to implement some of both alternatives–but possibly not enough law enforcement to satisfy conservatives, and not enough police improvement to satisfy liberals.

What may be needed especially in low-income minority communities is a more vigorous program to upgrade skills and job opportunities. People with good jobs or good job prospects are more likely to be law-abiding, rather than risk losing those opportunities. They are also more likely to be treated with more respect by the police. Thus this alternative can promote both the conservative and liberal goals. This contrasts to having more severe law enforcement which may score well on the conservative goal but not the liberal goal, and having more sensitive police which may score well on the liberal goal but not the conservative goal.

This SOS table involves a set of weights for each goal which is different from the usual SOS table. Here the conservative and liberal weights are only one unit apart at either 3 versus 2 or vice versa, as contrasted to 3 versus 1. The explanation is that conservatives and liberals do not differ as much on the relative importance they assign these goals as they do on the goals in an economic policy controversy.

Chapter 4

Pretrial Procedures

Pretrial Release

Evaluating Policies toward Pretrial Release

The SOS alternative involves a five-part package that includes (1) better screening out of persons posing high risks to release, (2) reporting to the courthouse every week or so before trial, (3) notifying defendants with reminders to appear at trial, (4) prosecuting at least some of those who skip out, rather than waiting for them to commit another crime, and (5) especially reducing delay from the time of arrest to the time of trial.

Evaluating Alternative Ways of Handling Pretrial Release

The conservative position is to set relatively high bonds in order to generate a high holding rate. Doing so increases the likelihood that arrested defendants will show up for trial and not commit another crime between arrest and trial.

The liberal position is to set relatively low bonds in order to generate a low holding rate. Doing so increases the likelihood that arrested defendants will be able to continue their jobs, avoid the bitterness of being held in jail prior to trial, and avoid expensive incarceration costs.

The compromise position in many states such as Illinois is to set relatively high bonds but require the defendant to provide only 10 percent of the total bond. This results in more defendants being

Table 4.1   (Simple) Pretrial Release

| | GOALS | |
ALTERNATIVES	Conservative Increase shows and non-crime.	Liberal Increase release productivity.
Conservative High bond.	+	−
Liberal Low bond or no bond.	−	+
Neutral 10 percent bond.	0	0
SOS or Win-Win 1. Screen. 2. Report. 3. Notify. 4. Prosecute. 5. Decrease delay.	++	++

released than does the conservative alternative, but fewer than does the liberal alternative.

The SOS alternative is designed to increase the release rate, possibly even higher than liberals advocate, but at the same time raise the rate of defendants showing up for trial without committing crimes in the meantime. This might be done by the five alternatives outlined previously.

Plea Bargaining

Evaluating Policies toward Plea Bargaining

Lenient plea bargains tend to occur when a defendant is capable of paying for a defense that will greatly tie up the prosecutor's scarce resources in motions, trial time, and appeals.

Severe plea bargains tend to occur when a defendant is held in jail pending trial and is willing to plead guilty to a crime for which jail time already is being served in order to be able to go home, even

Table 4.2   Plea Bargaining

	GOALS	
ALTERNATIVES	**Conservative** Deserving of sentences.	**Liberal** Separate innocent.
Conservative Abolish lenient plea bargains.	+	–
Liberal Abolish severe plea bargains.	–	+
Neutral Maintain as is.	0	0
SOS or Win-Win Settlements with jury results.	++	++

though waiting for a trial might result in an acquittal or a lighter sentence if the defendant were not being held in jail.

Plea bargaining that results in sentences approximating those that might occur from a bench trial or a jury trial can be obtained through a five-part package that includes (1) special funding to the prosecutor to deal with difficult defendants, (2) special services like appellate services enabling a public defender to effectively defend and bargain, (3) a higher rate of pretrial release, with provision for decreasing no-shows and crime-committing, (4) flat sentencing, so both sides know what sentences are likely to be given, and (5) access to data showing probabilities of conviction and average sentences so that both sides are less likely to be fooled into thinking the likely probability or sentence will be substantially higher or lower.

A Simplified SOS Analysis of Plea Bargaining

The analysis in Table 4.3 is simplified in the sense of having only three goals rather than five goals, but also in clarifying the differences between conservative and liberal goals.

Both conservatives and liberals endorse sentencing that is

deserved by the convicted defendant. Conservatives tend to believe more severe sentences are deserved, and liberals tend to believe less severe sentences are deserved. Both would like to see money saved as a result of reducing the number of trials when out-of-court settlements can produce results similar to those of trials.

If overly lenient bargains can be lessened, conservatives would be pleased. Those are the bargains arrived at by defendants who may be able to afford expensive legal counsel and threaten to tie up the prosecutor if a bargain is not struck. If overly severe bargains can be lessened, liberals would be pleased. Those are the bargains that are arrived at by defendants who have no funds for private counsel and possibly no funds for bail. These defendants are thus highly vulnerable to pleading guilty and accepting a sentence although they might not be found guilty if better represented.

The SOS alternative described in Table 4.3 should please conservatives by providing special funding from the state to country prosecutors to deal with defendants who are well-financed. The SOS alternative should please liberals by providing special funding to the public defender to represent defendants, at least on appeal, if the

Table 4.3   (Simple) Plea Bargaining

	GOALS	
ALTERNATIVES	**Conservative** More severe sentences as deserved.	**Liberal** Less severe sentences as deserved.
Conservative Abolish overly lenient bargains.	+	−
Liberal Abolish overly severe bargains.	−	+
Neutral Keep as is.	0	0
SOS or Win-Win Sentences that juries would give.	++	++

public defender feels an innocent person might otherwise be convicted. The liberal position should also welcome a higher rate of pretrial release since being held in jail prior to trial makes defendants especially vulnerable to offers from prosecutors. Both conservatives and liberals should welcome sentencing guidelines and access to prior data. Those procedures enable both sides to predict better how cases will be decided, and thus arrive at plea bargains which better reflect those likely decisions.

Exercising the Right to Trial

The problem on this issue is that defendants who ask for a trial to try to establish their innocence may receive a more severe sentence if they are convicted than if they had pleaded guilty.

The conservative alternative is to keep things as they are in order to aid the prosecutor to be able to get favorable plea bargains and reduced trials.

The liberal alternative seeks to abolish plea bargaining, but that is not feasible for implicit plea bargaining in which defendants plead guilty without negotiating because they anticipate receiving a lighter sentence.

Table 4.4   Penalty for Trial

	GOALS	
ALTERNATIVES	**Conservative** Reduce trials.	**Liberal** No penalty for trial.
Conservative As is.	+	−
Liberal Abolish plea-bargaining.	−	+
Neutral Increase release on recognizance.	0	0
SOS or Win-Win Flat sentencing.	++	++

The neutral alternative is to reduce the worst abuses of plea bargaining, which involve defendants being held in jail prior to trial who will plead guilty to weak charges in order to be released because of the time they have already served in jail or on probation.

Flat sentencing can slightly reduce trials by clarifying the probable sentence without having to go to trial to find out, while at the same time providing no penalty for going to trial.

A SOS Allocation of Cases to Plea Bargains versus Trials

Table 4.5 is designed to supplement the previous table. It provides a super-optimizing perspective on the same problem.

The object of the SOS allocation is to adopt the neutral allocation to plea bargains versus trials, but to achieve even more cost-saving than the conservative allocation, and even more due process than a liberal allocation.

Greater cost-saving can be achieved by reducing the quantity of trials as a result of a reduction in cases filed, rather than an increased allocation to plea bargains or out-of-court settlements. The main proposals of reducing cases filed relate to converting many drug cases from being legal problems into being medical-treatment problems,

Table 4.5   Allocation of Cases

| | GOALS | |
| | Conservative | Liberal |
ALTERNATIVES	Cost saving.	Due process.
Conservative Pleas.	+	−
Liberal Trials.	−	+
Neutral	0	0
SOS or Win-Win See text.	++	++

and converting many automobile accident cases from being litigation disputes into being no-fault insurance problems.

Greater due process can be achieved in plea bargaining by (1) providing adequate resources to prosecutors and public defenders, (2) more pretrial release, (3) access to data on prior cases, and (4) flat sentencing. Trials can provide greater due process or more accurate separation of the innocent from the guilty by providing for (1) right to counsel, (2) right to appeal, and (3) videotaping of testimony for use by judges or juries in reaching decisions.

Chapter 5

The Trial Process

Out-of-Court Settlements in Civil Cases

Resolving Litigation Disputes through Super-Optimum Solutions

The conservative alternative in most civil litigation is for the defendant to win at trial. The defendant is often an insurance company or type of business firm. The liberal alternative is generally for the plaintiff to win at trial. The plaintiff is frequently someone injured in an automobile accident, an on-the-job accident, or an accident involving a consumer product. The neutral alternative is a compromise settlement between what the plaintiff is asking and what the defendant is offering.

The criteria for determining the best alternative include benefits to the defendant, benefits to the plaintiff, costs to the defendant, and costs to the plaintiff. The conservative alternative does well on the conservative totals, with higher weight to the conservative goal. The liberal alternative does well on the liberal totals, with higher weight to the liberal goal.

The object is to develop an alternative whereby both the plaintiff and defendant can come out ahead of their best initial expectations simultaneously. Such an alternative may involve the defendant giving the plaintiff valuable insurance or other products. Those products may be worth a lot to the plaintiff in terms of market prices. They may, however, cost the defendant little if they are products which he or she manufactures or sells.

Table 5.1   Resolving Litigation

| | GOALS | |
ALTERNATIVES	Conservative Benefits to defendant.	Liberal Benefits to plaintiff.
Conservative Defendant wins on trial.	+	−
Liberal Plaintiff wins on trial.	−	+
Neutral Settle.	**0**	**0**
SOS or Win-Win 1. Insurance. 2. Products. 3. Credit unions, etc.	++	++

Whether to Require Mediation

The conservative position is to allow for, or even encourage, voluntary mediation or arbitration in disputes between business firms, labor and management, or government and business, but not make it compulsory. The liberal position tends to endorse mediation more strongly, including compulsory mediation.

Mediation is this context refers to a third party seeking to resolve a dispute between a plaintiff and a defendant by arriving at a compromise settlement without litigation. Arbitration refers to a third party seeking to resolve such a dispute by determining who is right and who is wrong, rather than facilitating a compromise settlement. Adjudication refers to formal litigation, generally with a win-lose solution, regular court personnel, and more formal rules.

Voluntary mediation or arbitration tends to favor the party that is likely to win if the case were to go to court. The dominant party is not likely to agree to a mediation compromise if the dominant party can win on all-or nothing basis. Compulsory mediation is more likely to favor the underdog side or probable loser if the case were to go to court.

Table 5.2 Require Mediation

ALTERNATIVES	GOALS	
	Conservative Dominant party wins (business, landlords, creditors).	**Liberal** Underdog wins (labor, tenants, debtors).
Conservative Free market voluntary.	+	–
Liberal Compulsory mediation.	–	+
Neutral Mediation forced sometimes.	0	0
SOS or Win-Win 1. Insurance. 2. Products. 3. Credit unions, etc.	++	++

The SOS alternative in this situation might be to train lawyers who are involved in negotiating as to how to facilitate win-win dispute resolution or super-optimum solutions, whereby both sides can come out ahead of their best initial expectations simultaneously.

Super-Optimizing Litigation Analysis (Using *Traveler's Insurance v. Sanyo Electronics* as an Illustrative Example)

Table 5.3 illustrates one approach to generating super-optimum solutions. It generates big benefits for one side and low costs for the other. SOS solutions enable plaintiffs, defendants, conservatives, liberals, and other major interests to all come out ahead of their best initial expectations simultaneously. Such solutions are facilitated by spreadsheet-based decision-aiding computer software.

Table 5.3   Sanyo Case

	GOALS	
ALTERNATIVES	**Conservative** Pro defendant (pay as little as possible).	**Liberal** Pro plaintiff (receive as much as possible).
Conservative Defendant's initial offer: $300.	+	−
Liberal Plaintiff's initial demand: $900.	−	+
Neutral Likely compromise settlement: $600.	0	0
SOS or Win-Win 1. Computers from defendant to plaintiff. 2. Big-screen TV sets from defendant to plaintiff. 3. Insurance claims from defendant to plaintiff.	++	++

Super-Optimizing Litigation Analysis
(Using *Ramirez v. Rousonelos* as an Illustrative Examples)

The data in Table 5.4 comes from "Finding a Super-Optimum Solution in a Labor-Management Dispute," in Nagel and Mills, *Multi-Criteria Methods for Alternative Dispute Resolution: With Microcomputer Software Applications* (Quorum Books, 1990).

The plaintiff's initial expectation is to be repaid approximately $1 million in wages. That is a wild expectation since the money was deducted for goods, services, and advances provided to the workers by the employer, but not in accordance with the proper paperwork procedures.

The defendant's initial expectation is to have to pay nothing. That, too, is a wild expectation since the defendant admittedly failed to comply with the proper deduction procedures with no good defense other than that the money was owed. The defendant would thus be likely to lose on the issue of compliance with proper procedures. A

Table 5.4   Ramirez Case

ALTERNATIVES	GOALS	
	Conservative Pro defendant (pay as little as possible).	**Liberal** Pro plaintiff (receive as much as possible).
Conservative Defendant's best expectation: $0.	+	−
Liberal Plaintiff's best expectation: $1,000.	−	+
Neutral Likely compromise settlement: $500.	0	0
SOS or Win-Win 1. Community development credit union, rental housing, and business. 2. Grievance procedure. 3. Payment to plaintiffs. 4. Compliance information.	++	++

penalty is likely to be assessed to deter such improprieties on the part of this defendant and other potential defendants. The penalty is likely to be substantial in order to have deterrent value. There is also likely to be compensation assessed to the defendant, plus considerable litigation cost if the case goes to trial.

The object is to arrive at a super-optimum solution whereby the workers receive more than $1 million and the defendant pays less than nothing.

The key element in the super-optimum solution is the establishment of a credit union funded mainly by $100,000 from the defendant to be deposited with interest for five years.

That $100,000 could quickly generate $2 million worth of housing by serving as a 10 percent down payment on mortgages for existing or new housing units for the workers. The housing might be used as collateral for additional capital. It is also possible that a federal or state government agency would match the $100,000 as part of an economic development plan, thereby further increasing the lending opportunities.

The workers thereby obtain multiple-family housing and a

lending source for business opportunities that may be worth at least $2 million, plus the benefits of an improved grievance procedure, payments to the plaintiffs, and compliance information. The total value is worth more than their wildest expectation.

The employer thereby obtains the benefits of not having to provide housing for the workers, as well as interest on savings and a subsequent return of the principal if requested. The grievance procedures can decrease friction. The compliance information can increase credibility. Payment to the plaintiffs is a cost rather than a benefit, but it is more than offset by the benefits from the other relevant items of value. Therefore the employer is making a net gain as a result of this SOS settlement, which is the same a paying less than nothing.

Determining Liability in Civil Cases

Evaluating Tort Liability Systems

Table 5.5 is especially concerned with the conservative goal of avoiding liability and the liberal goal of compensating the injured. The SOS solution is to concentrate on reducing accidents, rather than on the liability rules.

Table 5.6 is especially concerned with the conservative goal of stimulating innovation in the development of products and the liberal goals of safety and compensation. The SOS solution is to have the government be an insurer on liability for the first three years of new products or allow the common-law defenses during that time.

The first table (5.5) contains more detail on the alternatives. It divides the conservative alternative of difficult liability into contributory negligence and comparative negligence. It also divides the liberal alternative of easy liability into no-fault and no-fault add-on–terms that are defined below.

Table 5.5 also includes the two neutral goals of deterring accidents and being politically feasible. Neutral goals are, however, less important in a simplified SOS table that seeks to bring out

Table 5.5   Tort Liability

ALTERNATIVES	GOALS	
	Conservative 1. Decrease litigation costs. 2. Decrease lawyer fees. 3. Avoid liability.	**Liberal** Injured recover compensation.
Conservative Contributory negligence.	+	−
Liberal Pure no-fault.	−	+
Neutral 1. Comparative negligence. 2. No-fault add-on.	0	0
SOS or Win-Win Reduce accidents by improving cars, roads, and drivers.	++	++

Table 5.6   (Simple) Tort Liability

ALTERNATIVES	GOALS	
	Conservative Avoid liability and lawyers.	**Liberal** Compensate the injured.
Conservative Difficult liability.	+	−
Liberal Easy liability.	−	+
Neutral In between.	0	0
SOS or Win-Win Reduce accidents.	++	++

differences between conservatives and liberals on how to handle the public policy problem.

Allowing the injured person to be able to sue under either no-fault or the common law may be the best approach from the perspective of enabling the injured party to recover compensation. It may also be the best approach from the perspective of encouraging the defendant to take action to reduce accidents that involve on-the-job injuries, defective products, or other injuries by introducing greater safety.

Tort Liability and Simplified SOS Table

Under contributory negligence, the plaintiff collects nothing if the plaintiff has been partly negligent–even less than 10 percent so.

Under comparative negligence, the plaintiff collects only 60 percent of the damages if the plaintiff was 40 percent responsible, and likewise with other percentages of responsibility. In some states, the plaintiff collects nothing if the plaintiff is more than 50 percent responsible.

No-fault liability means that the plaintiff collects even if the plaintiff is more than 90 percent responsible. Such systems are advocated by insurance companies to reduce the need for lawyers and expensive litigation.

No-fault add-on allows the plaintiff in a no-fault state to reject the maximum limits that are generally provided for, and to sue under the old rules of contributory or comparative negligence.

Reducing accidents by improving cars particularly refers to installing airbags to protect drivers. Improving roads refers especially to building more median strips to prevent head-on collisions. Improving drivers refers especially to imposingmore severe penalties for drunk drivers.

Alternatives for Product Liability

Common-law defenses enable manufacturers to escape liability by arguing (1) they did not sell directly to the consumer, (2) contributory negligence by the consumer, (3) a third party is partially responsible, and (4) implicit waiver of the right to sue.

Strict liability means the manufacturer is liable for damages to the consumer if the product injured the consumer, regardless of the above common-law defenses.

Comparative negligence means the consumer collects even if the consumer is partly negligent, as long as the level of responsibility is less than 50 percent.

The SOS alternative given in Table 5.7 provides for strict liability only after three years of marketing, in order to stimulate product innovation and provide a period for eliminating product defects. A better SOS alternative might be to make the government an insurer for the first three years so as to provide better compensation to injured persons while freeing product innovators from liability if they exercise reasonable care.

Table 5.7   Product Liability

	GOALS	
ALTERNATIVES	**Conservative** Stimulate innovation of product.	**Liberal** Safety and compensation.
Conservative Common-law defenses.	+	−
Liberal Strict liability.	−	+
Neutral Common-law defenses with exceptions or comparative negligence.	0	0
SOS or Win-Win Strict liability after three years of marketing.	++	++

Determining Guilt in Criminal Cases

Admissibility of Relevant but Prejudicial Evidence

A concrete example of this issue is whether the jury in the O. J. Simpson case should view the pictures of Nicole Simpson's battered body from a previous beating by her husband. The evidence is relevant to show a previous similar wrongdoing by the defendant. The evidence, however, would be highly prejudicial in possibly causing the jury to consider convicting on the basis of that evidence alone. In 1994, O. J. Simpson was arrested and charged with the murders of his ex-wife, Nicole Brown Simpson, and her friend Ronald Goldman. Simpson pleaded not guilty and was placed on trial by the state of California later that year. The televised trial received an enormous amount of publicity. In 1995, the jury found Simpson not guilty of the charges against him.

Conservatives in the criminal justice process would generally favor admitting such evidence because it leads to convicting the guilty. Liberals would favor rejecting such evidence in order to facilitate acquitting the innocent. A compromise might permit oral testimony without pictures, or allow only some of the pictures.

Table 5.8   Admissibility

	GOALS	
ALTERNATIVES	**Conservative** Convict guilty.	**Liberal** Acquit innocent.
Conservative Admit.	+	−
Liberal Reject.	−	+
Neutral Testimony but not pictures.	0	0
SOS or Win-Win Admit with warnings.	++	++

A super-optimum solution that might help achieve both goals would be to admit or compromise the relevant evidence but require the judge to instruct the jury. The instructions would advise that the evidence not be given great weight because the victim is not available to testify or be cross-examined. A previous wrongdoing by the defendant it would be pointed out, does not necessarily prove guilt in the present instance.

Television in the Courtroom

The issue here is whether the Supreme Court or the Federal Judicial Conference should allow television coverage of trials. Some coverage is now permitted in forty-seven states, but not yet in the federal courts. A three-year experiment is now part of the information available to federal judges in reaching their decision.

Those who favor or oppose television in the courtroom do not necessarily divide into being prosecution-oriented or defense-oriented. Television could help or handicap either side.

The presence of television can help the prosecution by making judges more sensitive to public opinion, which may demand more convictions and harsher sentences. Television can also educate the public about the importance of crime reduction and respect for the legal system.

The presence of television can help the defense by discouraging judges from being abusive toward defendants in criminal cases. It can also educate the public about the purposes of defendants' rights.

Neutral aspects of television include educating the public about how the courts operate. Television can promote democracy by making judges more sensitive to public opinion. That may be particularly desirable in civil cases involving alternative interpretations of economic statues. It may not be so desirable in cases involving constitutional rights or minority rights which should not be subject to majority rule.

Table 5.9   Television in the Courtroom

ALTERNATIVES	GOALS	
	Conservative Decorum.	**Liberal** 1. Free speech. 2. Informed public.
Conservative No television.	+	−
Liberal Television.	−	+
Neutral Civil, but not criminal.	0	0
SOS or Win-Win Decorum television.	++	++

Other than being prosecution-oriented or defense-oriented, the goal of excluding television is to promote traditional decorum in the courtroom. The goal of allowing television is to promote freedom of the press and an informed public.

A compromise proposed for the federal courts is to allow television in civil cases but not in criminal cases. That could be considered an incremental super-optimum solution if it would lead to appropriate television in all cases. It is difficult to get judges to approve public scrutiny of themselves on television. The issue apparently is not salient enough for legislatures to pass laws requiring television in the courtroom.

A super-optimum solution might be to allow television in all cases, but only if the cameras are invisible in the courtroom so as to preserve traditional decorum. That might be done through the use of one-way mirrors or small slits or portholes just big enough for a camera lens to be able to observe the courtroom, but not to be observed in return. Such a solution might be used in all cases, thereby promoting free speech and an informed public without disrupting the proceedings.

The behavior of the judge may change with the presence of television even if the camera is hidden. The judge may improve as a result of being observed, such as staying awake and looking alert. The judge's behavior may, however, worsen as a result of wanting to appear tough in criminal cases. Those two effects may balance out.

Press Coverage of the O. J. Simpson Case

The issue here is how to deal with the press coverage of the O. J. Simpson case. The defense case is damaged more by the press coverage, which tends to make O. J. Simpson appear more guilty than the trial evidence might justify. The prosecution is also concerned about the press coverage because it could be the basis for reversing a conviction.

The conflict on this issue is not so much between the defense and prosecution, or between a liberal and conservative perspective. Instead it is between those who are especially sensitive to obtaining a fair trial that is not prejudiced by press publicity versus those who are especially sensitive to freedom of the press to report on pending and ongoing trials.

Those who emphasize a fair trial want to restrict the press. Those restrictions include keeping most or all of the press out of the pretrial activities, such as jury selection and evidence motions. Restrictions

Table 5.10 Press Coverage

	GOALS	
ALTERNATIVES	**Conservative** Fair trial.	**Liberal** Free press.
Conservative Restrict press.	+	–
Liberal Do not restrict press.	–	+
Neutral Recommendations but not barring the press.	0	0
SOS or Win-Win 1. Sequester. 2. Free press.	++	++

might also include recommendations that the press refrain from reporting on books, articles, or other information that relates to the guilt or innocence of the defendant.

Those who emphasize free press oppose such restrictions. A neutral position might only include recommendations, but not barring the press from any of the proceedings.

A super-optimum solution that can provide for both fair trial and free press simultaneously would involve sequestering the potential jurors and placing no prohibitions on the press being present for any hearings.

Sequestering potential jurors who are rejected as actual jurors would be brief if the jury selection process were accelerated. That might be done by using a more random selection, questioning potential jurors only on any associations with participants in the case. Doing so might require eliminating preemptory challenges, which might, in turn, require amending California law.

Sequestering the actual jurors would not pose a big hardship since the only persons approved to serve on the jury would be those willing to be sequestered. The expense of sequestering would be a small percentage of the total cost of so expensive a trial–and worth the money if sequestering provides a verdict that is capable of being upheld on appeal.

If potential jurors are sequestered, then the newspaper reporting (even if prejudicial) would do no harm since the jurors would have no access to it. The alternative of moving the trial elsewhere in California might not make much difference in terms of the publicity, and doing so might be unfair to the defendant.

This is an unusual case. Usually, adverse local publicity can be handled by moving the case elsewhere in the state. The alternative of trying to find jurors who have read virtually nothing about the case would not generate a representative sample of jurors. The alternative of holding newspapers in contempt of court for reporting on the case would unduly restrict freedom of the press, although it is done in England for pretrial publicity. Newspapers then can report freely after the trial begins and the jury is sequestered, or after the trial is over if the jury is not sequestered.

Right to a Federal Appeal

The issue here is how much right to a federal appeal should be granted to a convicted defendant in a state case or a federal trial. The conservative position is that the right to an appeal has been satisfied by granting the defendant one appeal. That position is oriented toward the goal of preserving rightful convictions and reducing congestion of the courts.

The liberal position is that the right of appeal should be unlimited if new evidence or a new argument is offered. That position is oriented toward the goal of reversing wrongful convictions or sentences.

A neutral position might allow for one appeal, but provide a list of exceptions, especially if capital punishment is involved. Only defendants can appeal under the American constitutional system since a prosecution appeal would generally violate the principle of double jeopardy.

An SOS alternative should reduce appellate congestion, preserve rightful convictions, and facilitate the reversal of wrongful convic-

Table 5.11 Federal Appeal

	GOALS	
ALTERNATIVES	**Conservative** 1. Preserve rightful convictions. 2. Reduce court congestion.	**Liberal** Reverse wrongful convictions or sentences.
Conservative One appeal only.	+	−
Liberal Unlimited if new evidence or argument.	−	+
Neutral One appeal with exceptions.	0	0
SOS or Win-Win Pre-appeal hearings.	++	++

tions or sentences. An appropriate procedure might involve a pre-appeal hearing, analogous to a pretrial hearing at the trial level. Such a hearing before an experienced lawyer is designed to filter out the appeals with little merit and accelerate those with more merit.

Pre-appeal hearings can result in settlement of disputed matters without going to an appeal, just as pretrial hearings often result in a settlement without going to trial. A pre-appeal hearing can result in a narrowing of the issues so as to shorten the appeal process. It can also clarify for the defendant why an appeal is likely to be unsuccessful. Doing so can help make the trial court decision more acceptable.

Delay in the Courts

Evaluating Policies to Reduce Delays in Courts

Diverting personal-injury cases refers to instituting a no-fault system in which automobile accident cases can be resolved more easily through insurance companies than through litigation.

Table 5.12 Delay Reduction

	GOALS	
ALTERNATIVES	**Conservative**	**Liberal** Due process.
Conservative Less processing time.	+	−
Liberal Hiring more judges.	−	+
Neutral More settlements.	0	0
SOS or Win-Win 1. Divert personal injury cases. 2. Drug medicalization. 3. Use management science.	++	++

Drug medicalization refers to attempts to reduce the illegal drug market by treating drug addicts as medical patients with free treatment on demand. This might substantially reduce the caseload of criminal cases.

The use of management science refers to such techniques as having a special procedure for shorter cases, or docketing all civil cases in the order of their predicted trial times with the shortest cases heard first. The system also has to provide a maximum waiting time for longer cases.

Evaluating the "Loser Pays" Rule

The conservative position is that the loser in a court case should pay the litigation costs of the winner, regardless of whether the loser is the plaintiff or the defendant. Actually, a defendant-loser generally does cover the winner's litigation costs because the plaintiff's lawyer takes a portion of the damages collected.

Under the prevailing system, each side pays its own litigation costs. This is supported by liberals who do not want to see worthy plaintiffs discouraged from suing for fear they will not only lose, but

Table 5.13 Loser Pays

	GOALS	
ALTERNATIVES	Conservative Discourage damage suits.	Liberal Facilitate collecting proper damages.
Conservative Loser pays.	+	−
Liberal Each side pays own costs.	−	+
Neutral Loser pays half of winner costs.	0	0
SOS or Win-Win Loser does not pay unless unreasonable.	++	++

also go into debt for the defendant's costs.

A neutral position might involve the loser paying one-half of the winner's costs as a compromise between paying all of them or nothing.

The SOS position might be that the loser does not pay. That facilitates injured persons collecting the money to which they are entitled. An exception would occur when the loser has acted unreasonably. One test of unreasonableness would be whether the loser's case is so weak that the matter was decided at the pleadings before testimony was taken, or before the testimony was completed.

Special Issues

Whether Negligence Charges Should Be Made Public

The issue here is that defendant companies in damage cases may be reluctant to pay damages as part of a settlement because of the adverse publicity. Instead, they may prefer to go to trial hoping that no liability will be found.

The conservative position is to keep the negligence charges confidential so as to facilitate settlements and protect business interests. The liberal position is to allow the charges to be accessible to future plaintiffs in order to deter injuries.

The compromise position would be to make the charges accessible whenever public safety or health might be threatened. The charges would not be accessible if the damage suit involves libel or slander of a person rather than a product or some other matter unrelated to safety.

The SOS alternative involves trying to decrease the occurrence of injuries due to negligence of safety or health matters. One way is to require the defendant to prepare a health and safety report indicating how the situation will be remedied for the future. This can also apply in damage situations involving no-fault liability. Another aspect of the SOS alternative might be to provide government grants or tax credits designed to improve the health and safety or products.

Table 5.14 Negligence and the Public

ALTERNATIVES	GOALS	
	Conservative Facilitate settlement or non-litigation.	**Liberal** Decrease injuries.
Conservative Keep negligence charges confidential.	+	–
Liberal Allow negligence charges to be accessible.	–	+
Neutral Some charges public if public safety or health threatened.	0	0
SOS or Win-Win 1. Health and safety report. 2. Grants to improve health and safety of product.	++	++

Such an SOS alternative helps achieve the conservative goal of avoiding litigation, while at the same time achieving the liberal goal of decreasing injuries.

Medical Malpractice

Conservatives want to keep damages low in medical malpractice cases, partly to preserve profits which they see as stimulating entry into the profession.

Liberals advocate higher damages in order to provide adequate compensation and punishment for wrongdoing. A compromise position would be to encourage more out-of-court settlements–an idea advocated by President Clinton.

Table 5.15 Medical Malpractice

	GOALS	
	Conservative Doctor profits high.	**Liberal** Compensation and pun- ishment for wrongdoing.
ALTERNATIVES		
Conservative Damages low.	+	−
Liberal Damages high.	−	+
Neutral Damages middling.	0	0
SOS or Win-Win Improve procedures and doctors.	++	++

An SOS alternative might involve suggesting ideas to decrease negligence and injured patients. Doing so would mean no damages imposed for those cases in which there is no negligence or injury. That should please liberals who presumably would rather see no wrongdoing than compensation and punishment.

Decreasing negligence and injury might require research on improving the medical procedures in which negligence and injury are most likely. It may also be necessary to improve the skills of doctors through better training and continuing medical education, especially in the specialities in which malpractice is more prevalent.

Only a small percentage of doctors are responsible for a high percentage of malpractice actions. That suggests that their licenses should be removed or they should pay higher insurance premiums. The punishments approach, however, may deter doctors from being willing to operate or medicate in risky situations. For further material on medical malpractice and related topics, see Milton Fisk, *Toward a Healthy Society: The Morality and Politics of American Health Care Reform* (University Press of Kansas, 2000), and Walter Olson (ed.), *New Directions in Liability Law* (Academy of Political Science, 1988).

Other reforms might include (1) requiring malpractice insurance,

(2) publicizing malpractice records of doctors, (3) opening disciplinary proceedings to the public, and (4) appointing medical-care consumers to disciplinary boards along with doctors. Those ideas are, however, less likely to please both conservatives and liberals than improving medical technology and skills so as to reduce malpractice. The funding for such improvements might come from a tax on doctors or a percentage of higher license fees.

Chapter 6

Criminal Sentences and Civil Damages

Criminal Sentences

Evaluating Policies toward Sentencing

The conservative alternative of long to middling sentences wins with the conservative weights, before introducing the SOS alternative. The liberal alternative of short to middling sentences wins with the liberal weights, before introducing the SOS alternative. The SOS alternative emphasizing sentencing guidelines wins on either the liberal or the conservative weights.

Sentencing guidelines refer to tables that indicate the sentence appropriate to the severity of the crime and of the defendant's prior criminal record.

Table 6.1   Sentencing

	GOALS	
ALTERNATIVES	Conservative Deterrence.	Liberal Equity.
Conservative Long sentences.	+	−
Liberal Short sentences.	−	+
Neutral Middling sentences.	0	0
SOS or Win-Win Sentencing guidelines.	++	++

Such guidelines appeal to liberals because they provide for greater equality across demographic groups and do not penalize for exercising one's right to trial.

Such guidelines appeal to conservatives because they are usually based upon determining the average past sentence for a given severity and prior record, with about 10 percent sentencing time added in order to get conservative legislators to adopt such guidelines.

Validity versus Ethics in Experimental Social Science

The concrete example here is to try to determine experimentally the effects of being incarcerated (versus being granted probation) on the probability of repeating one's crime.

Paid incarceration (rather than randomly forced incarceration) is needed to meet the ethical problems, but doing so can interfere with the meaningfulness of the experiment.

To offset the bias that has been introduced by paying those who consent to incarceration over probation, one needs to statistically adjust for differences in the demographic and attitudinal characteristics between the two groups.

Table 6.2   Validity versus Ethics

	GOALS	
ALTERNATIVES	**Conservative** Validity.	**Liberal** Ethics.
Conservative Random.	+	−
Liberal Do not conduct.	−	+
Neutral Compromise.	0	0
SOS or Win-Win Paid incarceration.	++	++

One also has to observe a lag in recidivism, since repetition of one's crime may be delayed as a result of funds available to those incarcerated.

Evaluating Intermediate Sanctions

Intermediate sanctions refer to new forms of sentencing that may subject a convicted person to a long or intensive relation with corrections personnel, short of a prison term. Examples include (1) electronic monitoring through a device worn by the convicted offender, (2) home detention, (3) intensive supervised probation, (4) payment of fines over a long period, (5) community-based corrections with numerous weekends spent in jail, and (6) shock incarceration or boot-camp confinement. The third and sixth approaches may not involve a long period of time, but they do involve more intensive control than traditional probation or jail time.

Conservatives traditionally favor long sentences to achieve the goal of deterring wrongdoing by others, as well as the person convicted. Liberals traditionally favor shorter sentences to facilitate rehabilitation into the community. A relatively neutral goal is to try to save tax money while reducing neither deterrence nor rehabilitation.

Table 6.3   Intermediate Sanctions

	GOALS	
ALTERNATIVES	**Conservative** Deterrence.	**Liberal** Rehabilitation.
Conservative Long sentences.	+	–
Liberal Short sentences.	–	+
Neutral In between.	0	0
SOS or Win-Win Long, but not in prison.	++	++

The so-called intermediate sanctions may have considerable deterrent effect because of their length of intensiveness. Likewise, they may have more rehabilitation potential by being more community-based than middling sentences. They may save more money than traditional sentencing.

This analysis of sentencing differs from that in which the conflicting goals are deterrence versus equity. That analysis leads to an SOS of objective guidelines with higher than average sentences. Here the conflicting goals are deterrence versus rehabilitation. This analysis leads to SOS sanctions that are long or intensive, but not in prison where expense is high and rehabilitation is low.

The Insanity Defense

The defense of insanity, if accepted, allows a defendant to avoid conviction by arguing that he or she was not mentally responsible for what otherwise would have been a crime.

The conservative position is to define insanity narrowly so as to facilitate convicting guilty defendant, then impose sentences which will deter others from committing similar crimes. The conservative definition of insanity emphasizes not knowing right from wrong at the time the crime was committed.

The liberal position is to define insanity broadly so as to facilitate acquitting mentally innocent defendants. They would then be returned to the community if temporary insanity were involved, or hospitalized if the insanity were continuing. The liberal definition of insanity emphasizes psychiatric disturbances, more than knowing right from wrong.

The neutral or compromise position is to go beyond knowing right from wrong into concepts such as irresistible impulse, while avoiding concepts that relate to psychiatric disturbances.

An SOS alternative might be to consider no insanity defense in determining whether the defendant did otherwise commit the crime. The insanity or psychiatric problems of the defendant would then only come up in determining what punishment or treatment to impose. The punishment or treatment would consider both deterrence

Table 6.4   Insanity Defense

ALTERNATIVES	GOALS	
	Conservative 1. Convict the guilty. 2. Deter.	Liberal 1. Acquit the innocent. 2. Rehabilitate.
Conservative Narrow defense.	+	−
Liberal Broad defense.	−	+
Neutral Middling defense.	0	0
SOS or Win-Win Relevant to sentencing not guilt.	++	++

to others and rehabilitation of the defendant.

Such an SOS alternative increases the likelihood of both convicting the guilty and acquitting the innocent by eliminating the subjectivity of the concept of insanity. The SOS alternative also can combine deterrence and rehabilitation in the sentencing by explicitly including the relevance of the insanity defense in these objectives.

Capital Punishment

Evaluating Capital Punishment

The first two goals are especially important. Conservatives emphasize the need to decrease murder and other crimes. Liberals emphasize the need to separate out the innocent and decrease executions.

There is only a small correlation, if any, between conducting capital punishment and decreasing murder or other crimes. There is a greater correlation, of course, between banning capital punishment and avoiding executions, including those of innocent defendants. For correlation between conducting capital punishment and decreasing murder or other crimes, see Samuel Walker, *Sense and Nonsense about Crime: A Policy Guide* (Brooks/Cole, 1989), 96-104.

Not allowing capital punishment saves the cost of expensive appeals and eliminates an especially undesirable form of discrimination. Allowing capital punishment scores well as an anti-murder symbol, which helps explain conservative support for it. Capital punishment involves multiple forms of discrimination. It discriminates against the poor who are more likely to be executed if one compares defendants who have court-appointed lawyers with defendants who are sentenced to die who hire their own lawyers. Likewise, blacks sentenced to die are more likely to be executed than whites sentenced to die. Males sentenced to die are more likely to be executed than females sentenced to die. Defendants who kill white victims are especially more likely to be executed than defendants who kill black victims. These statistics are given in *McClesky v. George,*

Table 6.5   Capital Punishment

	GOALS	
ALTERNATIVES	**Conservative** 1. Decrease crime and murder. 2. Anti-murder symbol.	**Liberal** 1. Separate innocent and decrease executions. 2. Decrease discrimination of poor and blacks.
Conservative Capital punishment for all murders.	+	−
Liberal No capital punishment.	−	+
Neutral Capital punishment with special murders and procedures.	0	0
SOS or Win-Win Decrease murder by gun control, drug medicalization, socialization.	++	++

107 Supreme Court Reports 1756, 1987, and Gregory Russell, *The Death Penalty and Racial Bias* (Greenwood, 1994).

Neutral positions on capital punishment allow it for special murders such as the killing of police officers or mass murder. Neutral positions may also allow it under special procedures such as a jury recommendation, automatic appeal, or specially qualified jurors.

The SOS alternative is to concentrate on greatly reducing murders through better gun control, drug treatment, and childhood socialization which encourages a negative attitude toward violence.

The Death Penalty Moratorium

Abolishing the death penalty outright is not so easy to do. Once there is a moratorium, however, the death penalty is unlikely to be restored.

Changing Reasoning

The moratorium is not arguing that the death penalty is cruel and unusual punishment. That argument does not appeal to people who like the cruelty. The moratorium people instead are arguing that the death penalty is being frequently imposed on innocent people. It is hard for the pro-cruelty people to argue that cruelty is good for innocent people. They also recognize it makes the death penalty look bad when applied to innocent people. The proof of innocence is a relatively new technological development, based largely on DNA testing.

The moratorium people are appealing to conservatives by arguing what a burden to the taxpayer it is to have to support death row arrangements, which may easily run up to $100,000 per year and go on indefinitely when all costs are figured in with regard to appeals. This runs contrary to the notion that the death penalty saves money.

The racist aspects of the death penalty are also getting some attention. A generation ago when racism was so prevalent, the fact that the death penalty was disproportionately applied to black murderers rather than white murderers would have meant less. Now racism is recognized as something to be ashamed of, especially when it can be so easily statistically established.

The argument is also being made that the death penalty is blatantly discriminatory on the basis of money.

The right to life people formerly tended to support capital punishment while opposing abortion. The apparent inconsistency was resolved by saying that fetuses were innocent, but murderers were not innocent. Now that some or many alleged murderers are being found (by DNA or other evidence) to have been wrongly convicted, the anti-abortion people, such as Pat Robertson are expressing a new negative reaction toward the death penalty.

Governors and Presidents

All those elements are working favorably to lead to moratoriums, as indicated by the moderately conservative Republican governor coming out in favor of a moratorium and being supported by both Democrats and Republicans in the legislature.

Also, one of the reasons that George W. Bush seems to be hypocritical with regard to his compassionate conservatism is that while governor, his state has executed more people, or close to it, than the other forty-nine states together with the possible exception of his brother's in Florida. He has even implied that he does not care if any of those people were innocent so long as they were executed before innocence could be proven. McCain, Gore, and Bradley are all less favorable toward the death penalty than George W. Bush. The important thing here is that George W. Bush's positive attitude toward the death penalty may be costing him votes when he thought the opposite was true. Times have indeed changed.

Attitudes toward and by Americans

The death penalty does not affect many people directly, but it indirectly affects the world's thinking toward the United States. It makes the United States look like a barbaric country, being the only industrial country so attached to the death penalty. This is not good for promoting American values of free speech, due process, free trade, or anything else. How can we argue for the sanctity of life when the United States may now be executing more people than all the rest of the world put together? The death penalty has been abolished in South Africa and all of Western Europe, and it is greatly lessening in Eastern Europe.

Likewise, the death penalty may affect other attitudes by Americans. The death penalty cheapens the value of life. Capital punishment is now opposed by the Catholic church to be consistent with opposing abortion. It is opposed by virtually all religions. By cheapening the value of life, we can thereby more easily tolerate genocide in Africa, Asia, Latin America, or wherever it occurs. It is a bad symbol on American thinking even if it only directly affects a few hundred executed people. It affects additional Americans indirectly by causing them to rationalize the deliberate killing of people by the government. This also fits with the fact that the U.S. has more hand gun killings than all the rest of the world combined. The two go together. They indicate a society in which killing is accepted by both hand guns and by lethal injections.

Causes and Possible Solutions

The explanation for the U.S. death penalty sometimes is historical in that it is part of our frontier mentality. That seems like nonsense. The frontier ended over 100 years ago. The explanation seems more likely that the U.S. has far more crime, especially drug-related crime, than all of Western Europe and industrialized countries. The presence of drug-related crime as a result of so badly handling the drug prohibition causes people to live in fear of being crime victims, and it is a reasonably accurate fear. They therefore endorse carrying guns to shoot armed robbers, and they endorse executing armed robbers.

The possible solution is to reduce the fear of being a crime victim by reducing the millions of people who are predators in order to get money for their drug habits. They should be treated as sick people who are in need of phase-out prescriptions instead of encouraging them to rob and kill in order to buy illegal drugs in the illegal drug market.

The Supreme Court is not likely to declare moratorium on the death penalty. That is a matter of the discretion of Congress, the president, state governors, and state legislators. The Supreme Court can only declare capital punishment constitutional or unconstitutional. It has refused to do so on the grounds that capital punishment violates the cruel and unusual punishment clause, even though such punishment seems to be cruel revenge rather than any meaningful deterrence, and it is highly unusual in an arbitrary way. The Supreme Court has also refused to find that capital punishment violates the equal protection clause, even though it seems to be highly discriminatory in terms of being especially applied when there is a white rather than a black victim. The moratorium approach seems to be the best way to bring an end to what many consider to be a form of medieval barbarism. The moratorium approach may, however, need to be stimulated by further reductions in crime, especially drug-related robberies and murders which are now the main kind of robberies and murders.

Broader Significance

The broader significance of this dramatic change in public policy includes the following:

1. Technological changes can bring policy changes, such as the development of DNA analysis.
2. Even such emotional values (such as those that relate to abortion) are subject to change when the facts sufficiently change.
3. It is easier to suspend a bad policy than to repeal it, although the effect may be the same.
4. Republicans can get away with being soft on crime easier than Democrats can. Just as Nixon could get away with being soft on Red China, or Reagan could get away with being soft on the Soviet Union. This is an important benefit that conservatives perform in bringing about changes in conservative policies.
5. Liberals are also capable of bringing about related changes by deciding that a relatively conservative approach may make more sense than the former liberal approach. This is so in the welfare field regarding welfare handouts rather than work facilitators and regarding concentrated public housing rather than housing vouchers.

It could also work regarding the illegal drug problem which is responsible for so many undesirable side effects repressing illegal drugs through police tactics rather than through medicalization. Those side effects include (1) corrupting the police, (2) corrupting the governments of developing nations in Latin America and Asia, (3) overburdening prisons, courts, police, and the taxpayer, (4) pauperizing the inner city by failing to deal effectively with the drug problem, and (5) being a big factor in the spread of AIDS through needle drugs. Some conservatives like William Buckley and Milton Friedman have advocated allowing phase-out cocaine prescriptions under medicaid, HMO insurance, or a fee-for-service doctor. That kind of medicalization could be a win-win for ending the drug cartels, gangs, and dealers, which conservatives especially oppose, and for ending the undesirable side effects which liberals especially oppose. There is, however, the political feasibility hurdle, which conservatives are better at overcoming than liberals like the capital punishment moratorium.

Postscript

One of the effects of the moratorium is the proposal of a new federal statute called "The Innocence Protection Act of 2000." The Act requires (1) competent counsel at every stage to defend those accused of capital crimes and improve respect for the legal system, (2) the use of DNA and other new technologies that can confirm or refute guilt or innocence, (3) requiring juries to be informed of the option of sentencing a capital defendant to life without parole, (4) compensation for those who have been wrongly convicted for capital crimes, and (5) annual reports from the Justice Department on the administration of capital punishment. This statute is a compromise between having a federal moratorium and continuing past execution procedures, although some of the provisions like counsel and DNA could be endorsed by both conservatives and liberals. A moratorium is a compromise between abolishing the death penalty and continuing those past procedures. Drastically decreasing drug-related capital crimes by medicalizing the drug problem might be a win-win solution by reducing both capital punishment and capital crimes.

Qualifications for Jurors in Capital Cases

The issue here is what special qualifications, if any, should jurors possess order to serve on cases in which the prosecutor is asking for the death penalty.

The conservative position is that all such jurors must indicate they are willing to invoke the death penalty if the circumstances merit it. Allowing that requirement facilitates capital punishment, and it may facilitate convicting the guilty.

The liberal position is that there should be no such qualification because that would bias the jury in favor of capital punishment and possibly in favor of convicting even an innocent person. Such a jury would also be unrepresentative of the general population.

The Supreme Court's position is somewhat neutral because the court has held that anybody who would automatically refuse to invoke the death penalty, regardless of the circumstances, can be excluded from the jury.

Table 6.6   Jurors in Capital Cases

	GOALS	
ALTERNATIVES	**Conservative** Convict guilty and facilitate capital punishment.	**Liberal** Acquit innocent and decrease capital punishment.
Conservative Favor death qualified jury.	+	−
Liberal Oppose death qualified jury.	−	+
Neutral Allow, but exclude automatics.	0	0
SOS or Win-Win One jury for guilty, one jury for sentence.	++	++

An SOS alternative might be to impanel two juries at the start of each capital case. One jury would decide only whether the defendant is guilty or innocent. That jury would be a roughly random sample of the general population and might include some people opposed to the death penalty. The second jury would decide only the sentence if there were a conviction. Members of the second jury would all be willing to invoke capital punishment if and only if the circumstances in this particular case merited it.

That kind of SOS alternative provides for a representative jury to decide guilt and innocence, rather than a potentially conviction-prone jury if all jurors are willing to invoke capital punishment. That part should please liberals.

The SOS alternative simultaneously provides for a jury that is willing to grant the death penalty depending on the circumstances. That part should please conservatives.

Having only one jury might antagonize liberals if the jury is conviction-prone and antagonize conservatives if it includes members opposed to capital punishment.

Another SOS alternative might be to have one jury that is a cross section, but let it decide the sentencing matter by majority vote even though it decides guilt unanimously. A majority vote would allow jurors to participate in the sentencing decision who are opposed to capital punishment. Still another SOS alternative might be to have one jury, but for it to decide only the guilt question, leaving the judge to decide the sentence. Either of the latter two SOS alternatives might be rejected as not preserving jury unanimity, or as not giving the jury sufficient participation in capital decisions.

Civil Damages:
A SOS Approach to Punitive Damages

The SOS in general seeks to (1) remove potential wrongdoers, (2) decrease the possibility of serious injury if wrongdoing occurs, (3) use the government as an insurer if serious injury occurs and society is reluctant to discourage entrepreneurial risk-taking.

Table 6.7   Punitive Damages

	GOALS	
ALTERNATIVES	**Conservative** Facilitate business risk-taking.	**Liberal** Deter business wrongdoing.
Conservative No punitive damages.	+	–
Liberal Unrestrained punitive damages.	–	+
Neutral Conditional punitive damages.	0	0
SOS or Win-Win Remove causes of punitive damages.	++	++

The government could serve as an insurer on liability for new products to facilitate business risk-taking, while at the same time guaranteeing compensation for injuries.

In automobile accident cases, the great need is to reduce injuries in or at least accidents. That might call for more median strips, required air bags, and removal of licenses for drunk drivers.

Corrections and Prisons

Prison Labor and the Minimum Wage

The issue here is whether or not to pay the minimum wage to prisoners in federal prisons.

In Table 6.8 liberals advocate paying prison labor the minimum wage. Conservatives advocate paying below the minimum wage like $1.00/hour or maybe virtually nothing. The neutral position is somewhere between the minimum wage and virtually nothing, or about $3.00/hour.

Table 6.8   Prison Labor

ALTERNATIVES	GOALS	
	Conservative 1. Reduce costs. 2. Increase deterrence.	**Liberal** Rehabilitation.
Conservative $1.00 an hour.	+	−
Liberal Minimum wage.	−	+
Neutral $3.00 an hour.	0	0
SOS or Win-Win Produce profitable products.	++	++

The conservative position is to pay as little as possible in order to keep prisons costs down and provide unappealing conditions to increase deterrence. The liberal position is to pay the minimum wage in order to provide better rehabilitation. Liberals also support broad coverage of the minimum wage so as not to depress the wages of non-prison workers. A compromise may lie somewhere between paying nothing and paying the minimum wage.

A super-optimum solution that would score well on both the conservative and liberal goals would be to put more emphasis on producing profitable products in prison. If the products were more profitable, the income generated could cover the minimum wage with money left over to further reduce costs. Producing profitable products also might enable prisoners to learn skills more useful in obtaining jobs outside prison.

Prison labor does potentially compete with non-prison labor, just as does the labor of developing nations or other countries. In both situations, the solution is not to repress efficient competing labor. Instead, public policy can upgrade the skills and technologies of American workers to better participate in whatever goods are being produced. The other workers who are viewed as competition might also be viewed as better customers if earning higher incomes. They might also be viewed as better suppliers of products to the American workers who are also consumers.

One might also view prison labor as analogous to increasing the productivity of the elderly, the disabled, mothers of preschool children, and other segments of the population who could add to the Gross National Product (GNP) and international competitiveness more so than they do.

Community Notification of Released Defendants

Community notification refers to notifying the police, school authorities, and others that a released convict is moving into the community, especially a sex offender.

The conservative position advocates notification in order to prevent repeat crimes. The liberal position opposes notification in order to facilitate rehabilitation.

A neutral position taken by the courts is to require registration with the police, but no notification of others. The requirement of notification can be included in the original sentence, so as to avoid the appearance of subsequent punishment.

Table 6.9   Community Notification

| | GOALS | |
ALTERNATIVES	Conservative Prevent repeat crimes.	Liberal Facilitate rehabilitation.
Conservative Notification.	+	−
Liberal No notification.	−	+

Neutral
1. Registration but not no-
   tification.
2. Put notification in sen-
   tence.
	0	0

SOS or Win-Win Conditional notification.	++	++

Conditional notification means the notification requirement is included at the time of sentencing, possibly applying only to registration with the police. The notification is only invoked, however, if the parole board, pardon board, or other relevant agency decides at the time of release that the defendant poses sufficient danger to merit the notification.

That SOS arrangement may help prevent repeat crimes if the defendant is a danger. It also may help facilitate rehabilitation if the defendant is not a danger. If the defendant commits no crimes for two years, then the notification could be withdrawn.

Section B

Legal System Personnel

Chapter 7

Right to Counsel

Alternative Ways of Providing Counsel to the Poor

Right-to-Counsel Matrix

The alternatives have the following meanings:

1. No right to free counsel for indigent defendants, only hired counsel, prior to 1932.
2. Right to free counsel in capital cases only, as of 1932.
3. Right to free counsel in capital and felony cases, as of 1963.
4. Right to free counsel in capital, felony, and misdemeanor cases, as of 1972.
5. Right to counsel in all three levels of cases and also pretrial and post-trial as of 1963, 1966, and 1972.

These dates represent years when the Supreme Court handed down landmark cases dealing with right to counsel. 1932 was the year of the Scottsboro case, 1963 was *Gideon v. Wainwright*, 1972 was the year of the Argersinger case. Those three cases established the rights mentioned in points 2, 3, and 4.

The criteria have the following meanings:

1. Acquit the innocent.
2. Convict the guilty.
3. Decrease governmental expense.

4. Increase respect for the legal system.
5. Facilitate adversary truth-finding.

The relations are scored on a ranking system of 1 to 5. Thus, no right to counsel ranks lowest on acquitting the innocent, and comprehensive right to counsel ranks highest, with the opposite rankings on convicting the guilty.

With those alternatives, criteria, and relations, comprehensive right to counsel is the winning alternative with the highest summation score, provided that the goals are given equal weight.

Any alternative involving less then comprehensive right to counsel could be the winner if enough extra weight were given to convicting the guilty and decreasing the expenses, while the other three goals are held at weights of 1.

The reason why comprehensive right to counsel was not adopted immediately is because the Supreme Court also sets a criterion that could be called "decrease deviation from the prevailing law." As of 1930, Alternative 5 would have a highly negative score on that goal,

Table 7.1   Right to Counsel

	GOALS	
ALTERNATIVES	**Conservative** 1. Convict. 2. Expense. 3. Respect. 4. Adversary.	**Liberal** Acquit.
Conservative 1. No right to counsel. 2. Capital cases.	+	−
Liberal 1. Capital, felony, and misdemeanor. 2. Appeals and pretrials.	−	+
Neutral Capital and felony.	0	0
SOS or Win-Win See text.	++	++

but not as of 1965 in view of the intervening changes in the law. 1930 was the pre-Scottsboro time when there was only right to hired counsel, not court-appointed counsel for indigents. 1965 was subsequent to the Gideon case when the court declared a right to court-appointed counsel in all felony cases. The prevailing law in 1930 was no right to counsel. The prevailing law in 1965 was a well developed right to counsel, although it was further developed in 1972 to apply to misdemeanors.

Legal Counsel for the Poor

Alternative ways of providing legal counsel for the poor include:

1. Volunteer attorneys, favored by the Clinton administration.
2. Salaried government attorneys, favored by Congress.
3. A compromise that involves continuing the salaried system, but requiring that 10 percent of its funding go to making volunteers more accessible and competent.

Table 7.2   Counsel for the Poor

	GOALS	
ALTERNATIVES	**Conservative** Inexpensiveness.	**Liberal** Accessibility.
Conservative 1. Volunteer. 2. Salaried. 3. Compromise.	+	−
Liberal 1. Volunteer. 2. Salaried. 3. Compromise.	−	+
Neutral	0	0
SOS or Win-Win See text.	++	++

The criteria are inexpensiveness, accessibility, political feasibility, and competence. Each alternative is scored on each criterion on a scale of 1 to 2.

Conservative values involve giving a weight of 2 to inexpensiveness and political feasibility when the other criteria receive a weight of 1. Liberal values involve giving a weight of 2 to accessibility and competence when the other criteria receive a weight of 1.

With conservative values, the volunteer system wins over the salaried system, 10 points to 8. The compromise is an overall winner with 11½ points.

The "10 percent compromise" is thus a super-winner–better than the original best solution of both the conservatives and the liberals.

Evaluating Policies for the Right to Counsel

The SOS alternative refers to having a base of salaried government lawyers but with many volunteers, possibly under a mandatory *pro bono* rule that may someday be adopted by the American Bar Association.

Using the volunteers more effectively requires clearinghouse activities to determine their times of availability, their specialties, the clients who need their help, and then to schedule appointments at the regular legal aid offices.

Volunteers also need to be trained in the special problems facing poor people as tenants, consumers, family members, welfare recipients, and in other roles.

Mandatory *Pro Bono* Legal Work

Lawyers fall into two major groups on the issue of whether they should be required to work a certain number of hours per year on behalf of charities, legal aid, or non-commercial public-interest organizations. One group wants no requirement, mainly arguing free choice for lawyers. The second group wants a requirement of about twenty hours per year to maintain one's license. The compromise

Table 7.3 Right to Counsel

ALTERNATIVES	GOALS	
	Conservative Politically feasible.	Liberal 1. Accessible to the poor. 2. Competent attorneys.
Conservative No free counsel or only volunteers.	+	−
Liberal Salaried government lawyers.	−	+
Neutral 1. Reimbursed judicare. 2. Salaried criminal. 3. Volunteer civil.	0	0
SOS or Win-Win 1. Salaried base. 2. Clearinghouse. 3. Training program.	++	++

Table 7.4 (Simple) Mandatory *Pro Bono* Work

ALTERNATIVES	GOALS	
	Conservative Free choice.	Liberal Legal services for charities.
Conservative Zero hours.	+	−
Liberal 20 hours.	−	+
Neutral 10 hours.	0	0
SOS or Win-Win Required reporting.	++	++

position would be about ten hours.

The Florida Bar Association has instituted a reporting requirement which may be an SOS solution. Lawyers are not required to serve any hours, but twenty hours is recommended. The reporting requirement does give free choice to put in no hours. At the same time, it may encourage lawyers to put in even more than twenty hours, in order to have something to report and thereby avoid embarrassment.

The Florida rule also goes beyond free choice by allowing lawyers to donate $350 to a legal aid program, rather than put in the recommended twenty hours. Likewise, if a lawyer is a member of a firm of X number of lawyers, the twenty-hour recommendation can be satisfied by the firm contributing twenty-times-X hours, even if all the hours come from one member of the firm. The result would be both increased free choice and increased legal services for charities, in comparison to a compromise of a required ten hours for all lawyers.

This is a good example of an SOS solution because it does better on both conservative and liberal goals than the neutral compromise. It is thus able to outscore the conservative alternative on the conservative totals, and simultaneously outscore the liberal alternative on the liberal totals.

Encouraging Volunteers to Provide Counsel

Alternative Policies toward Mandatory
Public Interest Work by Lawyers

The SOS package involves five elements:

1. Increase the benefits of mandatory *pro bono* work by offering above-cost subsidies to the bar associations and providing them with favorable publicity.
2. Decrease the costs by covering the coordination expenses and by allowing conservative cases to be counted.

Table 7.5   Mandatory Public Interest Work

ALTERNATIVES	GOALS	
	Conservative Conservative causes.	Liberal Increase representation.
Conservative Not mandatory, 0 hours.	+	−
Liberal Mandatory, 40 hours.	−	+
Neutral Partly, 20 hours.	0	0
SOS or Win-Win Package. See text.	++	++

3. Increase the costs to non-compliers by threatening loss of one's license.

4. Decrease the benefits to non-compliers by welcoming the overcrowded bar which gives lawyers free time to take on cases of the poor. Overcrowded bar refers to having more members of the lawyer profession than there are business and individual customers.

5. Provide a good monitoring system so the benefits and costs can be better allocated.

Chapter 8

Society-Attorney-Client Relations

Relations between Society and Attorneys

Comparing the Adversary and Inquisitorial Systems

The traditional adversary system is undesirable because it tends to be unbalanced in favor of the side that is represented by counsel, which is the prosecutor in criminal cases and business interests in civil cases.

The inquisitorial system is undesirable because it is unbalanced

Table 8.1   Adversary and Inquisitorial Systems

	GOALS	
	Conservative 1. Increase class interest. 2. Increase national inter- est. 3. Decrease taxpayer cost.	Liberal 1. Decrease inequality. 2. Decrease arbitrariness.
ALTERNATIVES		
Conservative Adversary system.	+	−
Liberal Inquisitorial system.	−	+
Neutral Modified adversary sys- tem.	0	0
SOS or Win-Win See text.	++	++

131

in favor of arbitrary judicial decision-making without the checks and balances of adversary lawyers.

The most desirable system may be a modified adversary system with the following adjustments:

1. Right to free counsel for the poor in both criminal and civil cases.
2. Encouragement of out-of-court settlements in both criminal and civil cases in which both sides come out ahead.
3. Special tribunals for determining truth in technical, fact-finding matters.

Evaluating the Inquisitorial and Adversarial Judicial Systems

The traditional adversary system involves a hands-off approach by the government. The SOS alternative improves on the system by providing court-appointed counsel to the poor. Doing so provides more balanced competition between the plaintiff and the defendant in seeking a favorable decision from the judge.

Table 8.2   New Adversarial System

| | GOALS | |
ALTERNATIVES	**Conservative** Favor those with money.	**Liberal** Separate innocent from guilty or liable.
Conservative Pre-1960 adversarial.	+	−
Liberal Inquisitorial or paternal-istic.	−	+
Neutral Some of both.	0	0
SOS or Win-Win 1. Free counsel. 2. Encourage settlement.	++	++

The traditional adversary system emphasizes that one side wins and the other side loses in trial. The SOS alternative improves on the system by encouraging mediated settlements which may even result in both sides coming out ahead of their best initial expectations simultaneously.

Table 8.2 refers to the adversarial system prior to 1960. At that time there was no constitutional right to counsel in felony criminal cases. There was also no legal services program to provide counsel to the poor in civil cases. Likewise, there was no organized movement toward out-of-court settlements or alternative dispute resolution as developed later.

Relations between Attorneys and Clients

Dealing with Attorney-Client Conflicts

The conservative alternative of no government regulation has in the past resulted in reducing competition in the legal profession by

Table 8.3 Attorney-Client Conflicts

	GOALS	
ALTERNATIVES	Conservative Profit.	Liberal Client.
Conservative No government regulation.	+	–
Liberal Government regulation.	–	+
Neutral Regulation of outright theft.	0	0
SOS or Win-Win Free market, no price setting or advertising.	++	++

allowing bar associations to fix minimum fees and prohibit advertising.

The SOS alternative relies on competition among attorneys to promote the best interests of clients as consumers. That competition has resulted from intervention by the Supreme Court declaring minimum fee schedules to be anti-trust violations and prohibitions on advertising to be free speech infringements. See Geoffrey Hazard, *Ethics in the Practice of Law* (Yale University Press, 1979).

Dealing with the Contingency Fee

The issue here is that in the United States the most common fee arrangement in damage suits is a contingency fee, especially in personal injury cases. The lawyer agrees to represent the plaintiff with no payment if the lawyer loses the case. On the other hand, if the lawyer wins the case, then the usual arrangement is for the plaintiff to receive 67 percent of the damages and for the lawyer to receive 33 percent.

The conservative goal is to favor the defendant in personal injury cases since the defendant is usually an insurance company in an automobile accident case, a manufacturer in a product liability case, or an employer in an employee injury case. The justification given is that businesses will make better products and be more profitable if they are not subjected to expensive liability. They are less likely to be so if a would-be plaintiff cannot obtain a litigation-provoking lawyer so easily. The plaintiff should be willing to pay by the hour, which may require up-front money.

Those opposing the contingency fee are also likely to emphasize that it encourages lawyers to gamble their fees on the outcomes of cases. This is not a gamble, though, if the skills of the lawyer are involved in determining the likely outcome. The contingency fee also stimulates the lawyer to do a better job in order to get paid.

The liberal goal is to favor the plaintiff in personal injury cases. British and other European liberals advocate the alternative of socialistic law practice to enable the low-income defendant to be able to obtain an attorney in a personal injury case.

Table 8.4   Contingency Fees

ALTERNATIVES	GOALS	
	Conservative Pro defendant in civil cases.	Liberal Pro plaintiff in civil cases.
Conservative Prohibit contingency fee.	+	−
Liberal Socialistic law practice.	−	+
Neutral Dual system or contin- gency fee.	0	0
SOS or Win-Win Reduce accidents.	++	++

A compromise system would include both government-paid attorneys and privately-hired attorneys. That system does exist in the United States with government-paid attorneys, including public defenders in criminal cases and attorneys for the Legal Services Corporation in civil cases. The LSC, however, rejects personal injury cases because in the United States they can be handled privately through a contingency-fee arrangement.

The approach that may benefit both defendants and plaintiffs in civil cases is to seek to reduce personal-injury accidents through better cars, highways, and drivers. Both sides would also benefit from procedures that encourage out-of-court settlements. No-fault liability can also be considered as benefitting both sides. It helps the defendant by eliminating the one-third fee paid to lawyers and by setting a cap on what can be collected. It helps the plaintiff by increasing the likelihood that the plaintiff will collect something, even if the damages are less than in a common-law victory.

Windfall Contingency Fee

The issue here is whether personal-injury attorneys should be allowed to collect a 33 percent fee on damage awards that often require little legal time for large awards. This is a problem of the windfall contingency fee, not a question of whether there should be contingency fees at all.

Those who want to regulate the contingency fee to reduce windfalls say that the percentage should be no higher than 10 percent if there is a settlement within sixty days, no higher than 20 percent if there is a settlement thereafter, and no higher than 33 percent if the case goes to trial. There are other more complicated variations to discourage stalling by the plaintiff's lawyer.

Those who want no such regulations argue that the occasional windfall offsets the many cases in which the plaintiff's lawyer collects nothing because the case is lost, or collects virtually nothing because the lawyer's expenses have been so high. The plaintiff bar also argues that both the lawyers and the clients are better off without regulation. The total damages may then be higher, thereby resulting in more dollars for both lawyer and client. The size of the damages (especially punitive damages) is a separate issue.

The main justification for the contingency fee is that it enables poor clients to hire lawyers by promising a percentage of the damages. The main justification for high punitive damages is to deter outrageous wrongdoing that is not likely attract criminal prosecution.

Table 8.5   Windfall Fee

	GOALS	
ALTERNATIVES	**Conservative** Reduce windfalls.	**Liberal** Reward risk-taking.
Conservative Regulate contingency fee.	+	−
Liberal No regulation.	−	+
Neutral Some regulation.	0	0
SOS or Win-Win Encourage competition.	++	++

A compromise would involve raising the above caps from 10 percent, 20 percent, and 33 percent to higher amounts, but still retain caps on the contingency fee percentages.

An SOS alternative for reducing excessive percentages and contingency fees would be to encourage competition among plaintiff lawyers. That might be done partly by bar associations or government agencies encouraging lawyers to publicize sample fees in the yellow pages of telephone directories, in their ads, and post them in their offices. Such posting might stimulate competitive lawyers to offer lower contingency rates in the easier cases, bigger cases, or cases in general.

Competition can be beneficial to clients by reducing contingency fee rates. It can also be beneficial to lawyers, who can compete well by being more efficient. It may also reduce the damages that defendants pay by reducing the amount that goes to lawyers.

A better approach to reducing the damage awards and increasing the probability of collecting would be to institute a no-fault system. Perhaps even better would be to concentrate more on reducing the accidents that lead to high damages, especially punitive damages.

Chapter 9

Judicial Selection

Comparing Methods of Selecting Judges and Alternative Terms of Office

Scoring Relations

Each alternative method of judicial selection and tenure is scored on a scale of 1 to 3 on each goal. A 3 means relatively high compared to the other alternatives. A 1 means relatively low. A 2 means in the middle.

Elected judges receive a 3 on economic liberalism, and appointed judges receive a 1. Elected judges tend to be more liberal on economic matters because they tend to be more likely to have working-class backgrounds and to get nominated through political precinct work. Appointed judges are more likely to be appointed as a result of being party contributors. Length of term has no relation to economic liberalism. See Nagel, *Comparing Elected and Appointed Judicial Systems* (Sage, 1973).

The alternatives do not differ substantially on case output.

Weighting Goals

Conservatives place a negative weight on liberalism, and liberals place a positive weight on liberalism.

The complete liberal adds Columns 2 and 4, since those contain liberal weights. The best system from a liberal perspective is one having elected, long-term judges, although that is the worst from a

139

Table 9.1   Selecting Judges

ALTERNATIVES	GOALS	
	Conservative 1. Economic conservatism. 2. Civil-liberty conservatism.	**Liberal** 1. Economic liberalism. 2. Civil-liberty liberalism.
Conservative Appointed short-term.	+	−
Liberal Elected long-term.	−	+
Neutral 1. Appointed long-term. 2. Elected short-term.	0	0
SOS or Win-Win See text.	++	++

conservative perspective.

The complete conservative adds Columns 1 and 3, since these have conservative weights. The best system from a conservative perspective is appointed, short-term judges, although that is the worst from a liberal perspective.

"Hardhat" or "pocketbook" liberal adds Columns 2 and 3, since they are liberal on economic matters, but conservative on civil liberties. The best system from their perspective is elected, short-term judges.

Libertarian conservative adds Columns 1 and 4, since they are conservative on economic matters, but liberal on civil liberties. The best system from a libertarian perspective is appointed, long-term judges.

Overall

The best system depends on the weights assigned to the two ideological goals–whether one weights them negatively or positively.

The data for this table come from Nagel, *Comparing Elected and*

Appointed Judicial Systems (Sage Publications, 1973). There seems to be no difference among the four alternatives on case output or other measures of efficiency or judicial quality. That goal is thus not included in the summation scores.

New Judicial Selection

Elected judges tend to side with labor, tenants, and consumers more than management, landlords, and merchants, as compared to appointed judges, when political party is held constant.

Long-term judges tend to side with the civil liberties position in free speech, due process, and equal treatment cases, as compared to short-term judges.

The SOS alternative recommends professional judges who receive judicial training in law school and rise up through a judicial civil service as in France and other European countries.

Such a system may not be politically feasible for the United States because the political parties want to preserve their ability to award judgeships to loyal lawyers, and judicial selection is not so

Table 9.2   (New) Judicial Selection

	GOALS	
ALTERNATIVES	**Conservative** Conservative judges.	**Liberal** Liberal judges.
Conservative Appointed short-term.	+	−
Liberal Elected long-term.	−	+
Neutral 1. Appointed long-term. 2. Elected short-term.	0	0
SOS or Win-Win Career judges with training and promotion system.	++	++

salient a public issue to make reform easy.

As a result, judicial reform tends to emphasize limiting judicial discretion and arbitrariness rather than changing the selection process. That means more codification, flat sentencing, judicial-character committees, and no-fault liability.

Evaluating Policies toward Judicial Selection

Table 9.3 has more goals that the two preceding tables. The first four goals, however, could be considered as all relating to the neutral goal of competency.

This table leaves out the important goal of political feasibility. If that goal is considered, then the SOS of having professional judges may lack sufficient political feasibility to be an SOS alternative.

Table 9.3   Judicial Selection

ALTERNATIVES	GOALS	
	Conservative 1. Conform with the law. 2. Conservative values.	**Liberal** 1. Creativity. 2. Liberal values. 3. Response to public opinion.
Conservative Appointed short-term.	+	−
Liberal Elected long-term.	−	+
Neutral 1. Appointed long-term. 2. Elected short-term.	0	0
SOS or Win-Win Professional judges.	++	++

Chapter 10

Juries

Whether to Have Criminal Juries

Evaluating Alternatives for Criminal Jury Trials

The scoring of the relations is on a scale of 1 to 5, in which 1 equals – –, 2 equals –, 3 equals 0 or ?, 4 equals +, and 5 equals ++.

Table 10.1 Criminal Jury Trials

	GOALS	
	Conservative 1. Decrease crime. 2. Reduce delay and cost. 3. Predictability.	**Liberal** 1. Separate out the inno- cent. 2. Equal treatment, class,
ALTERNATIVES		and race.

Conservative
1. No jury trials (former
    conservative position).
2. Some kind of jury trial
    (current conservative
    position).
	+	–

Liberal Full jury trials.	–	+
Neutral Modified jury trials.	0	0
SOS or Win-Win See text.	++	++

143

Limited jury trials mainly refer to jury trials that allow for less than twelve jurors and/or less than unanimous decisions. They also must involve sentences of at least six months in jail and adult defendants.

Full jury trials are the winning alternative if extra weight is given to separating out the innocent and to public participation.

No jury trials is the winning alternative if extra weight is given to separating out the innocent and to public participation.

No jury trials are the winning alternative is most countries of the world. It is the most desirable alternative if extra weight is given to decreasing crime, reducing delay, and to increasing predictability of decisions.

L or C equals liberal or conservative goal, alternative, or total score. Liberals give liberal goals a weight of 3, middling goals a weight of 2, and conservative goals a weight of 1. Conservatives do the opposite.

SOS Analysis of the Criminal Jury

The full criminal jury involves twelve persons deciding by unanimous vote. The limited criminal jury involves fewer than twelve persons deciding by less than unanimous vote. The full criminal jury involves no exceptions for juvenile cases, contempt of court cases, courts-martial, or other special criminal cases.

Liberals tend to prefer trial by jury in criminal cases. Doing so makes it more difficult for the prosecutor to convict an innocent defendant because the prosecutor has to receive a favorable vote from twelve people deciding unanimously. Conservatives tend to prefer limited criminal juries or making the criminal jury inapplicable to the states or quasi-criminal proceedings. This is because the full jury system often makes it more difficult to convict guilty defendants.

The SOS alternative should be capable of (1) pleasing conservatives even more than limited juries or no criminal jury, and simultaneously (2) pleasing liberals even more than the full criminal jury. One SOS approach is to reduce crime so there are fewer guilty defendants to prosecute and fewer innocent defendants to defend.

Table 10.2 (Simple) Criminal Jury

ALTERNATIVES	GOALS	
	Conservative Pro-prosecution.	Liberal Pro-defense.
Conservative No criminal jury.	+	–
Liberal Full criminal jury.	–	+
Neutral Limited criminal jury.	0	0
SOS or Win-Win 1. Crime reduction. 2. Improve accuracy.	++	++

Reducing crime may involve more effective treatment and education for drug crimes, better gun control, and less depiction of violence in the mass media.

Another SOS approach is to increase the equitable outcome of trials regardless, whether bench trials or jury trials. Doing so may involve better training of judges and juries, more questioning by judges and juries, and access to a videotape of the trial to refresh memories and clarify testimony.

Whether to Have Civil Juries

Evaluating the Use of Juries in Civil Cases

Table 10.3 includes the less important goals, while Table 10.4 is a simplified SOS table containing the two key goals separating conservatives from liberals.

SOS Analysis of the Civil Jury

The full civil jury, like its criminal equivalent, involves twelve persons deciding by unanimous vote. The limited civil jury involves fewer than twelve persons deciding by less than unanimous vote. The limited civil jury may also require the plaintiff to cover some of the costs.

Liberals prefer trial by jury in civil cases, especially personal injury cases, because juries are more likely to decide in favor of the injured plaintiff than judges are. Juries tend to reflect popular justice, which may emphasize the relative ability of the defendant and plaintiff to pay damages, whereas judges tend to emphasize prior legal precedents. Conservatives tend to prefer no civil jury, meaning a preference for bench trials.

The SOS alternative should enable the defendant to do better in civil cases than at a bench trial, and simultaneously enable the plaintiff to do better than at a jury trial. Procedures that can bring about those results include an emphasis on (1) accident reduction through better cars, roads, and drivers, (2) alternative dispute

Table 10.3 Juries in Civil Cases

	GOALS	
	Conservative 1. Avoiding liability. 2. Reduce delay and cost.	**Liberal** 1. Liability determination. 2. Equal treatment.
ALTERNATIVES	3. Respect for the law.	
Conservative No civil jury.	+	−
Liberal Full civil jury.	−	+
Neutral Limited civil jury.	0	0
SOS or Win-Win Accident reduction and Alternative dispute reso- lution.	++	++

Table 10.4 (Simple) Civil Jury

ALTERNATIVES	GOALS	
	Conservative Pro-defense.	Liberal Pro-plaintiff.
Conservative No civil jury.	+	−
Liberal Full civil jury.	−	+
Neutral Limited civil jury.	0	0
SOS or Win-Win 1. Accident reduction. 2. Alternative dispute. 3. No fault liability. 4. Improve accuracy.	++	++

resolution (ADR) which facilitates out-of-court settlements, (3) no-fault liability which saves the defendant money by eliminating lawyers and big damage awards while greatly increasing the likelihood that the plaintiff will collect something, and (4) improving the accuracy of civil jury decisions by better training, more questions, access to a videotape of the trial, and taking notes.

Jury Size: Six versus Twelve Jurors

Videotaping allows judges and juries to view during deliberations what was said at the trial. Doing so facilitates accurately resolving disputes over the evidence, thereby increasing the probability of convicting the truly guilty and acquitting the truly innocent.

Notetaking may also improve recall and the accuracy of decision-making–as may allowing jurors to ask questions of the judge or the lawyers, and providing special training to jurors on meaning of relevant phrases and procedures.

Those matters are likely to do more for convicting the truly guilty than switching to smaller juries. They are also likely to do more for

Table 10.5 Six- or Twelve-Person Juries

	GOALS	
ALTERNATIVES	**Conservative** Convict the guilty.	**Liberal** Acquit the innocent.
Conservative Six-person juries.	+	−
Liberal Twelve-person juries.	−	+
Neutral Between six and twelve or unanimity.	0	0
SOS or Win-Win Videotaping or note taking.	++	++

acquitting the truly innocent than retaining the twelve-person jury. This is an example of redefining the problem in terms of the goals, rather than the alternatives.

Retrials after Hung Juries

This analysis was prompted by the discussion of the desirability of holding retrials, as requested by prosecution, after the hung juries of the Beckwith and Menendez cases in 1994. The Beckwith case involved the killer of Medgar Evers who was twice acquitted before finally being convicted in 1994. His case was the subject of the movie *Ghosts of Mississippi*. The Menendez case refers to the two sons who killed their parents and were convicted in a retrial in 1994 after a hung jury.

The conservative position is to allow a retrial since the previous hung jury does not constitute a trial because no unanimous decision was reached. That position gives the prosecutor a second chance to convict a guilty defendant. Allowing a retrial is currently accepted as being constitutional.

The liberal position is to deny a retrial. That position is based on

Table 10.6 Hung Juries

ALTERNATIVES	GOALS	
	Conservative Convict the guilty.	Liberal Acquit the innocent.
Conservative Allow retrial if hung jury.	+	–
Liberal No retrial if hung jury.	–	+
Neutral Retrial if hung jury and new evidence.	0	0
SOS or Win-Win Neutral alternative plus methods for improving jury accuracy.	++	++

the concept that retrials increase the probability of convicting an innocent defendant or over-convicting a guilty defendant. A retrial also may be seen as harassing a defendant until the defense resources are worn down. A further argument is that when in doubt, the defendant should be considered not guilty. A hung jury which cannot decide is clearly in doubt.

A neutral or compromise position might be to allow a retrial after a hung jury, but only if important new evidence justifies reopening the case.

A neutral or compromise position might be to allow a retrial after a hung jury, but only if there is important new evidence to justify the prosecutor bringing the case again.

An SOS alternative designed to further both the conservative goal of convicting the guilty and the liberal goal of acquitting the innocent might involve adopting the neutral alternative, but supplementing it with methods for improving jury accuracy regarding both goals.

Some of the latest methods for improving the ability of juries to reach right decisions include (1) videotaping trials for instant playback during the deliberations to aid in accurate recall, (2) notetaking by jurors to increase paying attention and also aid in recall, (3) allowing jurors to ask questions of the judge and lawyers in order to clarify the meaning of instructions and evidence, and (4) pretrial training to improve the understanding of jurors as to the court procedures, principles of evidence, and other matters that will help them to be better jurors.

Section C

Law Compliance

Chapter 11

Traditional Criminal Behavior

Drug Crimes

Drug crimes or drug-related crimes include (1) selling and posses-sion, (2) crimes while under the influence of drugs, (3) robbery, burglary, and crimes to obtain money to buy drugs, (4) police wrongdoing in making arrests and searches as a result of the hostility felt toward people involved with drugs, and (5) corruption of people in government by wealthy drug dealers.

Law enforcement in the context of drug crimes means trying to reduce supply through more arrests, more severe penalties, more police, more prosecution, and more prisons. It also means stopping or decreasing the influx of drugs through air, sea, and land interdiction, as well as trying to change the practices of farmers of drug-producing plants in Latin America and elsewhere.

Treatment and education in the context of drug crimes means trying to reduce the demand for illegal drugs by providing free treatment for addicts, especially if the treatment results in some cures. Free treatment can also lessen the incentive for drug dealers to seek new addicts. A strong educational program could also reduce the percentage of potential addicts who become actual addicts.

The neutral position advocates law enforcement, but not as strongly as the conservatives. It also advocates treatment and education, but not as strongly as the liberals.

Law enforcement is directed toward deterrence and retribution. The effectiveness of such deterrence is questionable since it tends to increase the price and reduce the suppliers, thereby making drug dealing more profitable.

Table 11.1 Drug Crimes

| | GOALS | |
ALTERNATIVES	Conservative 1. Decrease crime. 2. Increase retribution.	Liberal Increase fair procedure and equity.
Conservative 1. Increase punishment. 2. Decrease loopholes. 3. Decrease bribery.	+	−

Liberal
1. Increase opportunity
  costs.
2. Increase professional-
  ism.
3. Decrease peer approval.
	−	+

Neutral Combination.	0	0
SOS or Win-Win 1. Medicalization. 2. Job opportunities.	++	++

Table 11.2 Drug Crimes No. 2

| | GOALS | |
ALTERNATIVES	Conservative Deterrence and retribu- tion.	Liberal Societal productivity.
Conservative Law enforcement.	+	−
Liberal Treatment and education.	−	+
Neutral Parts of both.	0	0
SOS or Win-Win All of both.	++	++

Treatment and education are directed toward increased societal productivity by (1) diverting law-enforcement money into more productive activities, (2) preventing wasteful drug addiction, and (3) decreasing drug crimes which interfere with societal productivity. "All of both" means strong law enforcement against illegal drugs. Most of the drugs that would be in circulation would be part of the free treatment for addicts. It also means more law enforcement and more treatment/education than the neutral position would provide.

Evaluating Policies for Dealing with the Drug Problem

Crackdown means trying to reduce supply through greater law enforcement and more effectively stemming the inflow of drugs.

Legalization means selling drugs the way liquor is sold. There would be a minimum age. There would be regulation to control unsanitary injection needles and impure products.

Medicalization means selling drugs only by prescription and only to confirmed addicts under a phase-out program.

Drug-related crimes include those mentioned previously.

Table 11.3 Drug Problem

	GOALS	
	Conservative Decrease crime.	**Liberal** Societal productivity.
ALTERNATIVES		
Conservative Crackdown.	+	−
Liberal Legalization.	−	+
Neutral Prohibit cocaine and her- oin, not marijuana.	0	0
SOS or Win-Win Medicalization.	++	++

A better SOS alternative might be one that emphasizes trying to reduce demand.

SOS Budget Allocation and Drug Policy

Table 11.4 is an example of an SOS table in which conservatives and liberals are roughly in agreement on at least the main goal. The disagreement is mainly over how each alternative relates to that goal.

The widely accepted goal is the need to reduce the use of drugs, especially cocaine. Conservatives emphasize law enforcement and reducing the supply of drugs as the main alternative policy. Liberals emphasize treatment, education, and reducing demand as the main alternative policy.

Conservatives see law enforcement as being potentially effective in reducing drugs. Liberals see that approach as being largely ineffective, and that it may even make drug-selling more profitable by reducing the competition.

Liberals see treatment and education as being potentially effective in reducing drugs. That especially includes treatment by way of drugs by prescription to reduce the need for drug addicts to engage in crime

Table 11.4 Budget Allocation and Drug Policy

	GOALS	
ALTERNATIVES	**Conservative** Reduce drugs.	**Liberal** Reduce drugs.
Conservative Law enforcement (supply side).	+	−
Liberal Treatment and education (demand side).	−	+
Neutral	0	0
SOS or Win-Win See text.	++	++

to obtain funds to buy illegal drugs. Conservatives see such treatment as increasing the use of drugs and thereby worsening the problem.

With those relation scores, the neutral allocation to the two alternatives would be 50 percent of the budget to each alternative. The conservative allocation would be about 67 percent versus 33 percent. The liberal allocation would be about 33 percent versus 67 percent.

If the budget for combating drug abuse were 100 monetary units, then giving $68 to law enforcement and $68 to treatment-education would exceed the best expectations of both conservatives and liberals. That would mean obtaining 36 monetary units more than the original budget.

An alternative approach to exceeding the best expectations of both groups would be to increase the effectiveness of law enforcement or supply-side reduction in the eyes of liberals. That might be done through subsidies to cocaine farmers to induce them to shift to other crops. The funds for the farmer subsidies could come from funds now being spent on traditional law enforcement. The result might be to improve the effectiveness of law enforcement within the budget of 100 monetary units.

A related alternative approach would be to increase the effectiveness of treatment-education in the eyes of conservatives. That might be done through developing a substitute drug for cocaine, just as methadone is a substitute for heroin. That could also improve the effectiveness of treatment-education within the present budget.

Dealing with Mothers of Cocaine Babies

A cocaine baby is one who has ingested cocaine through the mother's drug usage. Ingesting cocaine at the pre-natal stage can cause permanent mental injury.

The conservative approach of prosecuting the mother may have little deterrent effect since the mothers are likely to be addicted. The prosecution, though, may serve to emphasize retribution or revenge against a person that society considers to be especially irresponsible.

The liberal approach of treating the mother as a medical case

Table 11.5 Cocaine Babies

	GOALS	
ALTERNATIVES	**Conservative** Deterrence and retribution.	**Liberal** Rehabilitation.
Conservative Prosecute as criminal case.	+	−
Liberal Treat as medical case.	−	+
Neutral Mild prosecution and some medical help.	0	0
SOS or Win-Win Decrease cocaine market.	++	++

might result in some rehabilitation. The success rate tends to be low, but rehabilitation is more likely to occur through medicalization than through prosecution.

The super-optimum solution of decreasing the cocaine market may involve a program of phase-out prescriptions for drug addicts under a free public-health program and an emphasis on educating children away from drugs. To the extent that the illegal cocaine market can thereby become substantially less profitable and less large, there would be a decrease in future cocaine babies. That would not focus the deterrence, retribution, or rehabilitation on cocaine mothers. It would place the cocaine problem in the larger context of decreasing demand, as contrasted to the less successful approach of decreasing supply.

It is assumed that a statute under which cocaine mothers are prosecuted provides that ingesting cocaine without a prescription is a crime, and the sentence will be increased if the user is pregnant at the time. Otherwise, there might be questions of constitutional or statutory vagueness.

One might argue that the SOS of decreasing the cocaine market might be improved by also prosecuting cocaine mothers, for whatever deterrent value that has. A counter argument might be that doing so distracts from the importance of prosecuting leaders in the cocaine trade, and especially getting at the economic forces which make the market so profitable.

Under a cocaine-maintenance medical program, women with a high risk of getting pregnant could be encouraged to have a skin implant to prevent pregnancy as a condition of receiving the cocaine prescription. That decreases both the cocaine market and the possibility of a cocaine baby.

Specific Crimes

A SOS Analysis of Terrorism

Severe law enforcement means relatively extensive security checks for entering public buildings. Also easier rules on wiretapping, searches, and arrests where suspected terrorism is involved.

Getting at the causes of the conflicts refers to eliminating or reducing friction between ethnic groups in the former Yugoslavia, the Middle East, and elsewhere. Doing so is likely to reduce both terror-

Table 11.6 Terrorism

	GOALS	
ALTERNATIVES	**Conservative** Reduce terrorism.	**Liberal** Minimize interference with civil liberties.
Conservative Severe law enforcement.	+	–
Liberal Less severe law enforcement.	–	+
Neutral In between.	0	0
SOS or Win-Win Getting at causes of conflict.	++	++

ism and the interference with civil liberties that is associated with severe anti-terrorist law enforcement.

Reducing Rape Crimes

The alternatives are referred to as no. 1 and no. 2. The alternatives referred to as no. 1 and no. 2 rather than as conservative or liberal because one side here involves a mixture of conservatives and liberals and so does the other side. The first group wants easier convictions and more severe sentences. This group may include feminists, who are normally liberal on other aspects of criminal procedure. Easier convictions include introducing evidence of a prior rape conviction, as recommended by Clinton administration sentences. More severe sentences include mandatory minimum, which do not exist for other forms of aggravated assault.

The second group wants the same due process applied to rape cases as to other felony cases. It also wants sentences as for other forms of aggravated assault, including mutilation.

Table 11.7 Reducing Rape Crimes

	GOALS	
ALTERNATIVES	**Conservative** Decrease rape.	**Liberal** Acquit innocent.
Conservative 1. Easier convictions. 2. More severe sentences.	+	−
Liberal 1. Due process. 2. Sentences as for aggra- vated assault.	−	+
Neutral 1. Procedural reform. 2. Middling sentences.	0	0
SOS or Win-Win Increasing respect for women.	++	++

Procedural reforms in the neutral context refer to excluding evidence of the prior sexual behavior of the complainant. Only her present interaction with the defendant would be deemed relevant. Middling sentences refer to sentences between those for aggravated assault and those that are substantially more severe.

Group no. 1 is very much concerned with decreasing rape. Group no. 2 is concerned with acquitting the innocent, although no more so in rape cases than in other felony cases.

Both goals might be achieved at a level above the compromise level if rape can be decreased by increasing respect for women. That might be done in part through education at the pre-school, elementary, and high-school levels, partly by showing the importance of women in science, history, and in the classroom. It might also be done by improving equal opportunity of the professions, traditional male jobs, and higher education. Those measures could be combined with the compromise alternative in order to generate a higher total score on either the conservative or liberal totals.

Presidential Assassination

Table 11.8 was stimulated by the 30th anniversary of the assassination of President John F. Kennedy in 1963. Assassination is not presently a serious problem in the United States. There has been no successful presidential assassination since 1965 and no attempt since 1981. There have been only four presidential assassinations in two hundred years, and they apparently have been the work of individuals rather than organized opposition.

One position is to keep the president isolated. Another position is to allow much mingling with the public but with more Secret Service protection than in the past. The first position emphasizes the goal of avoiding assassination. The second position emphasizes the goal of presidential interaction.

An SOS position might emphasize the reduction of societal violence in general, as well as Secret Service protection. Such reduction might be brought about through better gun control, less violence in the media, and reduction of drug-related crimes. Separate

Table 11.8 Presidential Assassination

	GOALS	
ALTERNATIVES	Conservative Avoid assassination.	Liberal Presidential interaction.
Conservative Isolate.	+	−
Liberal Mingle with more Secret Service protection.	−	+
Neutral	0	0
SOS or Win-Win Reduce societal violence.	++	++

SOS tables are to be presented on each of those problems. Anything that is done to reduce crime in general is also relevant to reducing violence and assassinations.

Prostitution Policy

In 1993, the city council of San Francisco discussed the possibility of having city-run brothels.

The conservative position is to prohibit prostitution in order to discourage sexual vice or sex outside of marriage. The liberal position is to allow prostitution by law as a victimless crime involving consenting adults. The neutral position is to maintain the prohibition, but not vigorously prosecute it.

An important neutral goal endorsed by both conservatives and liberals is to decrease disease, especially AIDS which is increasingly being spread by prostitutes.

A super-optimum solution that promotes the conservative, liberal, and neutral goals might be regulated prostitution. It promotes the conservative goal by decreasing sexual vice, which tends to be widespread even if prostitution is prohibited. A decrease might result

Table 11.9 Prostitution

	GOALS	
ALTERNATIVES	**Conservative** Decrease sexual vice.	**Liberal** No jail for victimless crimes.
Conservative Prohibit.	+	−
Liberal Allow by law.	−	+
Neutral Allow by practice.	0	0
SOS or Win-Win Regulated prostitution.	++	++

by concentrating prostitution in a narrowly-defined geographical area. A decrease also may result from by vigorously prosecuting prostitutes who are not part of the regulated system.

Such regulated prostitution is relevant to the liberal goal of no jail for victimless crimes. It is also relevant to the neutral goal of decreasing disease since the regulated prostitutes would be frequently inspected and tested for diseases, especially AIDS. The "other danger" of unregulated prostitution includes being mugged and robbed. That is unlikely to occur in regulated brothels.

The San Francisco idea of brothels owned and operated by the government may go too far–legalizing prostitution to the point where it is almost approved or encouraged, especially if the city uses brothels as a source of revenue. Regulated prostitution is not meant to encourage prostitution or bring in revenue.

Juvenile Crimes

Adult versus Juvenile Trials

The issue here is whether juveniles under the age of eighteen should be tried as adults when the charge is murder or another felony.

Being tried as an adult means being subjected to the possibility of a longer prison sentence. Being tried as a juvenile may be more likely to result in being placed in a reformatory for juveniles.

The issue overlaps the criminal justice controversy as to whether sentences should be substantially increased regardless of whether the defendant is a juvenile. The conservative position is that longer sentences serve to deter others from committing similar crimes. The liberal position is that sentences should depend on whether the defendant has matured and is capable of being safely returned to society.

Rehabilitation often does not work well with people who have committed felonies, although it may work better with juveniles than with adults. Deterrence of the individual defendant through a long sentence frequently does not work well, although it may have more of an impact in deterring others from committing similar crimes.

An SOS alternative might be to adopt a compromise position of lowering the age at which a juvenile can be tried as an adult, while at the same time pushing other policies more effective in crime reduction than a philosophy of either deterrence or rehabilitation. That may especially include decreasing or eliminating the drug market through medicalization of addicts. Many of the more serious

Table 11.10   Adult versus Juvenile Trials

	GOALS	
ALTERNATIVES	**Conservative** Punishment and deterrence.	**Liberal** Rehabilitation.
Conservative Try for murder at any age.	+	−
Liberal Try for murder at age eighteen.	−	+
Neutral Try for murder at age sixteen.	0	0
SOS or Win-Win Anti-crime package.	++	++

juvenile crimes are drug-related.

There is also a need, in the case of juveniles, to provide monetary or other incentives to keep them in school until about age eighteen and to facilitate their getting legitimate jobs. Violence in the media may need to be controlled for impressionable juveniles, although without violating freedom of speech.

This example illustrates how seeking a compromise on a public policy issue may suggest that both the conservative and liberal positions are largely irrelevant to the problem that needs solving. The analysis may then lead one into thinking about more relevant policies that both conservatives and liberals could endorse.

Juvenile Crime

The problem of reducing juvenile crime is not greatly different from reducing adult crime. The main difference is that juveniles are generally not such hardened criminals or as hopeless as many adult criminals. The same methods can apply to adults and juveniles, but they generally work better with juveniles.

The conservative approach when dealing with juveniles is to treat them like adults as much as possible, including in prison sentences. The key goal is punishment and deterrence.

The liberal approach tends to treat juveniles paternalistically. The results are often supervised probation, rather than prison. The goal is mainly rehabilitation.

The neutral position tends to advocate incarceration rather than probation, but incarceration in special reformatories rather than prisons.

The super-optimizing approach seeks to combine punishment and rehabilitation, but in the context of prevention prior to committing crime, rather than in treatment subsequent to committing crime. The key punishment is to make juveniles suffer lost opportunities for realistic careers if they commit crimes. That requires making the careers more realistic by providing better education, more jobs, and reduced teenage pregnancy. Those are subjects for other policy analysis.

Table 11.11   Juvenile Crime

ALTERNATIVES	GOALS	
	Conservative Punishment and deterrence.	**Liberal** Rehabilitation.
Conservative Treat juveniles as adults (prison).	+	−
Liberal Treat paternalistically (supervised probation).	−	+
Neutral Reformatories.	0	0
SOS or Win-Win Changing costs, benefits, and causes.	++	++

Reducing the benefits of committing crime is also important. In the context of juvenile gangs, this may mean reducing the profits from drug-selling. Doing that may require arranging for drug addicts to receive phase-out prescription drugs through health-care insurance, rather than buying drugs from teenage gangs and other drug dealers.

Changing the hero models of juvenile gang members in the direction of people in sports, music, politics, and other fields might redirect their values and activities. Another remedy may be to increase the probability of apprehension by greater presence of police, especially police who are trained in juvenile crime reduction.

This package of policies is especially oriented toward increasing the costs and decreasing the benefits of juvenile crime, and increasing the probability that those costs will be incurred. The package also seeks to get at the causes of juvenile crime, which may mean going outside the criminal justice system into policies that relate to schools, jobs, and teenage pregnancy.

Allocating Anti-Crime Personnel

Budgeting Courthouse Personnel for Maximum Efficiency and Effectiveness

The relation scores are determined by asking which alternative is the least important on the goal. It is then given a relation score of 1. One then asks how much more important is the next alternative. If it is twice as important, it gets a relation score of 2, and a 3 if it is three times as important. Thus prospectors and public defenders are at the baseline on delay reduction, and judges are about twice as important as either of them.

The percentage of the budget for each alternative on each goal is proportionate to its relation score. Thus judges should get about 50 percent of the allocation that would go to delay reduction if it were the only goal, since judges have 50 percent of the total on the relation scores. Those scores are rough proxies for nonlinear elasticity coefficients. Such coefficients indicate how much of a change occurs in the goal to be achieved as a result of one unit change in the budget category. These coefficients are nonlinear because they take into consideration that additional funds cause additional goal achievement but at a diminishing or plateauing rate of return.

Adding the percentages and then dividing by three gives the neutral allocations for a budget of $200. Adding the percentages multiplied by the liberal weights and then dividing by the sum of the liberal weights gives the liberal allocations. Likewise with the conservative allocations, except substituting conservative for liberal.

The SOS allocation would give $73 to the prosecutors, which is a dollar more than the best expectation when only the conservative weights are used. The SOS allocation would also give $73 to the public defenders, which is a dollar more than the best expectation when only the conservative weights are used.

Thus the SOS conservative allocation gives more to the conservative alternative than the conservative allocation does. The SOS liberal allocation also gives more to the liberal alternative than the liberal allocation does.

Table 11.12   Courthouse Personnel

	GOALS	
ALTERNATIVES	**Conservative** Convict the guilty.	**Liberal** Acquit the innocent.
Conservative Prosecutors.	+	−
Liberal Public defenders.	−	+
Neutral Judges.	0	0
SOS or Win-Win See text.	++	++

The sum of the SOS allocations in the last column is $224, which is $24 more than the $200 budget. This means that ideas will need to be generated as to how the extra $24 is to be raised. Those ideas might include seeking charitable contributions from lawyers and others to cover the shortfall on prosecutors and public defenders. There also might be user fees on plaintiffs, loans through the bond market, and other fund-raising activities.

Allocating Police to Districts

This is a hypothetical problem to illustrate SOS allocation of personnel to places. One hundred police officers are to be assigned to two districts.

Conservatives tend to favor the rich district in order to protect property. Liberals tend to favor the poor district in order to protect people.

The rich district does well on the goal of protecting property, and the poor district does well on the goal of protecting people. If the two goals are treated equally, then half the police would go to the rich district and half to the poor district.

Table 11.13   Police to Districts

	GOALS	
ALTERNATIVES	Conservative Protect property.	Liberal Protect people.
Conservative Rich district.	+	–
Liberal Poor district.	–	+
Neutral	0	0
SOS or Win-Win See text.	++	++

If the conservative weights are used, then 58 percent of the police go to the rich district and 42 percent go to the poor district. The opposite occurs if the liberal weights are used.

The SOS allocation involves exceeding both the conservative and liberal best expectations simultaneously. That means sending fifty-nine police to the rich district, rather than just the fifty-eight advocated by the conservatives. It also means sending fifty-nine police to the poor district, rather than just the fifty-eight advocated by the liberals. The SOS budget thus requires finding money to hire eighteen additional police officers.

An alternative SOS approach is to adopt the neutral allocations. They need to be supplemented by finding ways of making the fifty officers in the rich district as efficient as if they were fifty-nine officers. Likewise, it means finding ways of making the fifty officers in the poor district as efficient as if they were fifty-nine officers.

Police in Squad Cars and on Foot

The issue here is whether police patrols should work mainly in squad cars or mainly on foot. The alternatives are not clearly conservative or liberal. In recent years, many have advocated that more black police officers patrol inner-city neighborhoods on foot.

Using squad cars does have the advantage of enabling police to observe a wider area and respond to calls with greater speed. Patrolling on foot increases the possibility of friendly contact, so long as the police are capable of using methods that win friends.

An SOS alternative might be to rely on surveillance cameras to broaden the observation of streets. The cameras would have to be hidden on lamp posts or telephone poles to keep them from being sabotaged. Dispatchers would watch the screens and send a beeper message to the officers on foot. They would then go to their nearby cars to respond to calls.

That kind of alternative could provide better surveillance and speed than squad cars and even more public contact than having a majority of the police on foot, or at least more contact than half on foot and half in squad cars.

This SOS alternative is an example of a technological fix that enables both conservative and liberal goals to be achieved better than the previous, more limited alternatives.

Table 11.14　　Police in Squad Cars and on Foot

	GOALS	
ALTERNATIVES	**Conservative** Surveillance and speed.	**Liberal** Friendly contacts.
Conservative Squad cars.	+	−
Liberal On foot.	−	+
Neutral Half and half.	0	0
SOS or Win-Win Camera and beepers.	++	++

Allocating Anti-Crime Money

A SOS Allocation Table Increasing the Budget

Each allocation is arrived at by (1) multiplying the percentages in the goal columns by the neutral, conservative, or liberal weights, (2) summing the products, (3) dividing the sum by the total of the appropriate weights to obtain a weighted average allocation percentage, and then (4) multiplying the total budget of $200 by that allocation percentage.

The super-optimum budget is $243, since that is the minimum amount that will allow for a bigger allocation than the best expectations of both the conservatives ($112 to the police) and the liberals ($129 to the courts).

The next step would be to analyze various ways of increasing the budget from $200 to $243, and then taking the best combination of those in light of various criteria.

Table 11.15   SOS Allocation on Increasing the Budget

	GOALS	
ALTERNATIVES	**Conservative** Crime reduction.	**Liberal** Fair procedure.
Conservative Money for police.	+	−
Liberal Money for courts.	−	+
Neutral	0	0
SOS or Win-Win See text.	++	++

A SOS Allocation Table on Increasing
the Relation Scores

The left side of each allocation indicates dollars for the police, and the right side shows dollars for the judiciary.

The relation scores are shown as decimal exponents in the neutral, conservative, and liberal allocations because they can be considered as relative proxies for non-linear elasticity coefficients. Working with decimal exponents (rather than whole numbers of multipliers) generates curves that show diminishing returns between budget dollars and goal achievement.

The super-optimum solution involves improving at least one of the two relation scores associated with crime reduction, and at least one of the two relations scores associated with fair procedure. Doing so will cause the goal achievement on crime reduction to exceed the conservative allocation, and the goal achievement on fair procedure to exceed the liberal allocation.

The next step is to analyze ways of making the police or the courts more efficient on crime reduction, and ways of making the police or the courts more efficient on fair procedure.

Table 11.16   SOS Allocation on Increasing the Relation Scores

	GOALS	
ALTERNATIVES	**Conservative** Crime reduction.	**Liberal** Fair procedure.
Conservative Money for police.	+	−
Liberal Money for judges.	−	+
Neutral	0	0
SOS or Win-Win See text.	++	++

Gun Control

Finding a SOS Solution to the Gun Control Problem

Conservatives advocate private gun ownership, or at least not severely restricting it. The main purpose is to prevent people from being victims of criminals. Statistics show that gun ownership may have little effect on preventing victimization but a substantial effect on accidental killings and the shooting of those other than would-be criminals. This was shown in an article in the 1980s in the *New England Journal of Medicine.*

Liberals advocate strong restrictions on gun ownership. The main purpose is to prevent accidental and other killings that are not designed to prevent victimization. The neutral position favors some restrictions but of a more moderate nature.

An important point is that owning handguns is perceived by the owners as preventing victimization even if it does not do so. Thus in order to increase receptiveness to gun control, it may be necessary to reduce that perception by reducing crime rates, as well as by providing more accurate information.

Reducing crime rates may require (1) more treatment and education for reducing drug-related crimes, (2) more childhood

Table 11.17   Gun Control

	GOALS	
ALTERNATIVES	**Conservative** Prevent victimization.	**Liberal** Prevent other killings.
Conservative No handgun control.	+	−
Liberal Prohibition.	−	+
Neutral Restrictions.	0	0
SOS or Win-Win Crime reduction and gun control.	++	++

socialization away from violent resolution of disputes, (3) more job opportunities and prosperity, and (4) incremental gun control since that may be necessary to reduce the murder rate, although the murder rate must also go down in order to enable gun control to have a better chance of being adopted.

Brady Gun Control Bill

Table 11.18 deals with a specific gun-control law rather than gun control in general. The law is the so-called Brady Bill which provides for a five-day waiting period for buying a gun to allow time to check on the buyer.

The conservative position prefers no waiting period or being able to buy gun on same day. The liberal position is a waiting period of five days. A compromise might be three days.

Another compromise relates to states that provide for more than five days, or more than the compromise of three days. This does run contrary to the usual conservative endorsement of states' rights.

Table 11.18   Brady Bill

	GOALS	
ALTERNATIVES	**Conservative** Freedom to own protective guns.	**Liberal** Reduce gun killings and wrongful gun use.
Conservative No waiting period or same day.	+	−
Liberal Five days waiting.	−	+
Neutral Three days waiting.	0	0
SOS or Win-Win Accelerate technology for fast checking.	++	++

The conservative goal is freedom to own protective guns. The liberal goal is to reduce gun killings and wrongful gun use. Such a goal seeks to decrease guns in the hands of robbers, rapists, suicidal people, negligent people, and others besides potential murderers.

The SOS solution might be to appropriate funds to accelerate the technology for faster checking. It would mean that all gun sellers would have access to a computer hooked into a national databank. The databank would provide relevant information on potential gun owners within the same day. The system might have the capacity for using fingerprints as inputs, not just names or driver's licenses.

Violence on Television and in Movies

The problem of violence on television and movies mainly concerns children watching it and thereby adopting a more favorable attitude toward violence than is socially desirable.

This issue does not lend itself so well to the usually conservative and liberal labels. The position of "anything goes" is supported by conservatives who endorse unregulated business and liberals who endorse free speech. The position of having "certain prohibitions" is

Table 11.19   Violence on Television and in Movies

	GOALS	
ALTERNATIVES	Conservative Unregulated business and/or free speech.	Liberal Decrease violent behavior.
Conservative "Anything goes."	+	−
Liberal Prohibitions.	−	+
Neutral In between.	0	0
SOS or Win-Win Package of positive action.	++	++

endorsed by conservatives who favor various kinds of censorship, and by liberals who take a paternalistic position on social problems.

The package of positive actions seeks to minimize restrictions while decreasing the viewing of violence by children. The package could include the following:

1. Requiring television stations to broadcast a certain number of hours of educational children's programming in order to get their licenses renewed.
2. Classifying television programs in terms of violence content, but not quality.
3. Showing the violence classification at the beginning of each program as a warning to parents.
4. Requiring programs with a high level of violence to be shown during hours when children are not likely to be watching.
5. If a violence-oriented television program or movie is found to be stimulating violent behavior, and the producers do not make changes, then they might be held liable for damages.

SOS Crime Reduction

The conservative alternative of increasing punishment to deter crime includes longer prison sentences, greater use of capital punishment, and more flexible procedures for obtaining convictions.

The liberal alternative of increasing opportunities to reward those who would avoid crime includes programs to upgrade skills of those living in crime-prone areas. It also includes providing seed money and well-placed subsidies to potential employers through programs such as the enterprise zones.

The neutral alternative advocates punishment, but not as strongly as the conservatives. It also advocates opportunities, but not as strongly as the liberals.

Table 11.20   (Simple) SOS Crime Reduction

	GOALS	
ALTERNATIVES	**Conservative** Deterrence and retribution.	**Liberal** Rewards and due process.
Conservative Punishment.	+	−
Liberal Opportunities.	−	+
Neutral Part punishment, part opportunities.	0	0
SOS or Win-Win Full punishment and full opportunities.	++	++

The SOS alternative advocates more punishment and more opportunities than the neutral position would provide. The SOS alternative would also concentrate special efforts on reducing drug-related crimes, since such crimes and drug addicts constitute a large part of the current street crime problem.

Chapter 12

Business Wrongdoing

Pollution that Jeopardizes Public Health

Anti-Pollution Incentives

Subsidies to provide rewards or reduce costs can be effective, but they are expensive. They include subsidies to businesses to encourage the adoption of measures to reduce pollution of the natural environment. More effective subsidies go to research entities to develop new methods to cut pollution while keeping manufacturing costs down.

Reward subsidies cover more than just costs, whereas cost subsidies only cover all or part of the costs.

Damage lawsuits are difficult to win. Fines and jail sentences are difficult to impose. Pollution taxes are quite difficult to get adopted. "Padlock" injunctions may cause unemployment. Loss of a government contract is not much of a threat if does not already have one. Publicizing wrongdoers does not help if they do not sell to ultimate consumers, and even then consumers may be more influenced by other considerations.

The government can issue marketable pollution rights. Firms that pollute relatively little would then have an excess of rights to sell to firms that pollute relatively much. The high prices they charge provide an incentive to reduce pollution.

Any item that is negative on political feasibility (which means a score of 1 or 2) is probably not worth emphasizing. The alternatives that have an overall score of 23 or higher that are politically feasible seem worth adopting, along with subsidies to develop less expensive

Table 12.1 Anti-Pollution Incentives

	GOALS	
	Conservative Cost to general taxpayers.	**Liberal** 1. Effectiveness in reducing pollution. 2. Cleanup funds. 3. Cost to consumers and workers.
ALTERNATIVES		4. Public participation.
Conservative 1. Increase benefits of right doing. 2. Reduce cost of right doing.	+	−
Liberal 1. Increase costs of wrongdoing. 2. Reduce benefits of wrongdoing.	−	+
Neutral Increase probability of benefits and costs.	**0**	**0**
SOS or Win-Win See text.	++	++

and cleaner manufacturing processes.

Evaluating Incentives for Reducing Pollution

The alternatives that score relatively high (meaning 23 points or higher) include:

1. Giving government contracts to business firms that satisfy or excel on meeting pollution requirements.
2. A pollution tax system, although it may not be able to meet a minimum political feasibility level.
3. The buying and selling of marketable pollution rights at a cost to polluters and an income reward to non-

polluters.

4. Bounties for reporting wrongdoing, whereby the general public shares in fines levied.

Table 12.2 (New) Incentives for Reducing Pollution

	GOALS	
	Conservative Stimulate business.	**Liberal** 1. Effectiveness in reduc- ing pollution. 2. Cleanup funds. 3. Cost to consumers and workers.
ALTERNATIVES		
Conservative 1. Reward subsidies to cities and business. 2. Pollution tax reduction. 3. New government con- tracts. 4. Selling marketable pol- lution rights. 5. Tax deductions. 6. Cost subsidies to cities and businesses.	+	−
Liberal 1. Damage suits. 2. Publicize wrongdoers. 3. Pollution tax. 4. Fines. 5. Jail. 6. Loss of government contracts. 7. Buying marketable pol- lution rights. 8. "Padlock" injunction. 9. Confiscate profits.	−	+
Neutral 1. Improve monitoring. 2. Bounties for reporting.	0	0
SOS or Win-Win Combine all.	++	++

The alternatives that score relatively low (meaning 20 or below) include:

1. Reward subsidies to business are opposed as being too expensive to taxpayers.
2. Fines tend to be treated as a petty business expenses that are passed on to taxpayers.
3. Jail sentences are unlikely to be imposed and thus relatively ineffective.
4. "Padlock" injunctions   are opposed because they result in loss of employment and production.

If the criteria are weighted differently, political feasibility can be considered a constraint so that any alternative with a double-minus is considered unfeasible. Of the other criteria, effectiveness in reducing pollution is probably the most important, followed by cost to the general taxpayers.

The alternatives relate to incentives for reducing pollution. One could do a similar analysis concerning government structures for reducing pollution. The structural alternatives might be divided into those that relate to federalism, separation of powers, and relations between government and people.

Predictability in this context tends to refer to the extent to which formulas determine the allocation of benefits or costs. Due process refers to the extent to which the alternatives allow for those who are denied benefits, or made to bear costs, to receive a formal hearing to air their case.

Stock Brokerage Swindles

This analysis was stimulated by news reports that the Prudential brokerage firm had swindled its customers out of billions of dollars by lying to them regarding stocks that Prudential was selling. The Security and Exchange Commission negotiated a settlement to compensate customers who had suffered losses. See "U.S. Judge Approves a Prudential Settlement" in *New York Times*, 18 November

Table 12.3 Stock Brokerage Swindles

ALTERNATIVES	GOALS	
	Conservative Minimize regulation.	**Liberal** Deterrence of business wrongdoing.
Conservative Be lenient.	+	–
Liberal Be severe.	–	+
Neutral In between.	0	0
SOS or Win-Win Encourage competition by banks.	++	++

1995, at page 36.

The conservative position is to be lenient. Doing so is conducive to the goals of minimizing regulation, leaving the matter to the marketplace, and letting the "buyer beware." The liberal position is to be more severe–a reversal of positions from the reactions to street crimes. In the Prudential case, liberals wanted criminal prosecution, or at least punitive damages.

The middling position was a settlement that provided no punitive damages, but waived the short statute of limitations that would otherwise exclude many customers from being compensated.

The amount of money likely to be repaid is substantially less than the amount swindled. This implies a double standard toward big business swindlers. One could, however, argue that it is a double standard against relatively rich customers.

It normally is not desirable for an SOS solution to involve criminal or near-criminal wrongdoing. It might reward the defendant and defeat the deterrent value of punishment.

An SOS approach to business wrongdoing that is sometimes effective is to institute government-stimulated competition. That could be done in this situation. The SEC could authorize ordinary commercial banks to buy and sell stock on behalf of their customers. Doing so would reduce the power of stock brokerage firms to mislead their customers. The threat of banks entering the brokerage industry might also cause more self-policing within the industry.

Chapter 13

Judicial Review, Constitutional Compliance, and Government Wrongdoing

Preventing Constitutional Violations

Constitutional Law: Judicial Review

The concepts of conservative and liberal are not so applicable to these alternatives or goals. Instead one might refer to the first three alternatives as no. 1, no. 2, and no. 3.

Table 13.1 (Old) Judicial Review

	GOALS	
ALTERNATIVES	**Conservative** Popular responsiveness.	**Liberal** Sensitivity to minority rights.
Conservative No constitutional review.	+	–
Liberal Concurrent constitutional review.	–	+
Neutral Judicial constitutional review.	0	0
SOS or Win-Win Sensitize legislators, administrators, and the public.	++	++

Likewise, popular responsiveness might be referred to as goal no. 2 because it is closely associated with legislative participation in judicial review. Sensitivity to minority rights might be referred to as goal no. 3 because it is closely associated with judicial review.

No constitutional review tends to mean that the chief executive or prime minister (with or without the legislature) can promulgate laws without having them subject to constitutional review by another government institution.

Concurrent review means the legislature and the courts, or the Supreme Court, have equal power in interpreting the constitution. Judicial review means the courts have the last word.

The super-optimum solution is to rely more on sensitization of government officials and decision-makers as an important supplement to formal-review institutions like the courts. There is a need, possibly even at the pre-school level for teachers to encourage a higher regard for constitutional rights such as freedom to disagree, fair procedure in determining wrongdoing, and rewards on the basis of individual merit.

SOS Analysis of Judicial Review

Judicial review means empowering the courts in a nation or province, especially the higher courts, to declare null and void governmental acts that the courts find to be contrary to the constitution.

No judicial review means that the legislators and chief executives decide for themselves whether they are complying with the constitution. As of 1993 in the United States, this issue tends to apply only to civil liberties cases. It formerly applied to economic regulation cases, but not since the 1930s. As of 1937, the Supreme Court stopped declaring economic regulation legislation of Congress and the states to be unconstitutional on the grounds of lacking authority under the Interstate Commerce Clause or substantive due process. The court said that business firms that are subject to economic regulation can adequately protect themselves by lobbying the legislature. Soapbox orders, arrested persons, and minority ethnic group members, however, cannot protect themselves so well by going to a majoritarian legislature. They need the help of the courts to protect their constitutional rights.

The conservative goal in civil liberties matters tends to endorse majority rule regarding free speech, due process for people accused of crimes, and equal treatment for groups that have been discriminated against. Conservatives as of 1993 therefore tend to advocate judicial restraint, rather than vigorous judicial review.

The liberal position advocates a more activist judicial review—nullifying governmental acts that conflict with constitutional rights.

A neutral position might advocate judicial review subject to having a two-thirds concurrence rule, elected judges on the Supreme Court, or fixed terms to make the courts more responsive to the majority.

An SOS solution might involve better educating the majority as to how the majority benefits from free speech, due process, and equal opportunity. By sensitizing legislators, administrators, and the general public to the importance of civil liberties, more might be done to protect these rights than can be done through judicial review alone.

This analysis assumes that both conservatives and liberals endorse constitutional rights, but differ on the need and desirability for judicial review to protect such rights. The idea of supplementing restrained judicial review with appropriate sensitization should appeal to both conservatives who emphasize majority rule in civil liberties and liberals who emphasize minority rights.

Restrained judicial review means that the courts follow rules such as refraining from declaring a law unconstitutional (1) if it can be found to be illegal on other grounds, (2) if the law is not presented in the form of a case involving a litigant adversely affected by the enforcement of the law, or (3) if the benefit of the doubt rests on the side of the legislature in a close case.

Table 13.2 emphasizes the American context in judicial review. The previous judicial review table is more applicable to other countries. The table provides for constitutional review by the chief executive, the legislature, or the courts as three separate alternatives. It is also not as simplified in terms of relation scores and ideological designations.

Table 13.2   (New) Judicial Review

ALTERNATIVES	GOALS	
	Conservative Majority rule in civil liberties.	**Liberal** Sensitivity to minority rights.
Conservative No judicial review.	+	−
Liberal Judicial review.	−	+
Neutral 1. Judicial review with two-thirds concurrence. 2. Elected judges or fixed terms.	0	0
SOS or Win-Win 1. Restrained judicial review. 2. Sensitize legislators, administrators, and the public.	++	++

Increasing Constitutional Compliance

To promote constitutional compliance, minimize deviation from custom, maximize clarity, have respected legal policymakers, have professional administrators with good sanctions, target those more likely to comply and do so when there are appropriate environmental conditions.

Increase the probability of wrongdoers being caught by less due process and more professionalism; decrease crime benefits by hardening the targets or changing peer values; increase crime costs by stiffer penalties and missed opportunities.

Child support might best be handled through social insurance with a broadened definition of survivorship, although allowing the insurance agency a right of reimbursement.

Table 13.3 Constitutional Compliance

	GOALS	
ALTERNATIVES	**Conservative** Cost.	**Liberal** Increase compliance.

Conservative
1. Decrease
    deviation/custom.
2. Increase
    clarity/standards.
	+	−

Liberal 1. Heavy sanctions. 2. Receptivity. 3. Institutional support.	−	+
Neutral A little of both.	0	0
SOS or Win-Win See text.	++	++

Legislative Corruption

Unrestricted campaign spending by legislative lobbyists may facilitate the spread of creative ideas, especially if it enables challengers to suggest better ideas than those of incumbents, or vice versa.

Restrictions on spending allow more equal opportunity for candidates to get elected, rather than favoring the rich.

A compromise is to have no restrictions on the amount of spending, but require visibility as to how the money is spent.

The SOS alternative involves full or partial government funding of elections. Doing so might provide enough money to advertise creative innovations, while at the same time providing a degree of equal funding for major candidates.

Table 13.4 Evaluating Policies toward Lobbies

	GOALS	
ALTERNATIVES	Conservative Creativity.	Liberal Equality.
Conservative Unrestricted and unreported spending.	+	−
Liberal Spending restrictions and reporting.	−	+
Neutral Reporting but no spending restrictions.	0	0
SOS or Win-Win Government funding of elections.	++	++

Administrative Efficiency

To increase the likelihood that time-saving decisions will be chosen:

1. Increase the benefits gained from making time-saving decisions (that is, increase Bs). For example, reward assistant state's attorneys with salary increases and promotions for reducing the average time consumption per case.
2. Decrease the costs of making time-saving decisions (that is, decrease Cs). For example, establish a computerized system that informs assistant state's attorneys concerning actual and predicted consumption of time at various stages of cases to facilitate keeping track of cases. Also, provide more investigative and preparation resources.
3. Increase the costs incurred from making time-lengthening decisions (that is, increase CL). For example, under the speedy-trial rules provide for

absolute discharge of a defendant whose case extends beyond the time limit rather than just release on recognizance.

4. Decrease the benefits from making time-lengthening decisions (that is, decrease BL). For example, increase release on recognizance so that lengthening the pretrial time will not make the jailed defendant more vulnerable to pleading guilty.

5. Raise the probability of the decision-maker being penalized for lengthening time (that is, increase P). For example, allow fewer exceptions to the speedy-trial rules, such as suspending an application "for good cause" or "exceptional circumstances."

Table 13.5 Increasing the Likelihood that Prosecutors Will Reach Time-Saving Decisions

		Alternative Occurrences		
		Being Penalized for Lengthening Time (P)	Not Being Penalized for Lengthening Time (1-P)	**Benefits Minus Costs**
Alternative Decisions	Time Saving Decision (S)	B_S Benefits from S	C_S Costs from S	$B_S - C_S$
	Time Lengthening Decision (L)	C_L Costs from L	B_L Benefits from L	$(B_L)(1-P) - (C_L)(P)$

Note: P = probability of being penalized; B = benefits; C = costs; S = time saving decision; L = time lengthening decision.

Section D
Constitutional Rights

Chapter 14

Free Speech

Free Speech in General

Alternative Ways of Treating Freedom of Speech

Government funding and facilities for minority viewpoints might promote creative ideas and constructive criticism of government, but seems politically unfeasible since the Supreme Court does not mandate it and a majoritarian Congress is unlikely to appropriate funds. The closest equivalent is probably the requirement that radio and television stations give minority political parties free broadcast time when the major parties receive it, and federal funding of presidential campaigns if the minority parties are substantial.

Unlimited free speech would allow invasions of privacy, prejudicial pretrial publicity, and unlimited campaign expenditures, which neither the courts nor Congress endorse. Those rights of privacy, due process, and minimum equality in political campaigning are the fundamental rights that allow free-speech limitations.

Examples of limitations include pornography, libel, false pretenses, and advocacy that leads to physical harm. All those free-speech exceptions have been substantially limited over the last twenty years or so.

Evaluating Ways of Treating Freedom of Speech

The neutral position does well on both the liberal totals and conservative totals–better than a more liberal or conservative

Table 14.1 (Old) Freedom of Speech

ALTERNATIVES	GOALS	
	Conservative No undue burden on the taxpayer.	**Liberal** 1. Allow creative ideas. 2. Encourage construc- tive criticism of government.
Conservative Limit free speech when no fundamental right of others is jeopardized, but when the speech does not improve society, or when it is critical of prevailing government, religion, or other established ideas.	+	−
Liberal 1. Provide funding and facilities for minority viewpoint. 2. Allow unlimited free speech.	−	+
Neutral Limit free speech only when another fundamental right is jeopardized.	0	0
SOS or Win-Win See text.	++	++

position. This may be so because free speech is not an issue that divides liberals and conservatives as economic issues do.

The super-optimum solution may be virtually unrestricted free speech with the exceptions under the neutral alternative emphasizing conflicts with other rights in the Bill of Rights. To win support from the conservative business community, it might be necessary to allow free speech in advertising products, prices, and services, especially among the professions, union organizing, and business competition.

Table 14.2 (New) Freedom of Speech

	GOALS	
	Conservative Government stability.	**Liberal** 1. Increase creative ideas. 2. Increase constructive criticism of government.
ALTERNATIVES		
Conservative Restricted free speech.	+	−
Liberal Unrestricted free speech.	−	+
Neutral Some restrictions for equal protection, due process, and privacy.	0	0
SOS or Win-Win Free speech for business and labor, with access.	++	++

Dealing with Abhorrent Speech

Abhorrent speech refers to speech that represents a minority viewpoint, so obnoxiously that even some free-speech advocates argue that it should be curbed by arrest and possibly even court injunction. Examples are pro-Nazi speeches in Skokie, Illinois, flag burning, hardcore pornography, or sacrilegious provocation.

The conservative position tends to advocate prohibiting abhorrent speech. The liberal position is willing to allow it unless it poses clear and present danger of inciting violence against others. Both positions favor discouraging it. Both oppose any steps that encourage it, including government funding of abhorrent activities in the arts. Such activities can be excluded from government funding programs if the criteria relate exclusively to artistic merit and not ideological orientation.

Table 14.3 Dealing with Abhorrent Speech

	GOALS	
ALTERNATIVES	**Conservative** Protect from disruption.	**Liberal** Increase creative ideas.
Conservative Prohibit abhorrent speech and no funding.	+	−
Liberal Allow abhorrent speech as any other speech and no funding.	−	+
Neutral No funding but tolerate unless riot.	0	0
SOS or Win-Win 1. Remove causes. 2. Decrease Nazism. 3. Decrease pornography.	++	++

Liberals are especially concerned with the goal of encouraging innovative ideas. They worry that making abhorrent speech an exception to free-speech protection could spread to ideas that most liberals would not consider abhorrent. Conservatives are especially concerned with protecting the stability of institutions from emotional attack.

The SOS alternative seeks to promote creative ideas and protect sensitive minds from abhorrent speech. That might mean removing the causes of truly abhorrent speech. Doing so might require childhood sensitization that emphasizes judging people on their individual merit, resolving disputes through peaceful means, and other values that make them less likely to become adults receptive to abhorrent speech. Without an audience such speech is not so likely to occur, which removes the issue of whether it should be prohibited or allowed.

Hate Speech and Hate Crimes

Ku Klux Klan Rallies

The terms conservative and liberal are used here to refer to narrowing free-speech rights versus broadening them. The terms have nothing to do with endorsing Klan purposes.

The conservative approach is to prohibit or attack a Klan rally to prevent it from occurring. The liberal approach is to hold a counter-rally or demonstration to show that anti-Klan feeling is stronger and more meaningful.

A neutral approach might be to try to ignore the rally. That might have the effect of allowing it to go unchallenged, and thereby to make it appear that pro-Klan opinion is stronger than anti-Klan opinion.

The conservative position seeks to minimize the extent to which the Klan has an audience or outlets to obtain an audience. The liberal position seeks to allow diverse ideas, concerned that prohibiting ideas on the basis of content can set a bad precedent.

The SOS position may endorse the counter-rally in the short run. As a long-run solution, the SOS position may seek to remove the causes of Klan support among either participants or the audience. That might be accomplished partly through a prosperous economy

Table 14.4 Ku Klux Klan Rallies

	GOALS	
ALTERNATIVES	**Conservative** Minimize disruption.	**Liberal** Allow diverse ideas.
Conservative Prohibit or attack.	a +	b −
Liberal Counter-rally.	c −	d +
Neutral Ignore.	0	0
SOS or Win-Win Remove causes.	++	++

that minimizes hatred against minorities as scapegoats for lack of jobs and other opportunities. It also may be done through childhood socialization and education.

A SOS Analysis of Hate Crime Statutes

A hate crime statute is one that adds an extra penalty, if a crime such as assault, murder, rape, or vandalism is directed toward blacks, homosexuals, Jews, or other members of an ethnic, racial, religious, or sexual-orientation group because the victim is a member of the group. An example would be a statute that provides for a 10 percent increase in the severity of the prison sentence if the crime is committed against a black person because of the person's race.

The main argument for such statutes is that an assault becomes more damaging to society if it involves inter-ethnic hatred. If minorities can be protected against discrimination in employment or housing, the argument is that they can and should be given similar protection from being murdered, assaulted, or otherwise criminally victimized.

The main argument against such statutes is that in order to prove that the defendant was motivated by hate, it may be necessary to introduce as evidence the speaking activities of the defendant. Thus the penalty becomes a penalty for abhorrent speech, rather than for the abhorrent behavior already covered by ordinary criminal statutes.

In considering the constitutionality of hate-crime statutes, one has to decide which clause in the Constitution is more important under these circumstances. The key clauses are the equal-protection clause of the fourteenth Amendment and the free-speech clause of the First Amendment.

The SOS solution is to try to adopt policies to simultaneously promote both free speech and equal treatment based on individual merit. This may require socialization in the values of those constitutional ideas at the pre-school, elementary, and high school levels. A prosperous society with good employment opportunities also simultaneously promotes greater tolerance for deviant free speech and for minority-group interests.

Table 14.5 Hate Crimes

	GOALS	
ALTERNATIVES	**Conservative** Equal protection.	**Liberal** Free speech.
Conservative Longer sentence when group hate involved.	+	–
Liberal Same sentence.	–	+
Neutral In between.	0	0
SOS or Win-Win 1. Employment opportu- nities. 2. Socialization.	++	++

Table 14.5 illustrates that the winning alternative between two alternatives depends on how well or how poorly each alternative scores on each goal and how the goals are weighted relative to each other. Just because the Supreme Court weights free speech higher than equal protection does not mean that the hate statute would be declared unconstitutional. It might be declared constitutional if it is perceived to have only a slightly negative effect on free speech, but a very positive effect on equal protection. This would be the case if the scores in cells a and c approach 5 and 1, while the scores in cells b and d approach 3 and 3. This may also occur if the weights of free speech versus equal protection are about 3 and 2 rather than 3 and 1 for the Supreme Court. The SOS alternative must receive the highest score in the two columns in order to be an SOS.

Media Regulation

The Broadcasting Fairness Doctrine

The fairness doctrine requires radio and television stations to "afford reasonable opportunity for the discussion of conflicting views on issues on public importance." It was repealed by the Federal Communications Commission (FCC) in 1987. There is now an attempt to restore it.

Those who oppose the fairness doctrine seem willing to tolerate high number of conservative talk shows and a low number of liberal talk shows. Those who favor the doctrine seem to want something close to an equal number of each. The compromise position is to allow an imbalance in a conservative direction as long as there is a substantial liberal offset.

The SOS alternative might be to require more political discussion on radio and television. It might produce more of both conservative and liberal talk shows than we now have. That is an SOS solution if it gives conservatives more than the status quo, which they are seeking to preserve, and also give liberals more air time.

This is a classic SOS in which conservatives and liberals are fighting over percentages of benefits. A meaningful SOS in such circumstances might be to increase the total scarce benefits. They can each then get more than they would have received with a high percentage of a small quantity of benefits.

Table 14.6 Broadcasting Fairness Doctrine

	GOALS	
ALTERNATIVES	**Conservative** Promote conservative ideas.	**Liberal** Promote liberal ideas.
Conservative Oppose fairness doctrine.	+	−
Liberal Favor fairness doctrine.	−	+
Neutral 75 percent conservative to 25 percent liberal.	0	0
SOS or Win-Win Require more political discussion on radio and television.	++	++

Generating more political discussion can be justified as being informative and provocative. The results could lead to improving government and public policy. The broadcasting stations might provide more balance in order to satisfy listeners and advertisers.

Diversity in Book Publishing

The issue here is that there are virtually no legal restrictions on what books can be published in the United States. There are, however, economic restrictions in the sense that it is expensive to publish one thousand copies of a book that runs three hundred pages. As a result, the books published tend to be those that are more commercially profitable. Books that may offer innovative ideas may be unable to find publishers.

The conservative approach to the economic problem is to rely on the marketplace to generate sufficient diversity in book publishing. The liberal approach may emphasize anti-trust regulation to break up monopolistic or oligarchic book-publishing companies that dominate the field. A compromise position might involve some anti-trust activity, but less vigorous than the liberal alternative.

Both conservatives and liberals favor free speech. Conservatives, however, complain that the publishing business is biased in favor of liberals, and liberals complain that it is biased in favor of conservatives. Relying on the private marketplace tends to favor conservative publishing in view of the high cost. Relying on anti-trust regulation tends to favor smaller firms that are less costly to operate.

The SOS alternative seeks to provide opportunities for innovative authors through public publishing by state universities or by a publisher comparable to the public broadcasting system. The SOS alternative also provides funding through agencies such as the National Science Foundation to subsidize the publication of innovative books that are not commercially profitable. The National Endowment for the Arts or Humanities may also provide seed money for innovative publishers, both conservative and liberal.

Table 14.7 Diversity in Book Publishing

	GOALS	
ALTERNATIVES	**Conservative** Free speech, especially for conservatives.	**Liberal** Free speech, especially for liberals.
Conservative Private marketplace.	+	–
Liberal Diversity regulation by anti-trust laws.	–	+
Neutral Anti-price fixing.	0	0
SOS or Win-Win 1. Public publishing. 2. Seed money for diverse publishers.	++	++

Dealing with Pirate Broadcasters

An increase in unlicensed pirate radio broadcasting was reported by *The New York Times* 24 October 1993, although this has been an occasional problem going back many years. The activity seeks to avoid expensive licenses and also restrictions on what one can broadcast.

The conservative position tends to side with licensed broadcasters in order to protect their profits and property rights. That position does, however, interfere with a more competitive open marketplace. The liberal position tends to be more sympathetic to allowing pirate radio mainly because of the free speech aspects. Liberals also have more favorable attitudes toward the small-station operator seeking to compete with big business. The compromise position would be to outlaw pirate radio, but avoid vigorous enforcement and high fines.

Table 14.8 Dealing with Pirate Broadcasters

	GOALS	
ALTERNATIVES	Conservative Protect licensed broad- casters.	Liberal Promote free speech.
Conservative Only licensed broadcast- ing.	+	−
Liberal Allow private radio.	−	+
Neutral Not allow, but low fines.	0	0
SOS or Win-Win Expand available wave- lengths.	++	++

The long-run solution (which is coming and may be presently available) is to expand the available wavelengths. Space could be given on the FM band for a combination of pirate broadcasters to share a twelve-hour period. The merger activities of cable television and telephone companies may greatly expand the spaces available.

The idea of expanding the total resources is an important SOS approach, as contrasted to fighting over what is wrongly perceived to be a fixed set of available resources.

Government Secrecy

Table 14.9 was stimulated by the secrecy that for thirty years has surrounded CIA records on the Kennedy assassination.

Secrecy protects the right to privacy and national security. Openness promotes freedom of information. That information leads to free speech and press, which is desirable in improving public policy.

A compromise would be to make some items secret and some open. A super-optimum solution might involve highly protective

Table 14.9 Government Secrecy

ALTERNATIVES	GOALS	
	Conservative Right to privacy and national security.	**Liberal** Freedom of information.
Conservative Secrecy.	+	−
Liberal Openness.	−	+
Neutral Partial secrecy.	0	0
SOS or Win-Win Sequential.	++	++

secrecy for a set number of years, then complete openness thereafter. This is an example of a sequential SOS solution. It provides more privacy and security at first than partial secrecy does. It then later provides more freedom of information than partial openness.

As for when the secrecy period should be considered expired, that might be done when (1) the key people consent or die, or (2) a generation of thirty years has passed, whichever comes first. Such a time period has expired for the Kennedy assassination.

Chapter 15

Government and Religion

Government and Religion in General

Like free speech, separation of church and state also is an issue that does not divides liberals and conservatives as economic issues do.

A pro-religion position is illustrated by governments that have a specific state religion or close to it such as contemporary Iran (Islam), Israel (Judaism), Ireland (Christianity), and medieval governments.

An anti-religion position is illustrated by governments that have sought to substantially decrease the influence of a dominant religion as part of a post-revolution activity, such as Turkey in the 1920s (Islam), the Soviet Union from 1920 to 1990 (Eastern Orthodox), and France and Italy after their revolutions (Catholic).

Table 15.1 Government and Religion

	GOALS	
ALTERNATIVES	**Conservative** Avoid resentment.	**Liberal** Increase creativity and diversity.
Conservative "Pro" religion.	+	−
Liberal "Anti" religion.	−	+
Neutral Some pro-aid, some anti-interference.	0	0
SOS or Win-Win No aid, no interference.	++	++

207

The neutral position attempts to support religion in general but not one religion over another. This includes aid like tax exemption and grants, religious blessings at public ceremonies, and generic religious symbols on money or other government displays.

The super-optimum position permits virtually no aid or interference with religious institutions. The concept of aid and interference is difficult to deal with in the abstract. It is better to discuss aid in terms of issues such as organized prayers and Bible reading in the public schools, or to discuss interference in terms of government resistance to the refusal of Jehovah's Witnesses to accept hospital blood transfusions.

Where the United States fits depends on what one means by virtually no aid or interference. The Supreme Court has clearly declared that aiding a religion is unconstitutional. Yet it tolerates many forms of aid on the grounds that it is directed to charitable activities rather than religious activities, or the aid is too minor to be objectionable.

Public School Prayers and Bible Reading

Organized Prayers and Bible Reading in Public Schools

Anybody may pray silently at any time in a public school, or read the Bible at any time when other reading has not been assigned. The problem concerns organized prayers or Bible reading conducted or encouraged by the school authorities, rather than just allowed on an individual basis.

The neutral position emphasizes the reading of religious literature from the major religions of the world as part of a social science course or a literature course. That kind of scholarly, non-indoctrination course is constitutionally acceptable and may be desirable for broadening backgrounds. Such a course, though, may be opposed by some conservative parents who do not want their children to learn about other religions. Such a course may also be opposed by some liberal parents who are afraid the course will be biased in a conservative direction.

Table 15.2 Organized Prayers

	GOALS	
ALTERNATIVES	Conservative Increase ethical behavior.	Liberal Increase creativity.
Conservative Prayers and Bible reading.	+	−
Liberal No prayers or Bibles.	−	+
Neutral Religious literature.	0	0
SOS or Win-Win Ethical training.	++	++

The super-optimum solution emphasizes ethical training, rather than theological material. Such training could include a series of case studies for discussion purposes dealing with situations that involve being a good Samaritan and helping needy people in general. It could also deal with such values as freedom to disagree, fair procedures, judging people on the basis of individual merit, and being a productive person.

Prayer and Bible Reading in Public Schools

Table 15.3 is an improvement over the previous table because it has a simpler set of goals. There is also internal consistency, with the conservative alternative winning on the conservative totals and the liberal alternative winning on the liberal totals.

Simplified SOS Analysis of School Prayers and Bible Reading

The conservative position is to allow organized prayers and Bible reading in the public schools. The liberal position is to prohibit both.

Table 15.3 (Simple) Prayers and Bible Reading in Public Schools

	GOALS	
ALTERNATIVES	**Conservative** Ethical behavior.	**Liberal** Secular knowledge of social institutions.
Conservative Allow.	+	–
Liberal Prohibit.	–	+
Neutral Neutral.	0	0
SOS or Win-Win 1. Ethical training. 2. Comparative religion.	++	++

Table 15.4 (New Simple) School Prayers

	GOALS	
ALTERNATIVES	**Conservative** Stimulate religiosity and ethical behavior.	**Liberal** 1. Avoid dogma. 2. Stimulate creativity.
Conservative Prayers and Bible reading.	+	–
Liberal No prayers or Bible reading.	–	+
Neutral Student-led prayers.	0	0
SOS or Win-Win Ethical training.	++	++

A compromise position might be to allow prayers when they are conducted by the students, not faculty or administrators, and then only on special occasions such as graduation ceremonies. The Supreme Court has not yet ruled on that practice, although lower federal courts have held that if the student-led prayers are held during school hours and on school property, then they are unconstitutional.

The conservative goal is to stimulate religiosity and ethical behavior. The liberal goal is to stimulate diversity and creativity, and to avoid dogma and divisiveness.

A super-optimum solution might be to include in the curriculum (at many levels) modules that emphasize ethical training. Such modules could be based on the Golden Rule and related concepts endorsed by both conservatives and liberals without including the theological aspects.

After-Hours Use of Public Schools by Churches

The conservative position is to allow churches to use schools after regular hours regardless of their purposes so long as they are legal. The liberal position is to deny churches the use of schools after hours regardless of their purposes. The neutral position would restrict the permissible purposes.

The SOS position would allow any legal purpose, but provide that the activities must be open to the public, involve no church services, no school sponsorship, and occur after hours.

Such a position might recognize that separation of church and state is more important than equal treatment, but still decide in favor of the church group. The reason is that separation is only slightly violated by the restrictions imposed. One the other hand, equal treatment would be greatly violated if all other legal groups were allowed to use the school after hours, but not church groups.

Table 15.5 After-Hours Use of Public Schools by Churches

ALTERNATIVES	GOALS	
	Conservative Equal treatment.	Liberal Separation of church and state.
Conservative Any legal purpose.	+	−
Liberal No purpose.	−	+
Neutral Some purposes.	0	0
SOS or Win-Win 1. Any legal purpose. 2. Open to the public. 3. No church services. 4. No school sponsorship. 5. After hours.	++	++

Priestly Celibacy

The celibacy issue is not a public policy issue. No government that adheres to separation of church and state is going to require or prohibit celibacy on the part of ministers. It is an issue primarily within the Catholic church, although many people find it interesting to discuss.

Those who favor celibacy tend to justify doing so on the grounds that it promotes more exclusive dedication. Those who favor allowing marriage tend to claim that it promotes better understanding of the problems of one's parishioners, while promoting diversity within the church.

A neutral position might be to allow marriage only at the parish level. Bishops and other such church officials would have to be celibate, or celibacy would at least be a preference.

Table 15.6 Priestly Celibacy

	GOALS	
ALTERNATIVES	**Conservative** Exclusive dedication.	**Liberal** Better understanding and diversity.
Conservative Preserve celibacy.	+	–
Liberal Allow and encourage marriage and families.	–	+
Neutral Allow only at parish level.	0	0
SOS or Win-Win 1. Marriage with dedication. 2. Training and screening.	++	++

The SOS might be to allow marriage, but with special training and screening to improve dedication. This might mean a well-conducted study of Catholic priests to determine what those who are more dedicated have in common in terms of their training and attitudes. The attitudinal information could be used to screen out those who seem less likely to be highly dedicated.

Government and Religion in Other Nations

Pre-Ayodha Incident

Table 15.7 refers to the issues facing the government of India as to what to do about the threats of the Hindu fundamentalists to tear down the Moslem mosque at Ayodha in northern India. See the post-Ayodha table and text which is Table 15.8 for what subsequently happened in the short run. The long run of friction between Indian, Hindus, and Moslems is still being decided.

The conservative law-and-order position was to suppress the

Table 15.7 Pre-Ayodha Incident

| | GOALS | |
ALTERNATIVES	Conservative Uphold law.	Liberal Save lives.
Conservative Suppress with shooting.	+	−
Liberal Avoid suppressing with shooting.	−	+
Neutral Try to suppress with some shooting.	0	0
SOS or Win-Win Suppress with hoses, rub- ber bullets, or tear gas.	++	++

rioters with military action, including gunfire if necessary. The liberal position was to avoid any shooting regardless of the circumstances. The neutral position was to allow for some use of firearms under extreme circumstances.

The SOS alternative might have been to make use of military or paramilitary forces well-equipped with high-pressure firefighters' hoses, rubber bullets, and tear gas, but no military armed with regular bullets.

The prime minister of India, in discussing the situation afterwards, only talked in terms of shooting or not shooting. He did not discuss the above-mentioned SOS alternative which could have upheld the law and saved lives simultaneously. He considered the situation to involve an inherent tradeoff between either upholding the law with a loss of lives, or saving lives and not upholding the law.

Post-Ayodha

Table 15.8 refers to the decision-making process of the government of India as to what to do with the Ayodha site after the Moslem mosque had been torn down.

Table 15.8 Post-Ayodha Incident

ALTERNATIVES	GOALS	
	Conservative Good for Hinduism and India.	**Liberal** Good for Islam.
Conservative Hindu temple.	+	−
Liberal Moslem mosque.	−	+
Neutral Neither.	0	0
SOS or Win-Win Adjacent.	++	++

The conservative position (especially of the Hindu fundamentalists) is to build only a Hindu temple on the site. The justification is that such a temple had stood there before the Moslem conquerors arrived long ago.

The liberal position (especially of those sympathetic to the Moslems) is to rebuild the Moslem mosque. The justification is that a mosque has existed at that place for over one thousand years, and it is questionable whether there once was a Hindu temple there.

The neutral position is to do neither. The SOS position is to build both religious structures adjacent to each other as part of a larger complex devoted to better relations between Hindus and Moslems.

Chapter 16

Equal Treatment under Law

Merit Treatment in General

Contemporary conservatives advocate merit hiring as a response to equal employment opportunity, although in the past they have generally been more tolerant of discrimination than have liberals.

Contemporary liberals often advocate at least temporary preferential hiring in order to redress past discrimination, especially if candidates are nearly equally qualified, tests are subjective, preferences are temporary, and the employers are private rather than governmental.

The compromise position is merit hiring, but affirmatively seeking qualified minority candidates through advertising in minority

Table 16.1 (Simple) Equal Employment Opportunity

ALTERNATIVES	GOALS	
	Conservative Productivity of work force.	Liberal Equity or fairness in distributing benefits.
Conservative Merit hiring.	+	−
Liberal Preferential hiring.	−	+
Neutral Seek qualified minorities.	0	0
SOS or Win-Win Upgrade skills.	++	++

217

newspapers, locating employers' physical plants in minority neighborhoods, and removing requirements that are correlated racially, but not with job performance.

The SOS alternative emphasizes upgrading skills so that minorities can qualify for merit hiring without needing preferences or even affirmative recruiting. The upgrading might include formal education, adult education, and especially on-the-job training.

That kind of SOS does well on a conservative goal of achieving a productive workforce, and well on a liberal goal of equity or fairness in distributing benefits in employment or education.

Merit Treatment Regardless of Race, Religion, or Economic Class

Alternative Public Policies on Race Relations

Discrimination in this context means requiring or allowing a white with an employment-test score of 40 to be preferred over a black with a score of 60, if 50 is the minimum score for qualifying, or if both qualify but the white is preferred even though the black applicant is substantially more qualified.

Affirmative action in this context means hiring only blacks who are qualified but actively seeking out qualified blacks through (1) advertising, (2) locating one's physical plant near black job-seekers, (3) removing requirements that are racially correlated, and (4) providing on-the-job training especially geared to overcome lack of training for blacks.

Preferential hiring means only hiring blacks who are qualified, but preferring qualified blacks over moderately less-qualified whites, generally as a temporary measure to offset prior discrimination.

Reverse racism is the same as discrimination, except blacks are favored.

The summation column tends to indicate that the optimum policy level for achieving the desired goals is to move away from discrimination to requiring affirmative action, but not to requiring preferential hiring except as a short-term remedy for prior discrimination.

Table 16.2 (Old) Race Relations

ALTERNATIVES	GOALS	
	Conservative Always favoring the one with the higher test score.	**Liberal** Stimulating minority advancement.
Conservative 1. Requiring segregation or discrimination. 2. Allowing discrimina- tion (same as doing nothing).	+	–
Liberal 1. Requiring preferential hiring. 2. Allowing reverse rac- ism.	–	+
Neutral 1. Outlawing discrimina- tion. 2. Requiring affirmative action.	0	0
SOS or Win-Win See text.	++	++

Evaluating Policies toward Race Relations

Race relations is also an issue on which liberals and conservatives tend to take a more joint position than on traditional economic controversies.

Discrimination, affirmative action, and preferential treatment in this context all mean the same as in the previous table.

The SOS alternative emphasizes upgrading skills so that blacks and other minorities can qualify for good jobs without needing any preferential hiring or even non-preferential affirmative action. "K-12" refers to elementary and secondary education. Opportunities industrialization centers are facilities that help in overcoming functional illiteracy, obtaining a General Education Development (GED or high

Table 16.3 (New) Race Relations

	GOALS	
ALTERNATIVES	**Conservative** Increase economy.	**Liberal** Equity.
Conservative No affirmative action, but outlaw discrimination.	+	−
Liberal Preferential hiring.	−	+
Neutral 1. Affirmative action. 2. Temporary preferential hiring.	0	0
SOS or Win-Win Upgrade skills in K-12, on-the-job training, and opportunities industrialization centers.	++	++

school equivalency test) certificate, interviewing and completing employment applications.

Merit Treatment Regardless of Gender

An SOS Approach to Comparable Worth

In a business firm, industry, or government agency, each job position is scored on a set of criteria to determine how much the job should be paid. The criteria may include education, dangerousness, supply of applicants, demand for the services, difficulty of passing qualifying tests, and others.

If comparable worth has been complied with, then the rank order of the scoring should correspond to the rank order of the wages paid. If those two rankings do not sufficiently correlate, then adjustments should be made to raise the pay of the positions that are paid less than what they should be.

Table 16.4 Comparable Worth

| | GOALS | |
ALTERNATIVES	Conservative Avoid overpayment.	Liberal Equitable wage.
Conservative Do nothing, i.e., leave to marketplace.	+	−
Liberal Assigned comparable worth.	−	+
Neutral In between.	0	0
SOS or Win-Win Multiple-criteria decision- making comparable worth.	++	++

This type of adjustment is designed to make adjustments for the lower wages of positions associated with women. The above system of adjustments is referred to as multiple-criteria decision-making or MCDM comparable worth.

The conservative position is to leave salary adjustments to the marketplace without any comparable-worth adjustments. The most liberal position is to make somewhat arbitrary adjustments upward for positions that are associated with women without going through the kind of MCDM comparable-worth analysis described above.

The MCDM approach scores positively as avoiding overpayment, especially if it considers supply-and-demand criteria, as well as others. The MCDM approach also scores positively on the liberal goal of providing an equitable wage, since it is likely to make adjustments for gender discrimination even if gender is not used as a criterion. Thus the MCDM approach has the characteristics of being an SOS alternative.

Excluding Women from Work Activities
Hazardous to Fetuses

This issue occurs in workplaces using x-rays, toxic chemicals, or other elements that are hazardous to fetuses, but not to adult females or adult males.

The conservative solution is to exclude women from such work activities, or at least women capable of becoming pregnant. The key conservative goal toward which that policy is directed is to avoid legal liability.

The liberal solution is to leave the matter up to the women employees. They would be given the right to decide for themselves whether they wished to assume the risk after they have been properly informed. The key liberal goal toward which the liberal policy is directed is to provide more employment opportunities for women.

A neutral compromise would be to include women, provided they would sign a waiver indicating they will not hold the company liable for damage that might occur.

The super-optimum solution is to emphasize safety devices. This may mean tax credits to cover the cost of inventing or adopting safety devices. Such a solution scores well on avoiding liability and providing safe employment, as contrasted to the conservative and

Table 16.5 Hazardous to Fetuses

	GOALS	
ALTERNATIVES	**Conservative** Avoid liability.	**Liberal** Provide safe employment.
Conservative Exclude women.	+	−
Liberal Include women.	−	+
Neutral Include with waivers.	0	0
SOS or Win-Win Emphasize safety devices.	++	++

liberal solutions which involve a tradeoff on those two goals. The compromise solution of allowing for binding waivers imposes a disincentive to develop appropriate safety devices.

Sexual Harassment

Here are two issues that are about to be decided by the Supreme Court regarding the definition of sexual harassment under the federal equal employment opportunity legislation.

A broad definition of sexual harassment specifies that the harassment needs only to be objectively vulgar, whereas a more narrow definition requires a showing of mental harm. A broad definition can include references to women in general as sex objects, whereas a more narrow definition requires a reference to a specific woman who is the complaining party.

An interesting aspect of these issues is that the Illinois American Civil Liberties Union (ACLU) affiliate has broken with the national ACLU over the second aspects of broad versus narrow definition. The Illinois affiliate argues that penalizing an employer for allowing the

Table 16.6 Sexual Harassment

	GOALS	
ALTERNATIVES	**Conservative** Equal treatment.	**Liberal** Free speech.
Conservative Broad definition of sexual harassment.	+	−
Liberal Narrow definition of sexual harassment.	−	+
Neutral Middling position.	0	0
SOS or Win-Win Socialization and education.	++	++

posting of a flyer referring to women in general as sex objects infringes on free speech.

The sexual harassment in this context means words and not behavior. A broad definition may thus promote equality and dignity, but may dampen some aspects of free speech.

If one places more weight on gender equality than free speech, then the broad definition is likely to be a winner. Even if one considers free speech to be more important, the broad definition might still be a winner on the grounds that there is virtually no free speech infringement here, but a substantial infringement on gender equality-dignity.

The object of an SOS solution is to develop ideas for simultaneously promoting a higher regard for both free speech and the dignity of women. That may mean the ACLU should be devoting more funds and time to developing childhood education materials as the Southern Poverty Law Center has been doing. Those materials are directed toward upgrading both goals among preschool and elementary school children.

The socialization approach, combined with either a broad, narrow, or middling definition, may do more for both equal treatment and free speech than any of those definitions by themselves.

There is a need for also educating employers, employees, and other adults as to the definitions of sexual harassment and their purposes.

Even the narrow definition of sexual harassment allows penalties for activities that only involve speech, as contrasted to behavior. An absolute free-speech advocate might argue that sexual harassment should only cover behavior such as touching, firing, or threatening to fire. The First Amendment, however, does not generally protect hardcore pornography, libel and slander, fraudulent speech, or privacy invasion that may only involve words or pictures, not behavior.

Merit Treatment Regardless of Sexual Orientation

An SOS Analysis of Discrimination against Homosexuals

In Table 16.7 "doing nothing" means leaving it to the marketplace to determine job opportunities for homosexuals even if the marketplace results in discrimination. Anti-discrimination refers to prohibiting the non-hiring of a qualified homosexual because he or she is a homosexual. The neutral position involves a government pronouncement against discrimination, but without active enforcement.

The SOS alternative involves childhood socialization regarding the importance of judging people on the basis of merit, without explicitly mentioning homosexuals. At the teenage level, socialization and education should also include judging people on the basis of merit with an explicit mention of groups traditionally discriminated against, including homosexuals.

The fourth goal of isolating and ostracizing homosexuals is held by some conservatives, but not all. Thus the conservative totals are shown two ways–one with the fourth goal and one without it.

Table 16.7 Discrimination against Homosexuals

ALTERNATIVES	GOALS	
	Conservative 1. Entrepreneurial free-dom. 2. Isolate and ostracize homosexuals.	**Liberal** 1. Equal opportunity. 2. High national produc-tivity.
Conservative Do nothing.	+	−
Liberal Anti-discrimination.	−	+
Neutral Pronouncement without enforcement.	0	0
SOS or Win-Win Socialization.	++	++

The socialization approach wins over the conservative approach of doing nothing, unless one considers the fourth goal. The socialization approach also wins over the liberal approach of anti-discrimination action by the government at least in the long run.

We usually assume that conservatives give conservative goals a weight of 3 on a scale of 1 to 3, and that liberals give such goals a weight of 1, with the opposite weighting for liberal goals. That does not necessarily have to be so. On the goal of high national productivity, conservatives and liberals may be closer together, even in the context of discrimination against homosexuals.

Gays in the Military

As with many policy issues, the solution arrived at depends partly on how the issue is stated. Here the issue is stated in terms of whether gays should be excluded from or included in the military. Those favoring exclusion might respond quite differently in wartime if the issue were whether gays should be drafted or given an exemption. Responses also might differ if the issue were stated in terms of what conditions or restrictions should be placed on gays in the military.

There seems to be a consensus that gays involved in illegal behavior can be removed from the military just as can heterosexuals. What constitutes illegal behavior could be left to the individual states where the behavior takes place, or it could be a consensus against excluding or removing gays who do nothing or say nothing to indicate that they are homosexual. A controversy concerns what statements, if any, should result in exclusion.

The main conservative goal in this context is to prevent disruption that might occur as a result of the inability of gays and "straights" to get along. The main liberal goal is to judge people on the basis of their individual merit and behavior and not on the basis of their beliefs or statements concerning their beliefs.

In other discrimination issues, the conservative position generally emphasizes the goal of judging people on the basis of merit or efficiency, and liberals tend to advocate equity considerations to compensate for past discrimination. Business-oriented conservatives

Table 16.8 Gays in the Military

	GOALS	
ALTERNATIVES	Conservative Prevent disruption.	Liberal Judge on merit and behavior.
Conservative Exclude gays.	+	−
Liberal Include gays.	−	+
Neutral Include with restrictions.	0	0
SOS or Win-Win 1. Retain ban. 2. Prohibit information. 3. Prosecute sexual behavior.	++	++

tend to emphasize merit in discussing discrimination against gays, whereas religious or cultural conservatives may be more likely to consider homosexuality as a disqualification regardless of merit.

Some of this controversy may become obsolete as a result of court cases which argue that it is a denial of free speech to exclude someone from the military who makes statements about his or her homosexuality. The argument is also being made in court that it denies equal treatment under law for the military to exclude gays who make statements about their status, but not to exclude "straights" who make statements about their status. The free-speech argument may be rejected on the grounds that it is not advocacy speech, but more closely related to being a confession of potential wrongdoing. The equal treatment argument might be rejected on the grounds that the differences in treatment are justified by a need for military cohesion.

The solution toward which the military is moving would allow gays into the military without asking applicants whether they are gay, so long as gays do not openly indicate they are gay by way of statements or acts. That solution improves on liberal goals by opening up the military and judging people more on the basis of individual merit. It is also improves on conservative goals by making more explicit the basis for exclusion. This could, however, be considered more in the nature of a compromise than a super-optimum solution. Both sides are making concessions. The conservatives might like to totally exclude gays, but are tolerating their inclusion so long as they keep quiet. The liberals might like to include gays without any restrictions on keeping quiet.

The "don't ask, don't tell" solution can be considered part of a sequential SOS. This can be considered a step toward judging military applicants and other people on the basis of their competence, experience, and individual merit. The issue may be too emotional and too new to go further now. Perhaps in a few years or so, the solution based on merit will appeal to both liberals and conservatives if it can be broadened to include other forms of anti-gay discrimination (which might also please liberals) and other groups such as blacks (which might please conservatives).

Merit Treatment Regardless of Disability or Health

Public Policy toward Obesity as a Disability

Table 16.9 is based on a 1993 federal court case on whether obesity should be considered a disability under the Americans with Disabilities Act. If obesity is included, then obese people could not legally be discriminated against and reasonable accommodations would need to be provided for them. There seems to be agreement that obesity means more than fifty pounds overweight.

The conservative position is to avoid declaring obesity a disability. The older conservative position might have opposed including any disabilities as being subject to anti-discrimination laws.

The liberal position is to have obesity considered a disability even if it is based on bad eating habits. This is the position taken by the Equal Employment Opportunity Commission (EEOC) against the state of Rhode Island for refusing to hire a three hundred pound woman as an attendant at a state school for the mentally retarded.

Table 16.9 Obesity

	GOALS	
ALTERNATIVES	**Conservative** 1. Avoid burden on business. 2. Deter obesity.	**Liberal** Broaden job opportunities.
Conservative Not a disability.	+	−
Liberal Always a disability.	−	+
Neutral Sometimes.	0	0
SOS or Win-Win Disability but possibly subject to improvement.	++	++

The neutral position is to declare obesity a disability only if it is disease-based, but not if it is based on poor eating habits.

Conservatives are interested in avoiding burdens on business and in deterring activities that cause obesity or other disabilities. Liberals are interested in broadening job opportunities.

The super-optimum position might be to consider obesity as a disability regardless of its cause, but make it a conditional matter. That means employers might be required to hire a qualified obese person, but they could establish a reasonable condition that progress must be made in weight reduction if the obesity were based on bad eating habits.

Policy toward Firing At-Home Smokers

The issue here is whether Congress or state legislatures should enact laws prohibiting employers from firing people who smoke, but who only do so off the job, generally at home.

The conservative position is that employers should be allowed to do so because smokers impose upon business firms large costs in health-care and absenteeism. Smoking may not be related to job performance, but it is related to depressing business profits.

The liberal position is that a right of privacy is infringed when employers fire people for at-home activities, although these are not political or sexual activities which would raise more serious free-speech and privacy questions.

A neutral compromise would be to allow employers to fire people who smoke in the workplace, or to pass laws prohibiting smoking in the workplace. Conservatives could justify it on the grounds of saving business expenses. Liberals could justify protecting others from secondary smoke.

The super-optimum solution that preserves both business profits and privacy might be the health-care program proposed by the Clinton Administration. It provides for equal premiums for all people regardless of health or preconditions. Under it, business firms would not have increased health-care costs for smokers.

Higher premiums for smokers has been in the past a way of discouraging smoking. That might be done better by higher taxes on cigarettes, which is part of the Clinton health-care program. It can also be done better by more information on the health dangers of smoking and by prohibiting smoking in public places.

Table 16.10 At-Home Smokers

	GOALS	
ALTERNATIVES	**Conservative** Profits.	**Liberal** Privacy.
Conservative Can fire home smokers.	+	−
Liberal Cannot fire.	−	+
Neutral Can fire workplace smokers.	0	0
SOS or Win-Win Clinton health-care program.	++	++

Merit Treatment Specifically in Voting, Criminal Justice, Education, and Employment

Black Legislative Districts

Conservative whites in the South, Chicago, and elsewhere would like as few black-majority legislative districts as possible. Liberals would prefer as much black influence in as many districts as possible. The goal of conservative whites is white political power, which is mainly defined in this context in terms of the proportion of legislative seats held by whites rather than blacks. The goal of liberals, especially blacks, is to increase black political power, which could be defined in terms of the proportion of districts in which blacks hold the controlling vote, although not necessarily the majority vote.

The super-optimum solution might be racially balanced districts. That means if blacks were to constitute 40 percent of the population, then they should compromise about 40 percent of each district, rather than 40 percent of the legislators. The 40 percent figure applies both in Mississippi and Chicago, as illustrative examples.

Table 16.11 (Old) Black Legislative Districts

	GOALS	
ALTERNATIVES	Conservative White political power.	Liberal Black political power.
Conservative No black districts.	+	−
Liberal Black influence in all districts.	−	+
Neutral 1. Some black districts. 2. Some black influence.	0	0
SOS or Win-Win Racially balanced districts.	++	++

The effect of such racially-balanced districts would be that blacks would be able to determine the white winner in every district, and thereby have great influence on the attitudes of the white legislators. This should please liberals. The effect would be that there would be fewer blacks in the legislature, since there would be no "safe" black district. This should please conservatives.

Racially-balanced voting districts are like racially-balanced school districts, whereas concentrated black voting districts are like segregated black school districts. Segregation in either context promotes divisiveness and decreases minority influence.

A compromise would be to have some black districts and some black influence. That would be a concession contrary to the conservative's desires. It would also be a concession contrary to the liberal's preferences in giving up some black influence by wasting black votes in some concentrated black districts.

Racially-balanced districts would produce much black influence (without black representation) only if the percentage of blacks in the state or the city reaches between 30 percent and 50 percent. There would be virtually no influence or representation if the percentage is between 0 and 10 percent. If the state percentage is over 55 percent, then a black candidate could represent every district. Thus a black district might be defined as one in which more than 55 percent of the registered voters are black. This allows for nonvoters and for some black votes for the white candidates. A black-controlled district might be defined as one in which 30 percent to 50 percent of the registered voters are black. This may be insufficient to elect a black candidate in a racially divisive district, but it may be plenty for influencing the platform of a winning white candidate.

A combination of some black districts and some districts that are black influenced or controlled can be a super-optimum solution. For example, suppose the best expectation of blacks is to have eight black seats, and the best expectation of whites is to hold the black seats down to six. Suppose further that blacks consider two black-controlled districts to be the equivalent of one black seat. If there are five black seats and ten black-controlled districts, then blacks have the equivalent of ten seats, which exceeds their best expectations. Likewise, with only five black seats, the best expectations of whites have been exceeded by holding blacks below the six-seat level.

SOS Analysis Relating Capital Punishment to Racial Discrimination

The issue here is that capital punishment has been disproportionately applied to defendants with white victims rather than black victims. Thus, approximately 55 percent of all the convicted defendants get the death penalty in cases involving white homicide victims, but only 40 percent of all the convicted defendants get the death penalty in cases involving black homicide victims. These statistics are given in *McClesky v. Georgia*, 107 Supreme Court Reports 1756, 1987, and Gregory Russell, *The Death Penalty and Racial Bias* (Greenwood, 1994).

Liberals treat these findings as a further reason for abolishing capital punishment, thereby ending that kind of discrimination. A conservative counter-argument might be that if statistical patterns could be so used, then the Supreme Court could well abolish all crime penalties. One might find a similar pattern with white robbery victims versus black robbery victims.

Table 16.12 Capital Punishment and Racial Discrimination

	GOALS	
ALTERNATIVES	**Conservative** Deter crime.	**Liberal** End discrimination.
Conservative Retain capital punishment.	+	−
Liberal Abolish capital punish- ment.	−	+
Neutral Modification by appeal.	**0**	**0**
SOS or Win-Win 10 percent difference.	++	++

In this context, conservatives are especially interested in deterring crime, including murder. Liberals are especially interested in ending racial discrimination, especially if state executions are involved as contrasted to jail sentences.

A compromise position would be to allow more commuting of death sentences on appeal based on the individual circumstances. That, however, may not be sufficiently directed toward changing these statistical patterns.

An SOS alternative might specify that if the percentage of death-sentenced defendants with white victims is more than 10 percent greater than the corresponding percentage of defendants with black victims, then capital punishment would be suspended in that state until the percentage difference is less than 10 percent. For example, if the figures were 55 percent and 40 percent as above, then capital punishment would be temporarily suspended. The state would have an incentive to bring the 55 percent figure down by commuting some of the death sentences, rather than raising the 40 percent figure by making more use of the death penalty. Either course could be acceptable of reducing racial discrimination below an unacceptable threshold (which should please liberals) while still retaining capital punishment (which should please conservatives).

A SOS Analysis of Affirmative Action
in Medical Schools

The hypothetical problem is alternative affirmative-action programs in a medical school. Policy A emphasizes the training function of the medical school by recruiting minority students from undergraduate schools. Policy B is also concerned with servicing patients in the hospital that is associated with the medical school. That policy emphasizes providing experience to young minority people working in the hospital.

A compromise would be to adopt half of each policy. An SOS solution would be to fully adopt both policies if that is possible.

The many dimensions of the problem of measuring incremental students trained or incremental patients treated can be handled

Table 16.13 Affirmative Action in Medical Schools

ALTERNATIVES	GOALS	
	Conservative Students.	Liberal Patients.
Conservative Policy A: recruiting undergraduate schools.	+	–
Liberal Policy B: pre-medical interns.	–	+
Neutral Half and half.	0	0
SOS or Win-Win Combine both policies.	++	++

through scales of 2 to 4. A 4 means a relatively high positive increment in this context. A 2 means a relatively low positive increment,
and a 3 means something in between. Such a scale is rough, but may
be sufficient for reaching a decision that the SOS combination
alternative should be adopted.

Instead of referring to the alternatives and goals as conservative
and liberal, they could be referred to as Group No. 1 and Group No.
2.

The No. 1 alternative could be made more acceptable to the No.
2 group by giving the students financial aid under which they are
required to do intern activities. The No. 2 alternative could be made
more acceptable to the No. 1 group by specifying that the interns
must be medical students or pre-medical students.

Dealing with Layoffs and Affirmative Action Simultaneously

The issue here is that if layoffs follow the general rule of laying
off those who are last hired, then that might lead to disproportionately
laying off blacks and other minorities. The problem is how to offset
the occurrence without disrupting the merit system.

Table 16.14 Layoffs and Affirmative Action

	GOALS	
	Conservative Merit hiring and firing.	Liberal Protect minorities.
ALTERNATIVES		
Conservative As is. No points.	+	−

Liberal
1. Preferential non-lay-
  offs.
2. Artificial seniority of
  10 years.
	−	+

Neutral One year.	0	0
SOS or Win-Win 1. Strict merit. 2. No seniority. 3. Upgrade skills. 4. Seniority within a range.	++	++

The conservative alternative might be to fully allow the rule of laying off those who were last hired, since they have the least experience. The liberal position might be to give blacks and other minorities artificial seniority to compensate for not having been hired sooner. Thus a black worker hired in 1992 might be assumed to have been hired in 1982 if ten years credit is used. The compromise position between no credit and ten years might be about one year of credit.

An SOS alternative might involve laying off those who score the lowest on a merit test regardless of seniority (which should please liberals) and regardless of race (which should please conservatives). The alternative could be supplemented with a program to upgrade the skills of new and old workers so they can score higher on the merit test. That should further please conservatives since the training could lead to better-paid workers. A third component which represents an SOS compromise would be to lay off workers on the basis of merit ranges or categories, with people in the lowest category being laid off first. Within each category, workers with the lowest seniority would be laid off first, thereby combining merit and seniority.

In this context, there may be two kinds of conservatives. One kind is the conservative businessperson who wants to hire and fire on the basis of merit since that is more predictable. The other kind is the conservative, older worker who wants seniority to be the main criterion in layoffs. There may also be two kinds of liberals in this context. One kind wants preferences in firing, such as seniority credit. The other kind is satisfied with merit firing, since that may help some of the younger black workers retain their jobs over the older white workers who may be less capable.

Merit Treatment in Other Nations

Dealing with Low-Income Ethnic Groups in Russia and Elsewhere

There are two conservative positions toward minority ethnic groups in Russia and elsewhere. One is to force assimilation so as to make the group disappear. Another is to allow the group to preserve its culture, but discriminate against members of the group in employment and educational opportunities.

There are basically two liberal positions toward minority ethnic groups. One is to allow voluntary separatism. The other is to give minority-group members affirmative action or preferences in employment or educational opportunities.

The professed conservative goal is judging people on the basis of their merit. Any policy that discriminates or shows preference runs contrary to that goal. Separatism also decreases the ability of minority members to move into positions for which they can qualify in the larger society.

The professed liberal goal is equity or fairness toward minority and majority groups, and also responsiveness to the desires of both groups. Policies that repress minority cultures are not responsive to their desires. Policies that discriminate or show preferences lack

Table 16.15 Low-Income Ethnic Groups in Russia

ALTERNATIVES	GOALS	
	Conservative Merit.	Liberal Equity and responsive- ness.
Conservative 1. Repress culture. 2. Discriminate.	+	−
Liberal 1. Autonomous voluntary separatism. 2. Preferences.	−	+

Neutral
1. Encourage integration,
  but preserve culture.
2. Non-preferential affir-
  mative action.
	0	0

SOS or Win-Win Upgrade skills.	++	++

equity, at least in the long run.

The SOS alternative is to upgrade the skills of members of low income ethnic groups so they can better qualify for employment and educational opportunities without preferences or affirmative action. They are also more likely to want to be part of a larger society if they can qualify for better opportunities.

Dispute over South Ossetia

In the context of a neighboring dispute between Armenia and Azerbaijan (to be examined below), South Ossetia is like Nagorno-Karabakh. Russia is analogous to Armenia, and Georgia is analogous to Azerbaijan.

One difference is that the SOS alternative proposes an independent Ossetia, which would join together the Ossetia of Russia and the Ossetia of Georgia into an independent nation. Both Russia and Georgia would lose an area.

Table 16.16 Dispute over South Ossetia

ALTERNATIVES	GOALS	
	Conservative What is best for Georgia.	**Liberal** What is best for Caucasus Russia.
Conservative South Ossetia to Russia.	+	−
Liberal South Ossetia to Georgia.	−	+
Neutral Partition.	0	0
SOS or Win-Win Independent Ossetia.	++	++

The alternatives would be to give all of South Ossetia to Russia as one alternative, or to give all of South Ossetia to Georgia as a second alternative. The third alternative would be to split South Ossetia in half. None of those alternatives may make as much sense in terms of reducing the fighting as creating an independent Ossetia.

Doing so would relieve Russia of an undesirable separatist conflict. An independent Ossetia also would provide similar relief to Georgia. The people of Ossetia would gain independent national status, with guaranteed rights for minority ethnic groups within Ossetia.

Dispute between Armenia and Azerbaijan

Nagorno-Karabakh (NK) is an enclave in Azerbaijan that is inhabited mainly by Armenians. The Armenians would like to annex NK as part of Armenia. The Azerbaijanis would like to retain NK as part of Azerbaijan.

A neutral alternative might be to partition NK, with half going to Armenia and half to Azerbaijan. That is frequently the way land compromises work. Both sides make concessions so that both come out ahead of their worst expectations, but not ahead of their best

Table 16.17 Dispute between Armenia and Azerbaijan

ALTERNATIVES	GOALS	
	Conservative What is best for Armenia.	**Liberal** What is best for Azerbaijan.
Conservative Nagorno-Karabakh to Armenia.	+	−
Liberal Nagorno-Karabakh to Azerbaijan.	−	+
Neutral Partition.	0	0
SOS or Win-Win Independent Nagorno-Karabakh	++	++

expectations.

If NK goes to Armenia, this might be undesirable for Armenia because it could mean continued fighting. Likewise, the fighting could continue indefinitely if NK remains a part of Azerbaijan. Thus giving all of NK to one nation or the other generates a lose-lose situation in which both sides come out behind.

A super-optimum solution in which both sides come out ahead, notably by ending the fighting, might involve NK becoming an independent nation. That would mean no loss on the part of Armenia. It could mean no loss of a large number of Azerbaijanis since most of NK consists of Armenians. It would be necessary to install guarantees for the minority Azerbaijanis living in NK. The people of NK would also come out ahead by ending the fighting and obtaining a new independent national status.

PART THREE

INTERNATIONAL PEACE

Chapter 17

World Peace in General

U.S. Foreign Policy

An SOS Analysis of American Foreign Policy

Conservative foreign policy places more emphasis on defense and less on domestic matters in comparison to liberal foreign policy.

Table 17.1 (Old) Foreign Policy

	GOALS	
ALTERNATIVES	**Conservative** U.S. military power.	**Liberal** Fulfill domestic needs.
Conservative 1. Pro-defense. 2. Favor right. 3. Disfavor left.	+	–
Liberal 1. Pro-domestic. 2. Favor left. 3. Disfavor right.	–	+
Neutral 1. Be friendly to all. 2. Isolationism or pacifism.	0	0
SOS or Win-Win 1. Favor democratic gov- ernment and forces. 2. Favor free trade.	++	++

Conservative foreign policy tends to favor right-wing governments overseas, whereas liberal foreign policy tends to favor left-wing governments. A neutral foreign policy is more even-handed or withdrawn.

A super-optimum alternative might favor democratic governments (whether right-wing or left-wing) and disfavor dictatorial governments. A super-optimum alternative might also emphasize free trade as part of a conservative program for aggressive international sales. At the same time, such an alternative would stress free trade as part of a liberal program for meeting domestic economic needs.

U.S. Foreign Policy Since Cold War

Cold War U.S. foreign policy divided conservatives and liberals. Conservatives tended to favor right-wing governments and large defense expenditures, whereas liberals tended to favor left-wing governments and lower defense expenditures. Now, both sides support lower defense expenditures and are less influenced by the economic ideology of foreign governments.

Table 17.2 (New) Foreign Policy

	GOALS	
ALTERNATIVES	**Conservative** Save taxes and promote business.	**Liberal** Promote employment and peace..
Conservative Isolationism.	+	−
Liberal Peacemaking.	−	+
Neutral Selective peacemaking.	0	0
SOS or Win-Win Peace as part of larger international package.	++	++

The prevailing conservative orientation seems more isolationist and less interventionist than the current liberal orientation. That is shown in the greater liberal support for intervention in Bosnia, Somalia, and other places where peacemaking or humanitarian aid might be appropriate. A compromise position would advocate greater selectivity in the application of isolationism or peacemaking.

The key conservative goal seems to be to save taxes and promote domestic business. The key liberal goal seems to be to promote peace in the workplace and domestic employment opportunities.

An SOS solution might be to see peace as part of a larger international package. That foreign-policy package would include the United States actively promoting peace, prosperity, and democracy throughout the world in order to help all nations become better customers for the United States, suppliers to the United States, places for investment, and better world citizens. That kind of pragmatic policy would be mutually beneficial in increasing the national incomes and quality of life in both the United States and elsewhere.

Separate analyses could be developed. An important factor in promoting peace is supporting the United Nations' peacemaking activities. An important factor in promoting prosperity is free trade in the movement of products, factories, and labor. An important factor in promoting democracy is the free movement of ideas through the mass media and providing financial and technical support for democratic forces inside and outside potentially dictatorial governments.

Purposes for CIA Since the Cold War

During the Cold War, a key purpose of the Central Intelligence Agency (CIA) was to support governments that would side with the United States in local, regional, or world disputes against the Soviet Union. That purpose also involved destabilizing governments that behaved favorably toward the Soviet Union, or at least not favorably toward the United States. Destabilizing practices as extreme as seeking to assassinate Cuban President Fidel Castro or arming the Contras against Sandinistas in Nicaragua, possibly in violation of congressional statutes.

Since the end of the Cold War, few major disputes in the world have found Russia and the United States on opposite sides. Both countries, for example, voted in the United Nations Security Council to support a U.S. invasion of Haiti to restore Jean-Bertrand Aristide as the elected president. In Cold War days, the United States probably would have supported the right-wing military, and Russia would have supported the left-wing President Aristide. There was no invasion in 1994 because the military agreed to retire to Panama and allow for free elections.

The conservative position on the current CIA is that the agency should support governments that endorse U.S. foreign policy, and try to change governments that do not. That position is not concerned with whether the government is democratic or dictatorial. For example, Saudi Arabia may receive CIA reports on dissident Saudis even though Saudi Arabia is an authoritarian monarchy.

Table 17.3 CIA

	GOALS	
ALTERNATIVES	**Conservative** Maximize U.S. allies.	**Liberal** Promote domestic and international well-being.
Conservative Support groups that endorse U.S. foreign policy.	+	–
Liberal Greatly reduce or abolish CIA.	–	+
Neutral 1. Abolish covert activities. 2. Retain intelligence.	0	0
SOS or Win-Win Support democratic political forces.	++	++

The liberal position on the CIA is to greatly reduce its budget, or even to abolish its existence. A more neutral position would be to abolish the CIA activities that seek to overthrow unfriendly governments and bolster friendly but unpopular governments. The neutral position would retain the intelligence or data-gathering activities of the CIA. The agency might be renamed something like the International Data Gathering Agency.

A key goal of conservatives in this context might be to maximize U.S. allies on foreign-policy issues, such as the need for supporting Israel-Arab peace treaties. A key goal of liberals in this context might be to promote domestic and international well-being. Domestic well-being might be promoted by diverting CIA money to domestic-policy problems. International well-being might be promoted by the CIA no longer interfering with foreign political parties that promote democracy and equalitarian policies.

A CIA purpose that could both maximize U.S. allies and promote domestic and international well-being would be for the CIA to support democratic political forces abroad. That might mean dividing the CIA into two new agencies. One might be the International Data Gathering Agency, for gathering military, economic, political, and other information useful for American foreign policy. The other agency might be a counterpart to the Agency for International Development, which supports economic rather than political development. The new agency might be called the Agency for Democratic Development.

Political development would mean supplying funding and expertise to democratic political forces in dictatorial countries to increase the influence of those forces. The new agency would also broadcast regular radio and television programs carrying objective news, debates, and discussions of public-policy controversies relevant to the regions and nations receiving the broadcasts. It might be desirable for the agency to be semi-private with representation from outside the government, although with substantial government funding. The outside representatives could come from various non-governmental organizations that endorse democratic procedures, while perhaps differing on economic solutions.

Those kinds of purposes for a post-Cold War CIA could do more

for maximizing U.S. allies than supporting undemocratic governments that endorse U.S. foreign policy. Democratic governments are
more likely to enjoy lasting popularity at home, and thus be more
stable U.S. allies. Democratic governments are also more likely to
arrive at public policies that promote prosperity, including trade with
the United States.

SOS Analysis of Policy toward Yugoslavia, Somalia, and Other Trouble Spots

Since the Cold War, conservatives have tended to take a hands-off
position toward trouble spots in which there is no conflict between
communism and capitalism.

Liberals, meanwhile, have tended to take an interventionist
position on behalf of underdog ethnic groups, civilians, poor people,
starving people, or other have-nots in various international trouble
spots.

The following analysis applies to the former Yugoslavia, Somalia,
Moslems in India, pro-democracy students in China, the Tamils in Sri
Lanka, and others elsewhere.

Table 17.4 Trouble Spots

	GOALS	
ALTERNATIVES	**Conservative** Save money.	**Liberal** Save people.
Conservative Hands off.	+	−
Liberal Intervention.	−	+
Neutral Partial aid.	0	0
SOS or Win-Win Developing better customers, suppliers, investments, and U.S. image.	++	++

The SOS alternative is to support international activities that help to develop better customers, suppliers, investments, and a better U.S. world image. Doing so can provide monetary gain to the United States, pleasing conservatives. It can also provide altruistic gain, pleasing liberals.

Arms Control

International Law: Arms Control

Table 17.5 originated in 1986. The numbers show changes in the scores as of 1988.

Table 17.5 (Old) Arms Control

	GOALS	
ALTERNATIVES	**Conservative** Avoid being conquered.	**Liberal** Avoid nuclear war.
Conservative 1. Encourage war to bring Armageddon. 2. First strike with no retaliation. 3. Arms buildup. 4. Wait for bilateral reduction without stimuli.	+	–
Liberal 1. Unilateral disarmament. 2. Permanent unilateral freeze. 3. Temporary unilateral freeze. 4. Supervisable freeze.	–	+
Neutral Wait for bilateral reduction with stimuli.	0	0
SOS or Win-Win See text.	++	++

The policy alternatives are ranked from the four most war-oriented at the top to the four most pacifist at the bottom. The criteria are arranged in random order.
See Table 17.6 and the text for a win-win alternative.

Evaluating Policies toward Arms Control

Table 17.6 is mainly of historical interest since it deals with arms-control issues as they existed in approximately 1985.

The conservative position was to further increase American nuclear arms and the Strategic Defense Initiative (SDI) to intercept Russian missiles. The liberal position was a unilateral freeze or unilateral disarmament on the part of the United States. The neutral position concluded that nuclear arms had reached saturation, but that conventional arms needed development.

The SOS alternative adopted by Presidents Gorbachev and Reagan in 1986 was a bilateral arms reduction. That alternative did more to satisfy the conservative goal of avoiding Russian conquest than a nuclear arms buildup. It did more to satisfy the neutral or liberal goals of avoiding nuclear war and making funds available for the domestic economy than a unilateral freeze.

Table 17.6 (New) Arms Control

	GOALS	
ALTERNATIVES	**Conservative** Avoid being conquered.	**Liberal** Avoid nuclear war.
Conservative Nuclear arms buildup and SDI.	+	−
Liberal Unilateral freeze or disarmament.	−	+
Neutral Conventional arms development.	0	0
SOS or Win-Win Bilateral arms reduction.	++	++

The SDI program became so expensive, and possibly unrealistic and provocative, as to lose its political feasibility. The unilateral freeze may also have been politically unfeasible for symbolic reasons, unless there had been similar action on the part of the Soviet Union. See also Table 2.1 and the accompanying text.

Non-Proliferation

The conservative position advocates that United States retain nuclear arms. That may mean reducing pressure on other countries to eliminate their nuclear arms.

The liberal position seeks universal disarmament regarding nuclear arms. The neutral position lies somewhere between retaining arms and total nuclear disarmament worldwide.

Conservatives are especially interested in peace through deterrence. Liberals are especially interested in using money for domestic purposes instead of for maintaining nuclear capability and other expensive defense purposes.

Peacetime conversion of nuclear arms to materials that can be used to supply energy for business firms and consumers should

Table 17.7 Non-Proliferation

	GOALS	
ALTERNATIVES	**Conservative** Peace through deterrence.	**Liberal** Prosperity.
Conservative Retain nuclear arms.	+	−
Liberal Disarm.	−	+
Neutral Partial disarm.	0	0
SOS or Win-Win Peacetime conversion.	++	++

appeal to both conservatives and liberals. Conservatives like cheap energy, including nuclear energy. Liberals welcome conversion of armaments to peacetime uses.

United Nations

The U.S. and UN Peacekeeping

The conservative U.S. position on United Nations peacekeeping is to have minimum U.S. involvement. This runs contrary to previous advocacy of intervention on behalf of anti-communist forces throughout the world.

The liberal U.S. position calls for substantial U.S. involvement. Peacekeeping in this context includes both helping to bring about a cease-fire and preserving a cease-fire after it has been established.

A key conservative goal is to save U.S. dollars and lives. A key liberal goal is to promote peace, prosperity, and democracy. Liberals are also interested in saving U.S. dollars and lives, but not, relatively speaking, as much as conservatives in the context of these two goals. Conservatives are also interested in promoting peace, prosperity, and

Table 17.8 UN Peacekeeping

	GOALS	
ALTERNATIVES	**Conservative** Save U.S. dollars and lives.	**Liberal** Promote peace, prosperity, and democracy.
Conservative Minimum U.S. involvement.	+	−
Liberal Substantial U.S. involvement.	−	+
Neutral In between.	0	0
SOS or Win-Win Volunteer UN forces.	++	++

democracy, but not as much as liberals in this context.

Minimum U.S. involvement does well on saving dollars and lives, but not so well on promoting peace, prosperity, and democracy. Substantial U.S. involvement does better on the liberal goal, but not so well on the conservative goal.

A super-optimum solution that may be capable of doing well on both goals is to make the UN force voluntary. This would contrast with present U.S. involvement, in which American troops participate along with troops of other countries. A volunteer UN force would be compromised of individuals who join it for money, idealism, or adventure–not drafted or ordered to do so. They would be under the command of UN officers who would also be volunteers, although possibly aided by advisors from the United States and other countries.

Such an SOS solution would probably save more U.S. dollars and lives than an involvement that is more direct, since the force would be multi-national. Such a solution would also probably do more for promoting peace, prosperity, and democracy than substantial U.S. involvement or an in-between position. The UN force would seek to obtain the best people possible in terms of prior experience, age, health, diversity, and other characteristics, specifically for peacekeeping purposes. Also see Table 2.7 and the accompanying text.

Peace-making Role of the United Nations

The issue here is what role should the UN play in promoting world peace. The conservative alternative emphasizes discussion rather than military action. The liberal alternative endorses a military role for the UN, either by units from various cooperating countries or by an independent military force.

The neutral compromise positions sees the UN as being most useful in preserving a cease-fire that has already been reached. This can be contrasted to imposing a cease-fire on the warring sides, which is part of the liberal alternative.

Conservatives are especially concerned that each member of the United Nations retain its sovereignty and not be ordered by the UN

Table 17.9 United Nations

	GOALS	
ALTERNATIVES	**Conservative** Sovereignty.	**Liberal** Peace.
Conservative Discussion only.	+	–
Liberal Military peace-making force.	–	+
Neutral Preserve cease-fire.	0	0
SOS or Win-Win Dispute prevention.	++	++

to cease fire or to take other action. Liberals are especially concerned with maintaining world peace, even if it means some loss of sovereignty to an international peace-making force.

A super-optimum solution might be to strengthen the dispute-prevention activities of the UN. These include mediation and arbitration. It would be desirable for as many countries as possible to agree in advance to settle disputes by binding mediation or arbitration. Dispute prevention also may include promoting prosperity and free trade among neighboring countries. Doing so is likely to help prevent war-oriented disputes without interfering with national sovereignty.

Defense and Military Activities

Defense Spending

The conservative position on defense spending is to maintain expenditures at their current levels. The justification is that substantial reductions would undercut national security and shrink profits and employment in defense industries.

The liberal position favors drastic reductions, mainly to provide money for domestic policy problems. Advocacy of reductions in defense activities was previously motivated more toward reducing the likelihood of war, especially world war. That likelihood, however, has been greatly reduced since the end of the Cold War.

If conservatives want to keep defense spending at approximately $250 billion and liberals would like a drastic reduction to $150 billion, then a neutral position would be a defense budget of about $200 billion.

A super-optimum solution would maintain profits for defense contractors and simultaneously divert much federal money to domestic needs such as education. That might be done by instituting a program to determine out of approximately four hundred non-military products produced in the world, which forty products score best on criteria of supply and demand and relevance to the capabilities of defense contractors.

The federal government could provide capital for converting to the production of most or all of those products while still preserving sufficient defense production. The result could be that the defense

Table 17.10   Defense Spending

	GOALS	
ALTERNATIVES	**Conservative** Profits for defense con- tractors.	**Liberal** Divert to domestic policy problems.
Conservative Keep defense spending as is ($250 billion).	+	−
Liberal Drastic reduction (to $150 billion).	−	+
Neutral Neutral reduction (to $200 billion).	0	0
SOS or Win-Win Massive replacement if less than $250 billion income or greater than $150 billion in federal government spending.	++	++

industry would gain an income even greater than its present $250 billion, while the federal government would spend less than $150 billion. The difference of $100 billion would be made up from civilian purchases. The federal conversion money would be a one-time investment.

This analysis could be considered analogous to finding jobs for public-aid recipients. Some defense spending is as unnecessary as some public aid. Both aid recipients and defense contractors need government-financed facilitators to make the transition from federal money to productivity in the private sector.

The Draft and National Service

Mandatory national service could please conservatives by providing personnel for the military. The system should also please liberals by providing people who would choose to perform service on behalf of the poor and civilian public-interest causes. Everyone would have an equal obligation, as contrasted to a voluntary military which disproportionately attracts low-income whites and blacks.

Table 17.11   The Draft

	GOALS	
ALTERNATIVES	**Conservative** 1. Pro-military. 2. Equal obligation.	**Liberal** 1. Anti-military. 2. Military quality.
Conservative Draft.	+	−
Liberal No draft.	−	+
Neutral None.	0	0
SOS or Win-Win Required national service.	++	++

Expanding NATO

Some officials in the Department of Defense advocate that Eastern European countries be allowed to join the North Atlantic Treaty Organization (NATO) to gain security from Russia if Russia comes under the influence of a nationalist party that advocates territorial expansion.

Others in the Defense Department prefer to exclude Eastern Europe to avoid antagonizing Russia and provoking the kind of warlike interaction that a wider NATO is designed to prevent.

A neutral compromise would be to invite both Eastern Europe and Russia to join NATO. Russia would probably reject the idea on the grounds that it is still a super-power and does not need to have the United States and Western Europe come to its military aid.

A super-optimum alternative might be to form a new entity, possibly called the European Security Organization. It would consist of the United States, the European Community, and Russia. It would invite other countries of Europe to join as associate members. This

Table 17.12 Expanding NATO

	GOALS	
ALTERNATIVES	**Conservative** Promote peace in Europe.	**Liberal** Promote peace in Europe.
Conservative Exclude.	+	−
Liberal Include Eastern Europe and Russia.	−	+
Neutral Include Eastern Europe, but not Russia.	0	0
SOS or Win-Win Form a European Security Organization (ESO) with United States, Western Europe, and Russia.	++	++

alternative would give Russia equality with the United States and the European Community rather than subordination. All countries of Europe would benefit if the new entity could increase peace among them.

Enabling Air Force Reconnaissance Planes to Evade Missiles

The issue here is how to enable Air Force reconnaissance aircraft to evade missiles. The traditional way of thinking might be to look upon the missile as super-airplane and either shoot it down or maneuver away from it. More innovative thinking might try to interfere electronically with the guidance system of the missile to redirect it elsewhere. A compromise position would be to do some of both.

One goal is to gather as much information as possible. A second goal is to reduce the cost involved in developing evasive technologies.

Table 17.13 Evading Missiles

	GOALS	
ALTERNATIVES	**Conservative** Low cost in terms of avoiding evasiveness expense.	**Liberal** High benefits in terms of information gathering.
Conservative Traditional: Shoot down or outrun the missile.	+	−
Liberal Innovative: Redirect the missile.	−	+
Neutral Compromise: Do both.	0	0
SOS or Win-Win Switch to satellites.	++	++

Both the traditional and innovative approaches are about equally good in gathering information until the plane is shot down. Both are about equally bad in terms of spending a lot of money on evasive technologies that are not so likely to work.

The super-optimum solution should provide more information-gathering and low cost for special evasive technology. The SOS might be to switch the function to reconnaissance satellites. Doing so might provide more information and low evasive cost. Hitting a satellite with a missile is difficult.

Here is a good example of solving a problem by redefining the problem. The original problem was how to enable a reconnaissance plane to evade a missile. The new problem is how to gather information on military movements through aerial reconnaissance in such a way that the equipment isn't vulnerable to missiles. The key is emphasizing the goals to be achieved, rather than trying to decide which alternative is best.

Chapter 18

Specific Trouble Spots

The Persian Gulf

A Possible SOS Solution to the Persian Gulf Crisis

Since 1990, the conservative approach has advocated military action against Iraq. The liberal approach has advocated economic sanctions and diplomatic action. The neutral approach has emphasized some of both.

The SOS has changed over time. In 1990, it might have involved Iraq guaranteeing the independence of Kuwait in return for Iraq being guaranteed security from Iran and participation in a Middle East

Table 18.1 (Simple) Persian Gulf Crisis

ALTERNATIVES	GOALS	
	Conservative Keep oil flowing.	**Liberal** 1. Avoid loss of life. 2. Preserve peace.
Conservative Military action.	+	−
Liberal Diplomatic action.	−	+
Neutral Compromise (both).	0	0
SOS or Win-Win 1. Iraq returns Kuwait. 2. Israel returns occupied territories.	++	++

conference designed to bring peace and prosperity to the region.

Iraq's bargaining power has substantially decreased since 1990. As of 1993, an SOS might have involved Iraq guaranteeing autonomy to the Kurdish provinces in northern Iraq and the Shiite provinces in southern Iraq. In return, Iraq could be given the same guarantees and participation as before.

Another Possible SOS Solution to the Persian Gulf Crisis

Table 18.2 a more detailed version of the previous table. It adds an additional goal of avoiding yielding to aggression.

Both tables were prepared before the 1991 Persian Gulf War. Both proposed an SOS solution that would guarantee some form of independence for Kuwait, Palestine, Iraq, Iran, and other Persian Gulf countries.

Both tables were rendered obsolete by the Persian Gulf War. Iraq lost the war, and there is now no need to make concessions to Iraq to guarantee the independence of Kuwait. The situation as of 1993 is better analyzed in Table 18.3. The SOS there emphasizes stimulating

Table 18.2 Persian Gulf Crisis

	GOALS	
	Conservative 1. Avoid yielding to aggression. 2. Keep oil flowing.	**Liberal** Avoid casualties.
ALTERNATIVES		
Conservative Military action.	+	−
Liberal Diplomatic action.	−	+
Neutral Compromise.	0	0
SOS or Win-Win Acceptable linkage and sanctions.	++	++

in the Iraqi government a change toward greater democracy, partly by providing financial and technical assistance to democratic forces inside and outside Iraq.

U.S.-Iraq Relations as of 1993

The problem here is that Iraqi leader Saddam Hussein has been insufficiently cooperative with the United Nations or the United States regarding inspection of military facilities.

The conservative alternative tends to emphasize military action, such as bombing Iraq into compliance. A key goal beyond compliance is to replace Hussein as the head of the Iraq government with a more accommodating leader.

The liberal alternative tends to emphasize reasoning and negotiation. The liberal goal is not only compliance, but also having the United States be a good world citizen.

A middling position would be to punish Hussein by an even stronger embargo than currently exists, but not military action.

Table 18.3 U.S.-Iraq Relations

	GOALS	
ALTERNATIVES	**Conservative** Replace Hussein.	**Liberal** United States as good world citizen.
Conservative Bombing and force.	+	−
Liberal Reasoning and compromise.	−	+
Neutral Embargo.	0	0
SOS or Win-Win 1. Humanitarian drop, deducted from Iraq funds. 2. Subvert Hussein.	++	++

The SOS alternative might involve dropping food and medical supplies into Iraq from American aircraft to win favor among the Iraqi people. The cost of that activity might be deducted from Iraqi bank funds in Europe and the United States.

The SOS alternative might also involve providing financial and technical assistance to democratic forces inside and outside Iraq to turn people against Hussein. That kind of SOS alternative could be capable of bringing about the replacement of Hussein while still preserving the United States as a good world citizen, rather than a military bully.

SOS Perspective on Iraq as of 1994

The issue here is how to deal with Iraq, when the country was massing troops on the border of Kuwait in October 1994.

The conservative position is to demand that Iraq pull back its troops or run the risk of being attacked. The liberal position seeks to get Iraq to make concessions on democratic institutions and not just military matters. A neutral position might involve a mild approach to obtaining both military and democratic concessions, but too mild to obtain any concessions at all.

Both conservatives and liberals are interested in peace in the Middle East. In addition to peace, conservatives are also interested in trade opportunities, especially conservatives in Western Europe. In addition to peace, liberals are interested in achieving democratic institutions as a goal.

A super-optimum solution would involve an agreement advancing peace, trade, and democracy. Such an agreement might offer Iraq a lifting of the embargo in return for a withdrawal of Iraqi troops and recognition of Kuwait as a sovereign state. Those two items would promote both peace and trade in the area, and trade with the United States, including the purchase of Iraqi oil.

A super-optimum solution agreement might also involve Iraq agreeing to a system of decentralized federalism, with more autonomy for the Kurds in the north and the Shiites in the south. The agreement could also provide for opposition political parties and

Table 18.4 Iraq 1994

ALTERNATIVES	GOALS	
	Conservative Trade.	Liberal Democracy.
Conservative Iraq concessions on troops.	+	–
Liberal Iraq concessions on democracy.	–	+
Neutral Mild pressure for concessions.	0	0
SOS or Win-Win 1. Withdraw troops. 2. Recognize Kuwait. 3. Decentralize. 4. Allow opposition. 5. Lift embargo.	++	++

interest groups to freely engage in the electoral process and legislative advocacy.

Such an agreement would facilitate more peace and trade than merely having Iraq make statements endorsing democracy without implementation. Thus the United States could use the tremendous bargaining power of lifting the embargo to obtain a package arrangement that is more conducive to peace, trade, and democracy than the best traditional conservative alternative and the best traditional liberal alternative.

Israel and Its Arab Neighbors

Traditional versus Military Jewishness

The alternatives here suggest four ways of approaching the Arab-Israeli problem. Table 18.5 and the accompanying text provide caricatures of differing personality types, rather than public-policy alternatives.

The first position is that of some highly religious Jews. They prefer to be left alone to engage in various practices without outside interference from Arabs, Israelis, or others. They would essentially prefer to live as have such Jews for the last few hundred years in Palestine. The second position is the opposite on a scale of passive versus active. It is reflected in the native-born Israelis who tend to be oriented toward military solutions to the Arab-Israeli problem.

The main goals that are used here as criteria for evaluating the alternatives are the goals of toughness and altruism. The traditional Jew scores high on altruism, especially in terms of giving charity to each other, but low on toughness. The military-oriented Jew scores high on toughness, but not so high on altruism.

The intellectual Jew lies about in the middle on both goals. He or she is concerned with doing research which may require perseverance that is close to toughness, but not necessarily physically dangerous. The research may involve an altruistic element of seeking to benefit the world, but it does not involve giving away one's possessions.

Table 18.5 Jewishness

	GOALS	
ALTERNATIVES	**Conservative** Toughness.	**Liberal** Altruism.
Conservative Military (Sgt. Rambowitz).	+	−
Liberal Traditional (Rabbi Rabinowitz).	−	+
Neutral Intellectual (Professor Rabin).	0	0
SOS or Win-Win SOS (Capt. Marowitz).	++	++

The SOS alternative is a character referred to as Captain Marowitz–a takeoff on Captain Marvel. He is very tough, possibly even to a supernatural extent. He is also very altruistic in the sense of almost making an occupation of saving lives and doing good. He or she is largely a fictional character somewhat like the hero of the book *Exodus* by Leon Uris. An example might be the peace activist, a former paratrooper, who was assassinated in 1983 during a Peace Now demonstration.

Approaches to the Arab-Israel problem are better handled in Table 18.6. The traditional and military Jew represent variations on the conservative position. The intellectual Jew is more likely to favor independence or autonomy, as in the liberal or neutral positions. That makes the SOS idea of an international economic community among Israel, Palestine, and other Arab countries, a job for someone like Captain Marowitz and/or his Arab counterpart.

Resolving the Israeli-Palestinian Conflict

The conservative goal, from an Israeli perspective, is security from military attack and the symbolic goal of having Israel recover its Biblical boundaries.

Table 18.6 Israeli-Palestinian Conflict

	GOALS	
ALTERNATIVES	**Conservative** Security from military attack.	**Liberal** Peace from violence.
Conservative Stay as is.	+	–
Liberal Independence from Palestine.	–	+
Neutral Autonomy.	0	0
SOS or Win-Win Economic union.	++	++

The liberal goal is peace and prosperity, plus the symbolic goal of having Israel show sensitivity to the hardships of others. Peace in this context means peace from the violence associated with rebellion and terrorism, as contrasted to military attack.

The conservative alternative is to continue Israeli occupation of the West Bank and the Gaza Strip. More extreme conservatives would expel the Arabs from those areas.

The liberal alternative is to grant independence to those areas. The more extreme left-wing alternative would restore all or portions of Israel to the Palestinians in some kind of a secular state.

The neutral position involves granting more autonomy to the West Bank and the Gaza Strip.

The SOS alternative might be to allow independence with military constraints such as those placed on Japan after World War II. The agreement might especially provide for an economic union enabling mutually-beneficial buying, selling, investing, and employment opportunities.

The Pollard Case

Table 18.7 relates to the controversy over the way President Clinton should handle the request for leniency in the case of Jonathan Pollard, who gave classified information to Israel and was sentenced to life imprisonment in 1985.

One position advocates freeing Pollard because Israel was and is an ally of the United States, and spies who have given secrets to U.S. enemies have sometimes received sentences shorter than his.

A second position advocates having Pollard serve the original sentence with the possibility of parole, in 1995 or later. That position is based on justice in light of the security damage allegedly done.

A compromise position is for Clinton to shorten the sentence to allow for earlier parole but not before 1995.

A super-optimum alternative on Clinton's part might involve three components. The first would be to shorten the sentence but do so in return for Israel agreeing to make some concessions to facilitate the implementation of the Israel-Palestinian Liberation Organization

Table 18.7 Pollard Case

ALTERNATIVES	GOALS	
	Conservative Justice in light of Israel as ally.	**Liberal** Justice in light of damage done.
Conservative Free Pollard.	+	−
Liberal Serve original sentence with possibility of parole.	−	+
Neutral Shorten sentence to allow for earlier parole.	0	0
SOS or Win-Win 1. Shorten sentence. 2. Aid to implement accord. 3. World peace, prosperity, and democracy.	++	++

accord.

A second component might be to offer economic aid to implement the accord. A third component would be to emphasize the promotion of world peace, prosperity, and democracy. Those variables might do more for Israel's security than any classified information that Pollard could give to Israel.

Jewish Perspectives on the Holocaust Trials: David, Solomon, and Moses

Table 18.8 is designed to analyze some alternative Jewish perspectives on the Holocaust trials. The overall goal is to prevent a recurrence of the Holocaust or anti-Semitism. The analysis may be illustrated using the Demjanjuk case. Dcmjanjuk was believed to be a guard at the Sobribor concentration camp. But he was accused of also being Ivan the Terrible at the Auschwitz camp. The eyewitness testimony, however, was not sufficient and he was found not guilty in Israel of being Ivan the Terrible. He was then deported from Israel to the United States where he was a resident.

There are four perspectives. One might be considered conservative. It advocates extraditing Demjanjuk to Israel and trying him on the charge of being a guard at the Sobribor concentration camp. That position emphasizes deterrence and retribution. It could be considered the position of David the warrior.

The liberal position advocates dropping further prosecution or deportation on the grounds that Demjanjuk has already served about eight years in prison and that the Sobribor evidence may not be capable of convicting beyond a reasonable doubt. That position emphasizes due process in resolving reasonable doubts in favor of the defendant, rather than the prosecution. It could be considered the position of Solomon the judge.

A compromise position might be to deport Demjanjuk to the Ukraine for having given false information when entering the United States.

Table 18.8 Holocaust Trials

	GOALS	
	Conservative Prevent a recurrence of the Holocaust or anti-Semitism.	**Liberal** Prevent a recurrence of the Holocaust or anti-Semitism.
ALTERNATIVES		
Conservative Extradite and try on Sobribor charges.	+	−
Liberal Drop further prosecution or deportation.	−	+
Neutra Deport to Ukraine for false entry.	0	0
SOS or Win-Win 1. Jewish due process. 2. Holocaust museums. 3. World peace, prosperity, and democracy.	++	++

A win-win dispute resolution, which can achieve the overall goal of decreasing a Holocaust recurrence or anti-Semitism possibly better than either the conservative or liberal solution, might involve three parts. The first part would be to drop further prosecution or deportation, but emphasize that the action accords with legal principles in the Talmud teaching that it is worse to wrongfully convict or oversentence than to wrongfully acquit or under-sentence.

The second part of a win-win or synthesizing perspective on the Holocaust trials is to promote the development of Holocaust museums to communicate ideas on what happened, why it happened, and how a recurrence might be prevented.

The third part of the perspective is to emphasize the need for promoting world peace, prosperity, and democracy since fascism and anti-Semitism thrive in environments of lost wars, runaway inflation, economic depression, and dictatorship.

The win-win dispute resolution in this context could be considered a position that combines being both a warrior and a lawmaker like Moses. There is a need for both a fighting spirit to deter wrongdoing and a judge-like spirit to separate wrongdoers from rightdoers.

There are reciprocal relations among peace, prosperity, and democracy in that each of those three variables has a causal influence on the other two. The three variables collectively promote a higher quality of life for Jews and everybody else. Thus, Jews and all others have a self-interest as well as an altruistic interest in promoting the three variables by being better informed and more active participants in political activities.

This material was presented on a New Year's Eve at the Friday night services of Temple Sinai in Champaign, Illinois. That was an appropriate time for wishing a good new year and a future of peace, prosperity, and democracy for the world, the United States, and Jews everywhere in the spirit of David the warrior, Solomon the judge, and Moses who combined a tradition of fighting for what is right with a tradition of law and justice.

Immigration between Israel and Palestine

Allowing free movement of Jewish settlers to the West Bank is not politically feasible. It would probably end the Israel-PLO accord as a result of rejection by the PLO.

Allowing free movement of Palestinians into Israel is also not politically feasible. It would probably mean rejection of the accord by Israel.

Allowing no immigration in either direction would probably be acceptable to both sides, but might miss some mutual benefits. Even banning immigration in either direction would allow workers to go from the West Bank and Gaza to Israel. Israel benefits from their work, and they benefit from the wages paid.

Allowing controlled immigration in both directions could be mutually beneficial. Controlled immigration means enacting immigration laws that specify criteria for people who can move into a country as resident aliens. Perhaps Israel might benefit from having some highly skilled Palestinians living in Israel and vice versa. Both sides would also benefit from the interchange of products and ideas.

Table 18.9 Immigration between Israel and Palestine

	GOALS	
ALTERNATIVES	**Conservative** Pro-settlers and pro-Israel.	**Liberal** Pro-Arabs.
Conservative Allow settlements but not Arab immigrants.	+	–
Liberal Allow immigration in both directions.	–	+
Neutral Allow immigration in neither direction.	0	0
SOS or Win-Win Allow controlled immi- gration in both directions and products and ideas.	++	++

Implementing Israel-PLO Accord

The problem here is how to implement more smoothly the Israeli-PLO accord. The accord provides for autonomy in 1994 to Jericho and the Gaza Strip, with autonomy for the rest of the West Bank within about five years. Progress toward those targets has been substantially delayed or derailed by killings on both sides.

The Palestinians would like autonomy quickly, with a goal of achieving a higher level of prosperity and national recognition. The Israelis want autonomy slowly out of fear that a Palestinian autonomous region might threaten with Israel's national security.

The object is to develop an implementation program that can combine a higher standard of living for the Palestinians with greater national security for the Israelis. That might involve economic interaction.

Such interaction would reach beyond just Israel and the PLO. It should involve Israel interacting with all the Arab states in the Middle East who might be willing to participate. The United States could provide leadership in bringing the countries together to form a Middle East economic union.

Table 18.10 Israel-PLO Accord

	GOALS	
ALTERNATIVES	**Conservative** Palestinian prosperity.	**Liberal** Israel national security.
Conservative Fast Palestinian auton-omy.	+	−
Liberal Slow Palestinian autonomy.	−	+
Neutral Middling speed.	0	0
SOS or Win-Win Israel-Arab economic interaction.	++	++

Such an economic union would eliminate tariff barriers among all the countries and develop a division of labor in exporting and importing.

The results could score well on both goals. They could also score well on a third goal of Palestinian stature and a fourth goal of Israeli prosperity.

Too much negative emotion now exists between Israel and its Arab neighbors to achieve that kind of implementation without an outside country like the United States serving as facilitator. The United States performed that role in improving relations between Egypt and Israel. What is now needed is to expand that bilateral success into a multilateral success–including Israel and all the frontline Arab countries, as well as those farther away.

Settlers on the West Bank

The conservative Israeli position on Jewish settlers (as represented by the Likud Party) is basically to leave things as they are.

The liberal position (as presented by Peace Now) is to remove the settlers unless they are willing to accept the autonomy arrangements. That means operating under a Palestinian government, although with some at least transitional protection from the Israeli Army.

The neutral or compromise position (as represented by most of the Labor Party) is to remove the most dangerous settlers. That position was proposed by Prime Minister Yitzak Rabin the day after the Hebron massacre in 1994.

The key conservative goal is annexation or at least control of the West Bank. Conservatives are also more willing to appease the settlers than the liberals are. They key goal of the liberals is to develop a mutually beneficial peace.

An SOS alternative might be to leave the settlers who want to do so, while removing the most dangerous ones. The SOS involves disarming the settlers provided that the Israeli Army remains to provide armed protection. This is a gun-control approach to the dangerousness of the settlers.

Disarming the settlers might be conducive to a mutually benefi-

Table 18.11 Settlers on West Bank

	GOALS	
ALTERNATIVES	Conservative 1. Annexation or control. 2. Appease settlers.	Liberal Mutually beneficial peace.
Conservative As is.	+	−
Liberal Remove settlers unless they are willing to accept autonomy.	−	+
Neutral Remove most dangerous settlers.	0	0
SOS or Win-Win Disarm settlers.	++	++

cial peace. It also would allow the settlers and the army protectors to remain. The SOS thus provides Israel with at least some control over the settlement on the West Bank.

The idea of disarming the settlers has been proposed by both Arabs and Jews who are seeking to promote progress toward peace. The Arabs on the West Bank are mainly armed with rocks, not automatic weapons, as are some settlers. No country allows civilians such easy access to automatic weapons capable of firing as many as 175 bullets a minute, which was the capability of the automatic rifle used in the Hebron massacre.

A possible defect in the idea of disarming the settlers is that even if it applies only to automatic rifles and only outside the settlements, then the settlers might be able to argue that their lives would be in danger when they leave the settlements to go to work or to buy in the market. An alternative would be to consider disarming, rather than removing, as the key alternative. The liberals would then talk about disarming settlers of their weapons, including those kept in the settlements. The neutral position would then be a partial disarmament only for automatic weapons and/or only outside the settlements. The SOS would then be to remove (from the West Bank and Gaza) the most dangerous settlers, which may be more politically and administratively feasible than a program of disarmaments.

Eastern Europe

A 1993 SOS Analysis of U.S. Relations with Russia

There are three types of conservatives in dealing with Russia as of 1993. One group sees the Cold War as still continuing, and advocates defense activities in preparation for a possible renewal of hostilities with Russia. A second group takes an isolationist position of increased withdrawal from the concerns of the world in order to concentrate on developing American industry. A third group advocates aid to Russia, especially to promote free-market institutions.

There are three corresponding types of liberals. One group sees the Cold War as still continuing, and advocates support for the

Table 18.12 Russia

	GOALS	
ALTERNATIVES	**Conservative** Free markets in Russia.	**Liberal** Democracy in Russia.
Conservative 1. Cold War. 2. Isolation. 3. Aid.	+	−
Liberal 1. Cold War. 2. Isolation. 3. Aid.	−	+
Neutral In between.	0	0
SOS or Win-Win Conservative and liberal aid.	++	++

Russian hard-line left. A second group takes an isolationist position in order to concentrate on America's social problems, especially those in the inner-city. A third group advocates aid to Russia, especially to promote democratic institutions.

The compromise position would be a little aid to provide some support for prosperity and democracy, but not long enough to make much of a difference. A compromise position might also be more neutral on the Cold War perspective. A compromise might also argue isolation to assist both industry and the inner cities.

An SOS position would provide sufficient aid for both prosperity and democracy. It would probably optimistically assume the Cold War is over, but be prepared for preventive action. An SOS would also advocate that the country can afford both foreign and domestic aid, especially with a growing economy partly stimulated by foreign trade.

The symbols for Table 18.12 can be translated into 1-5 relation scores, in which 5 equals ++, 4 equals +, 3 equals 0, 2 equals –, and 1 equals – –. Continuing the Cold War is likely to have an adverse effect on prosperity and democracy in Russia and the United States. Isolation is likely to neither help nor handicap those goals, but more likely to handicap.

Aid will help those goals, especially the goal of international trade. Conservative aid is weighted toward helping free markets. Liberal aid is slanted toward helping democracy, depending on what strings are attached.

Whatever helps trade between Russia and the United States is good for U.S. interests in the short and long run. Thus the scores on the trade goals are the same as the scores on the U.S. interests goals.

The SOS approach (emphasizing both kinds of aid) is likely to produce the most international trade and thus do more for U.S. interests. The SOS alternative is therefore likely to win on both the conservative and liberal totals.

SOS on Serbia, Croatia, Slovenia

The first war in Yugoslavia in 1993 (after the Cold War) mainly involved Serbia, Croatia, and Slovenia, rather than Bosnia. The chief issue was whether Croatia and Slovenia should be allowed to secede from Yugoslavia and become independent nations.

The conservative position was to preserve a united Yugoslavia, with Serbia being the leading province. The capital was at Belgrade, which is in Serbia. The liberal position was to allow self-determination of each province, which meant allowing Croatia and Slovenia to secede.

The neutral compromise was a confederation. It was to be similar to the American system under Articles of Confederation before adoption of the federal Constitution, or to the Commonwealth of Independent States which replaced the Soviet Union.

A key conservative goal was business prosperity. A key liberal goal was peace and independence. Preserving the unity of Yugoslavia would promote prosperous interaction among the provinces, provided that preserving it did not require warfare. Seeking to preserve Yugoslavia through military action by Serbia against Croatia and Slovenia was clearly adverse to peace and independence. The confederation idea soon ceased to be a meaningful compromise because it lacked sufficient support to be politically feasible.

Table 18.13 Serbia, Croatia, Slovenia

	GOALS	
ALTERNATIVES	**Conservative** Business property.	**Liberal** Peace and independence.
Conservative Unitary or federal Yugo-slavia.	+	–
Liberal Independent states.	–	+
Neutral Confederation.	0	0
SOS or Win-Win Economic union.	++	++

The SOS solution should (in the intermediate or long run) bring prosperity, peace, and independence to the region. It might involve the establishment of an economic community similar to the European Community. Such an entity does not involve a government as does a confederation. It emphasizes free trade in goods, labor, and ideas. It can score well on both goals, after the emotional friction lessens enough for all three countries to be able to trade with each other to their mutual benefit.

SOS on Bosnia

The situation in Bosnia has been changing. Therefore any analysis may become obsolete as a result of new changes. A key issue in 1993 concerned whether to divide the country into ethnic regions or into economic regions.

The conservative forces (meaning the Serbs and Croats) favored three ethnic regions. Each would be dominated by Serbs, Croats, or Muslims. That would be conducive to ethnic prosperity but divisive to the point that the Serb portion might eventually join Serbia, and the Croat portion might eventually join Croatia.

The liberal forces tend to favor economic regions. They would promote peaceful coexistence among ethnic groups living together.

A compromise would be a mixture of ethnic and economic regions. That would require both sides to make concessions.

An SOS alternative with all sides coming out ahead of their best expectations might involve a mixture of ethnic and economic regions, but with the compromise made more acceptable by an agreement like the Camp David Agreement settling the dispute between Israel and Egypt over the Sinai Desert.

Such an arrangement might be supported by a kind of Marshall Plan for the former Yugoslavia. The arrangement would also involve lifting the arms embargo and enacting a Bosnian constitution with strong provisions for protecting the rights of each ethnic group.

Other proposals for settling the war in Bosnia emphasize intervention by NATO or the United States, at least by bombing

Table 18.14 Bosnia (1)

	GOALS	
ALTERNATIVES	**Conservative** Ethnic property.	**Liberal** Peaceful coexistence.
Conservative Ethnic regions.	+	−
Liberal Economic regions.	−	+
Neutral Both.	**0**	**0**

SOS or Win-Win
1. Camp David
   arrangement.
2. Lift embargo.
3. Constitution with
   strong rights.
	++	++

artillery placements. That kind of alternative could produce a lose-lose result rather than a win-win result since it might accelerate the killing on all sides.

Settling the War in Bosnia

The Serbian position is to acquire 70 percent of Bosnia. The Muslim position is for the Serbs to get only 49 percent. A compromise would be about 60 percent. An SOS would promote both Serbian unity and Bosnian unity. It might involve a combination of the 49 percent division. Serbian confederation, the right of displaced residents to return or be compensated, reconstruction aid, and Croat confederation.

Table 18.15 Bosnia (2)

ALTERNATIVES	GOALS	
	Conservative Serbian unity.	Liberal Bosnian unity.
Conservative 1. Pro-Serbian. 2. 70 percent.	+	–
Liberal 1. Pro-Muslim. 2. 49 percent.	–	+
Neutral 1. Compromise. 2. 60 percent.	**0**	**0**
SOS or Win-Win None.	**++**	**++**

Dispute Resolution in Yugoslavia

Table 18.16 analyzes the situation in Yugoslavia between the successful secession of Croatia and Slovenia and the attempted secession of Bosnia. Some of the notes from the two previous tables apply here.

The essence of this table is to emphasize the role of military intervention in bringing peace to Bosnia. One position is to have no UN military force. A second position is for the UN to impose a cease-fire using the military force supplied by nations that volunteer military units.

The compromise position is to provide no land troops to impose a cease-fire, but to provide aircraft to bomb Serbian artillery. The compromise also provides for arming the Bosnians to fight more effectively, rather than impose an arms boycott against the Serbs, Croats, and Bosnians.

The main goal of continuing matters as they are (with a relatively passive role for the UN) is to reduce loss of life among the UN participants. The main goal for imposing a UN cease-fire is to reduce loss of life by the combatants and especially the civilians.

Table 18.16 Yugoslavia

| | GOALS | |
ALTERNATIVES	Conservative Reduce UN loss of life.	Liberal Reduce Bosnian loss of life.
Conservative Continue as is.	+	−
Liberal UN impose a cease fire.	−	+
Neutral 1. Provide arms to Bosnia. 2. Bomb the artillery.	0	0
SOS or Win-Win Peace plan backed by military action.	++	++

The SOS alternative adds a peace plan to the military action. The peace plan might be a combination of ethnic and economic regions, as discussed above. The plan might not be able to go into effect though until a cease-fire is imposed and enforced by UN military action.

China and the Far East

SOS Approach to Uniting China Pre-1990

In the past, a Nationalist takeover of China has meant a military takeover. As of the 1990s, it means having capitalism and democracy prevail over the Communist system.

In the past, a Communist takeover of Taiwan has meant a military takeover. As of the 1990s, it means having the mainland control Taiwan through diplomatic negotiation.

The middle position is keeping the present ambiguous status for Taiwan, somewhere between being an independent country and being a province of China.

Table 18.17 (Old) Uniting China

	GOALS	
ALTERNATIVES	Conservative Pro-Taiwan.	Liberal Pro-China.
Conservative Nationalist takeover.	+	−
Liberal Communist takeover.	−	+
Neutral Two countries.	**0**	**0**
SOS or Win-Win 1. Hong Kong solution. 2. Guandong.	++	++

The SOS involves Taiwan becoming a special province such as Hong Kong or Guandong in southern China. The Hong Kong solution involves highly autonomous government for fifty years without having to pay taxes to the mainland. Both sides would receive considerable economic benefits from buying and selling goods, services, and investment.

China Unification

Table 18.18 differs significantly from the previous table. The two tables illustrate important changes resulting from the ending of the Cold War.

In the pre-1990 table, being pro-Taiwan meant favoring the conservative Nationalist Party. Being pro-China meant being sympathetic toward the Communist Party of the People's Republic of China. In the second table, reflecting conditions in 1992, the goal of doing what is good for China refers to China as a nation, whether the Communist Party or Nationalist Party is in control. The goal of doing what is good for Taiwan refers to the native-born Taiwanese, rather than the Nationalist Party members who took over Taiwan in 1950.

As of 1992, the conservative or traditional position is to unify

Table 18.18 (New) China Unification

ALTERNATIVES	GOALS	
	Conservative Good for China.	**Liberal** Good for Taiwan.
Conservative Unity.	+	−
Liberal 1. Independence. 2. Separate.	−	+
Neutral Status quo.	0	0
SOS or Win-Win Hong Kong solution.	++	++

China. Unity is supported now by both the Communists and the Nationalists, provided appropriate terms can be worked out. The radical position is for Taiwan to become an independent sovereign state, which is opposed by both Communists and Nationalists.

The neutral position is to preserve the status quo–that is, practically two countries, in fact if not in law.

The super-optimum solution should be better than the status quo for both China and Taiwan. It might still be the Hong Kong situation, as mentioned in the pre-1990 table. Such a solution might benefit China with better access to the wealth, technology, and resources of Taiwan, while giving Taiwan better access to the customers on the mainland.

Super-Optimizing China: Reunification as an Example

The mainland's four principles refer to upholding (1) the socialist road, (2) the people's democratic dictatorship, (3) leadership of the Communist Party, and (4) Marxism-Leninism and Mao Zedong's thought.

Sun Yat-sen's three principles called for the establishment of a (1) free, (2) democratic, and (3) equitable nation-state. The neutral position proposes one country with two systems, like the Hong Kong solution.

The SOS alternative includes National Awards of Public Service, especially to Communist Party leaders for improving political conditions. It also includes establishing a new political order, under which democratization can be realized while stability and predictability can be maintained. The funding for the awards would come from contributions to a special foundation, mainly from Taiwan business people.

This SOS analysis of China unification was developed by Professor King Chow of the University of Hong Kong. It comes close to the pre-1990 SOS table. The alternatives correspond to the Communist and Nationalist alternatives, rather than to the China versus Taiwan alternatives subsequent to 1990. The Hong Kong solution may be a more realistic SOS, but the above SOS does represent imaginative thinking.

Table 18.19 Super-Optimizing China

	GOALS	
ALTERNATIVES	**Conservative** Interests of mainland leaders.	**Liberal** Interests of Taiwan leaders.
Conservative Mainland's four principles.	+	−
Liberal Sun Yat-Sen's three principles.	−	+
Neutral One country, two systems.	**0**	**0**
SOS or Win-Win 1. National awards. 2. Democratization.	**++**	**++**

U.S. Policy toward China

Perhaps a more meaningful SOS alternative would be to offer increased access for Chinese exporters to the American market and increased access to American technology, in return for (1) lowering Chinese tariffs, (2) more openness to American investment, and (3) more freedom to criticize the government and to form opposition political parties.

SOS Applied to North and South Korea

In the past, having South Korea prevail in the long conflict on the Korean peninsula tended to mean through military means or an internal overthrow of the government of North Korea. By the 1990s, it meant capitalism and democracy prevailing over the Communist system.

In the past, having North Korea prevail tended to mean through military means or an internal overthrow of the government of South Korea. Today, it may still mean that, but the probability of its occurrence has been greatly reduced by the growth of South Korea as an economic power with the backing of the United States. In the meantime, North Korea has lagged behind and lost much of its previous backing from Russia and China.

The middle position would retain matters as they are, with South Korea and North Korea two separate countries.

The SOS involves a unification of North and South Korea similar to the unification of East and West Germany, provided that North Korea undergoes changes like those of East Germany or Eastern Europe. There could also be a unification SOS resembling the joining of Hong Kong and China, in which each partner pursues it own economic system but under an overall federal or confederate form of government.

Table 18.20 U.S.-China Relations

	GOALS	
ALTERNATIVES	**Conservative** Free markets.	**Liberal** Democratic government.
Conservative Support economy ("most favored nation") status.	+	−
Liberal Support democratic government (strings attached).	−	+
Neutral None.	**0**	**0**
SOS or Win-Win 1. Wait for changes. 2. Higher education for China students. 3. Spread books and ideas in China.	++	++

Table 18.21 Korea

	GOALS	
ALTERNATIVES	**Conservative** Promote capitalism and well-being of Republic of Korea.	**Liberal** Promote communism and well-being of Democratic People's Republic of Korea.
Conservative South Korea prevail.	+	−
Liberal North Korea prevail.	−	+
Neutral Two Koreas.	**0**	**0**
SOS or Win-Win Unification.	++	++

South Asia

The United States currently tends to favor trade over aid, since trade is more mutually beneficial than aid, which tends to mainly benefit the recipient nation unless there is a Cold War return. Developing nations tend to favor aid with no strings attached at least in the past, since they are fearful that (1) buying from the United States will disrupt local industries, and that (2) they have little to sell the United States. Skills and technology transfer greatly benefit the United States by improving places for (1) United States investment, (2) the buying of American products, and (3) selling the United States products needed by the American people. Skills and technology transfer benefit developing nations by enabling them to upgrade their international competitiveness even more than offering them either trade or aid.

The United States tends to favor self-determination out of a regard for democratic decision-making and emphasizing the majority

Table 18.22 India

	GOALS	
ALTERNATIVES	**Conservative** Customers and free market.	**Liberal** Peace: external and internal.
Conservative 1. Tariff reduction. 2. Outside investment.	+	–
Liberal Secular government and corruption free.	–	+
Neutral Federalism and peace with Pakistan.	0	0
SOS or Win-Win Technology transfer for increased GNP and middle class.	++	++

will within the rebellious provinces. Developing nations tend to favor retaining their own rebellious provinces, emphasizing the majority will within the larger political entity. Autonomy like a United States state refers to states having their own constitutions and governors that cannot be removed by Washington. States in India do not have their own constitutions and their governors can be removed by New Delhi.

The United States tends to favor removal of nuclear arms from South Asia for fear that their presence may lead to nuclear warfare which might involve the United States through international disruption. Countries which have nuclear capability like India and Pakistan are reluctant to weaken their deterrent power against each other. Peaceful conversion in this context means providing India and Pakistan with the skills and technologies for converting their nuclear capability into peaceful and safe nuclear energy with the aid of American investment funding.

Latin America

SOS Analysis of U.S.-Cuba Relations

The conservative American position has been to invade Cuba and replace Castro, although there has been little effort to do so since the abortive Bay of Pigs invasion in 1961.

The left-wing position has been to support or apologize for Castro, although that support has been diminishing.

The neutral position is to leave circumstances largely as they are. That has been the prevailing position since the 1960s. It could lead to changes that would be desirable to both the United States and Cuba (1) if Castro were to institute reforms like the Gorbachev reforms in Russia or (2) if Castro were to retire or be replaced. But these possibilities appear unlikely.

If the United States wants to accelerate change in Cuba, then encouraging more international trade and visiting might do more good than embargoes and military threats. Eastern Europe instituted economic and political reforms more as a result of increased educa-

Table 18.23 U.S.-Cuba Relations

	GOALS	
ALTERNATIVES	**Conservative** Pro-United States.	**Liberal** Pro-Cuba.
Conservative Invade Cuba and replace Castro.	+	−
Liberal Support or apologize for Castro.	−	+
Neutral Leave as is.	0	0
SOS or Win-Win Win over Castro through diplomacy.	++	++

tion and middle-class desires than as a result of attempts at isolation and deprivation. The same may be true of China, at least regarding economic reforms, with political reforms to come later. Perhaps Cuba, the Caribbean, and Central America could become part of the North America Free Trade Agreement in return for opening up their economic and political systems.

The idea of negotiating with Castro would have been virtually unthinkable during the Cold War when Castro was actively supporting anti-American forces in Central America and Africa. The possibility of negotiating a mutually-beneficial agreement with Castro today is no more absurd than the Reagan-Gorbachev agreements in the 1980s or the Nixon-Mao agreements in the 1970s.

U.S. Policy toward Haiti

The alternatives and goals are numbered rather than labeled "conservative" and "liberal," since the ideologies seem somewhat unclear. Raoul Cedras has many characteristics of a right-wing military dictator but with a strain of populism. Aristide has the characteristics of an intellectual, elected president, but with a record

Table 18.24 Haiti

ALTERNATIVES	GOALS	
	Conservative Influence of Cedras.	Liberal 1. Peace. 2. Prosperity. 3. Democracy.
Conservative Cedras for president.	+	−
Liberal Aristide for president.	−	+
Neutral A neutral position.	0	0
SOS or Win-Win 1. Aristide for president. 2. Cedras for defense 　minister.	++	++

of human-rights abuse.

Supporting Aristide for president was the U.S. position in October 1993. He was viewed as more likely to produce peace, prosperity, and democracy in Haiti than could Cedras. A neutral position on which both sides could agree did not seem to exist.

An SOS position in which both sides could come out ahead of the neutral alternative might involve Aristide serving as president with Cedras as defense minister. That is the type of solution developed in Nicaragua between the Contras and the Sandinistas. It has not worked perfectly, but it has brought more peace, prosperity, and democracy than previously existed.

Africa

U.S. Policy toward Somalia

The alternatives and goals numbered rather than labeled "conservative" and "liberal." General Mohammed Farah Aidid and his opposition seem to differ more in terms of personalities than ideology.

Opposing Aidid for president, or even as a national leader, was the U.S. position in 1993. The warlord was viewed as interfering with peace, prosperity, and democracy in Somalia.

An SOS position might have been to arrange for national elections as soon as possible with Aidid and others as candidates for president. Running for president should have pleased Aidid, who seemed to want influence and prestige. He might even have won.

Holding national elections would have been a substantial move toward furthering peace, prosperity, and democracy in Somalia, which should have pleased the Clinton administration.

Promoting peace, prosperity, and democracy is good for Somalia. It is also good for the United States in facilitating more customers for American products, suppliers to American consumers, and outlets for American investment.

Table 18.25 Somalia

	GOALS	
	Conservative Influence of Aidid.	**Liberal** 1. Peace. 2. Prosperity.
ALTERNATIVES		3. Democracy.
Conservative Aidid for president.	+	−
Liberal Aidid not for president.	−	+
Neutral Aidid ally for president.	0	0
SOS or Win-Win Arrange for national elections.	++	++

Chapter 19

International Trade and Development

Improving America's International Competitiveness

The conservative position (as held by in the Bush administration) has been to contend that government regulation increases business expenses and thereby reduces international competitiveness.

The liberal position (as held by the Carter administration) has been to seek to lower tariffs, break up monopolies, and encourage greater labor-management teamwork.

Table 19.1 International Competitiveness

ALTERNATIVES	GOALS	
	Conservative Business profits.	Liberal Benefit labor and consumers.
Conservative Decrease government regulations.	+	−
Liberal 1. Lower tariffs. 2. Anti-trust action. 3. Labor-management teamwork.	−	+
Neutral Keep as is.	0	0
SOS or Win-Win 1. Government investment in technology diffusion. 2. Upgrading of skills.	++	++

The neutral position has been to avoid substantial changes in regulation, tariffs, and other such matters.

The SOS alternative (as advocated by some in the Clinton administration) is to emphasize government investment in technological diffusion and the upgrading of skills. Doing so might be capable of increasing the profits of business and the wages of labor. It could also result in better products at lower prices for both domestic and international markets.

Tariffs

Evaluating Alternative Positions on Tariffs

On the issue of tariffs, conservatives who believe in free competitive markets both internationally and domestically tend to favor low tariffs. So do liberals who have an internationalist orientation and who recognize the mutual benefits of buying overseas goods that have low prices, high quality, and that stimulate economic competition back home.

On the other hand, conservatives who support monopolistic American businesses with unreasonable profits favor high tariffs. Likewise, pro-union liberals who do not want foreign competition also favor high tariffs.

The new SOS position is to support low tariffs or none at all, to stimulate worldwide competition to promote more efficient production and greater consumption.

The object is to develop plans for well-placed subsidies and tax breaks that will enable the United States to compete effectively for world market shares without the interference and high tariffs. That means encouraging the adoption and diffusion of new technologies, and the upgrading of worker skills to put the new technologies to good use. The result, at least in the long run, is likely to be high business profits, high workers' wages, low consumer prices, high consumer quality, and lower tax rates through an enlarged tax base.

Table 19.2 Tariffs

	GOALS	
ALTERNATIVES	**Conservative** High business profits.	**Liberal** High wages.
Conservative 1. Pro-business conserva- tives, high tariffs. 2. Free world market conser- vatives, low tariffs.	+	−
Liberal 1. Pro-union liberals, high tariffs. 2. Internationalist liberals, low tariffs.	−	+
Neutral Middling tariffs.	0	0
SOS or Win-Win Well-placed subsidies and tax breaks.	++	++

Inducing Japan and Other Countries to Reduce Tariffs

On this policy problem, conservatives and liberals share the same general goal of reducing foreign tariffs. In order to be a controversy, there must be a difference of opinion as to the best alternative for achieving that goal.

The conservative position advocates retaliatory raising of tariffs as the most effective way of reducing foreign tariffs. The liberal position prefers negotiation and bargaining without explicit threats, but with promises of mutual tariff reduction. The neutral position includes some of both approaches.

There is a controversy here because conservatives and liberals perceive differently the relations between the alternatives and their shared goal. The conservative perception is that threats will succeed, but conciliatory negotiation will fail. The liberal perceives that negotiating is more likely to succeed, but that threats will not.

In calculating the total scores, conservatives give more weight to their perceptions than to the perceptions of liberals. Likewise, liberals give more weight to their perceptions. On a scale of 1 to 3, each group gives a weight or multiplier of about 3 to its own perceptions, and a weight of about 1 to the other group's perceptions.

The super-optimum solution should be perceived as doing better than the neutral alternative by both conservatives and liberals. That enables the SOS to score higher on the conservative totals than the conservative alternative, and higher on the liberal totals than the liberal alternative.

The SOS might include a subsidy to enable efficient domestic producers to bypass the foreign tariff. For example, if U.S. rice producers are unable to sell to Japanese consumers because of a $1 tariff on each bushel of rice, then it might be worthwhile for the U.S. government to subsidize the rice farmers to the extent of $.90 per bushel. This might be enough to enable them to make a profit in spite of the Japanese tariff. The subsidy might keep many people employed and increase national income. Otherwise, the subsidy might not be cost-effective. Such a subsidy is more likely to make sense if the

Table 19.3 Reducing Foreign Tariffs

	GOALS	

	Conservative
	1. Reducing foreign tar-
	   iffs.
	2. Conservative percep-
		Liberal
		1. Reducing foreign tar-
		   iffs.
		2. Liberal perception.

ALTERNATIVES	tion.	
Conservative Threaten retaliatory tariff increase.	+	−
Liberal Negotiate mutual tariff reduction.	−	+
Neutral Some of both.	0	0
SOS or Win-Win 1. Subsidy to bypass for- eign tariffs. 2. Positive incentives.	++	++

Japanese government were under intense pressure from a politically-powerful Japanese industry to retain the tariff.

The SOS could also include positive incentives. As an example, the United States might agree to share in developing or marketing a new technology with Japan in return for a lowering of the tariff on rice. That positive incentive might be enough to stimulate the Japanese government to find a different way to subsidize Japanese rice farmers.

Negotiating Free Trade in Farm Products

Table 19.4 is based on a news report in September 1993 that the United States is seeking to have the French government reduce its subsidies to French soybean farmers. A $1 subsidy can have the same effect as a $1 tariff. In the case of a $1 tariff, a $2 quantity of U.S. soybeans costs the French consumer $3, which is higher than the $2.50 that the French farmer charges. In the case of a $1 subsidy, the French farmer can make a profit by charging $1.50, which undercuts the $2 charged by the American farmer.

Table 19.4 Negotiating Farm Products

	GOALS	
ALTERNATIVES	**Conservative** Aid U.S. producers (raise profits).	**Liberal** Aid U.S. consumers (lower prices).
Conservative Retaliatory tariff increases (+ 20 percent).	+	−
Liberal Lower U.S. tariffs without return (− 20 percent).	−	+
Neutral Keep tariffs as they are.	0	0
SOS or Win-Win Reciprocal tariff reduction.	++	++

A conservative U.S. negotiator may threaten a big tariff increase on French wines to force the soybean subsidy down. That may profit American wine producers, but cost American wine consumers.

A liberal U.S. negotiator may lower U.S. wine tariffs without receiving much in return. That may cost U.S. wine producers, but profit American wine consumers.

The SOS may be to agree to lower the U.S. tariff on French wines if France would lower the subsidy on French soybeans. The result may mutually benefit U.S. soybean producers, U.S. wine consumers, and French soybean consumers.

The reciprocal arrangement might produce a net gain to the United States if the nation has more soybean producers than wine producers, and if the U.S. wine producers can be diverted into growing something more profitable. The arrangement might also be a net plus to France if it has more wine producers than soybean producers, and the French soybean producers can be diverted into growing something more profitable.

This kind of mutually beneficial reciprocal tariff reduction is a good example of an SOS solution in which all sides come out ahead. This can be contrasted to a neutral compromise between a retaliatory increase and a unilateral decrease. Such a compromise of retaining the tariffs might disadvantage U.S. soybean producers, U.S. wine consumers, French wine producers, and French soybean consumers. The harm might be greater than a reciprocal reduction, although not so great as a retaliatory tariff increase on French wines, which might even increase French farm subsidies, rather than reduce them.

NAFTA

U.S. exporters and investors benefit from free trade with Mexico and other places because (1) Mexicans can buy more U.S. products if there are no Mexican tariffs artificially raising the price of American products, (2) Mexicans can buy more U.S. products if they have more income as a result of working in factories that have expanded as a result of American capital, and (3) U.S. investors can make money and boost the American economy by investing in Mexican factories whose exports are increased by lower U.S. tariffs.

U.S. consumers are helped by free trade with Mexico and other places because (1) they can buy products made in Mexico at lower prices because a U.S. tariff no longer artificially raises the prices, (2) they can benefit from low prices that should result from decreased labor expenses associated with some products made in Mexico, possibly stimulated with American capital, and (3) the consumers include U.S. business firms that buy producer goods less expensively from Mexico, making American firms more internationally competitive.

U.S. firms and workers that are not sufficiently competitive would be harmed by the North American Free Trade Agreement (NAFTA), but this can be minimized by (1) retraining workers and firms to make them more competitive, (2) side agreements that require upgrading of labor standards in Mexico, and (3) helping disrupted workers and firms share in the benefits.

Table 19.5 NAFTA

	GOALS	
	Conservative	**Liberal**
ALTERNATIVES	Benefit non-competitive U.S. firms and workers.	Benefit U.S. consumers.
Conservative 1. Opponents. 2. Labor unions and weak business firms.	+	–
Liberal 1. Advocates. 2. Intellectual liberals. 3. Most business interests.	–	+
Neutral Middling.	0	0
SOS or Win-Win 1. Free trade. 2. Retraining. 3. Side agreements. 4. Expanding economy.	++	++

Mexicans can benefit in the same way as Americans by substituting in the "goal"column (1) Mexican exporters and investors, (2) noncompetitive Mexican firms and workers, and (3) Mexican consumers.

The opponents of NAFTA are referred to in this table as conservatives, and the advocates are referred to as liberals. This is done partly to simplify the calculation of the tools. It also reflects that conservatives have traditionally favored high tariffs, although less so in recent years.

Immigration and Refugee Policy

U.S. Immigration Policy

Assuming that conservatives favor more restrictions on immigration than do liberals is not quite accurate. Those who favor restrictions do tend to be people who emphasize racial purity, but also include working people who resist immigrant competition. Likewise, those who favor relaxing restrictions may be liberals who want to provide opportunities to minority people from developing nations, but also conservative business people who welcome cheap labor.

Greatly restricting immigration could refer to setting very low quotas. It could refer to requiring immigrants to arrange jobs in advance or have relatives in the United States. Mildly restricting immigration means allowing much greater immigration and not requiring jobs in advance. Greatly restricting immigration might decrease unemployment of American workers, at least in the short run. In the long run, ambitious immigrants may enhance the economy and thereby increase employment opportunities. Mildly restricting immigration welcomes ambitious people, although it may also welcome those who could be a drain on the economy.

An SOS solution that enables all sides to come out ahead might emphasize jobs for displaced workers. That would mean special programs to upgrade the skills of workers in areas of high immigration. An SOS solution might also emphasize ambition criteria in determining who is eligible to come to the United States. Such criteria might favor those seeking higher education for themselves or

Table 19.6 Immigration

	GOALS	
ALTERNATIVES	**Conservative** Avoid unemployment.	**Liberal** Welcome ambitious people.
Conservative Greatly restrict immigration.	+	−
Liberal Mildly restrict immigration.	−	+
Neutral In between.	**0**	**0**
SOS or Win-Win Jobs for displaced workers and ambition criteria.	++	++

educational opportunities for their children. Such criteria might exclude people with a high probability of becoming recipients of public aid.

International Refugees and Super-Optimum Solutions

International refugees are people who have been forced out of their nations by war or natural disasters, and who are waiting to return or to go elsewhere. Emigrants are people who are voluntarily leaving their homes and going to other nations where they are considered immigrants.

The conservative position seeks to keep refugees out, partly to protect national purity but also to avoid competition for jobs. The liberal position is to let refugees in, partly to help them in a spirit of humanitarianism but also in recognition that they may provide useful labor and innovative ideas through themselves or their children. The compromise is to let some refugees in, but on a selective basis with restrictions.

Table 19.7 Refugees

	GOALS	
ALTERNATIVES	**Conservative** Protect national purity.	**Liberal** Promote quality of life of refugees and society.
Conservative Refugees out.	+	−
Liberal Refugees in.	−	+
Neutral In between.	0	0
SOS or Win-Win Upgrade skills.	++	++

The SOS solution might be to upgrade the skills of refugees through organized international efforts, possibly under the direction of the United Nations. With greater skills, the refugees might become more acceptable to both conservatives and liberals, given their increased productivity and ability to enhance the economies of their host countries.

Factory Transplants

Foreign Factories in the United States

The basic issue here is whether encouraging foreign factories to relocate in the United States provides more benefits than costs in terms of the national employment and income.

The benefits mainly consist of providing jobs for Americans who work in the factories. The costs mainly consist of increasing the competitiveness of foreign firms to attract American customers from American firms and thereby decrease employment in those American firms.

Relocation incentives include tax benefits and subsidies, or simply being allowed in on an equal basis with American factories.

The issue is similar to that of allowing foreign products into the United States on an equal basis with American products–meaning without tariffs or other restrictions. Doing so may be good for the American consumer. It also may stimulate American business to operate more efficiently. It also may help American firms to sell products overseas.

In addition to the consumer benefits of tariff-free foreign products, the entry of foreign factories may provide American job opportunities. It may, however, increase foreign competitiveness by reducing transportation costs. It may also make American consumers more willing to buy, knowing that the products have been made in the United States, even though the firm is headquartered elsewhere.

The Clinton administration has been divided on this issue, but those in favor of encouraging foreign factories are winning on the grounds that there may be a net increase in jobs and other benefits.

The Clinton compromise may indeed result in a net increase in jobs, but (at least in the short run) it also may result in a decrease in the profits of competing American business firms. The net increase in jobs, though, may result in an overall increase in the GNP, more than offsetting the decrease in profits.

Table 19.8 Foreign Factories

	GOALS	
ALTERNATIVES	**Conservative** U.S. profits.	**Liberal** U.S. jobs.
Conservative No encouragement for foreign factories in United States.	+	–
Liberal Substantial encouragement.	–	+
Neutral In between.	0	0
SOS or Win-Win Improve competitiveness of U.S. firms.	++	++

An SOS solution would seek to increase both U.S. jobs and U.S. profits, if possible. Providing encouragement or at least equal access scores reasonably well in generating jobs. To develop a policy that also scores reasonably well on profits, it would be helpful to incorporate a program to aid American business firms that face increased competition from the foreign factories relocating in the United States. That does not mean a bailout or handout. It means seed money or investment money to improve their technologies and upgrade the skills of their workers so they can be truly more competitive.

An SOS solution might also provide temporary investment money to enable American firms to build factories overseas closer to foreign markets. That may be a separate issue, although related. Doing so would provide jobs for foreign workers. There may still be a net gain to the U.S. economy if the foreign sales brought income that more than offset the loss of jobs to foreign workers. This might be especially so if U.S. factories overseas were supplemented by an expansion of related factories in the United States to supply those overseas factories with parts and related products.

U.S. Factories Moving Abroad

The issue here is whether there should be any restrictions or encouragement relating to American companies relocating factories abroad.

The conservative position seeks no restrictions. The liberal position is to prohibit U.S. firms from locating abroad if doing so involves undercutting federal fair labor standards. A compromise position would be to allow companies to relocate factories abroad and relaxing labor standards, but still making them at least partly applicable.

Conservatives are interested in promoting business profits. Liberals are interested in promoting employment for American labor under good wages and working conditions.

Business profits are promoted if an overseas factory has closer access to customers, raw materials, or skilled, inexpensive labor. Those profits become part of an increased U.S. national income.

Relocating factories overseas can also facilitate selling products abroad, reducing the trade deficit. The U.S. factories operating abroad may be producing products especially for the American market, which can be sold at a lower price than if the products were made in factories located in the United States where labor and resources might be more expensive.

Disruption in American employment can be reduced in various ways. One is to secure free trade agreements with foreign countries whereby they agree to establish and enforce fair labor standards on American companies and other firms. Another approach is to subsidize the upgrading of relevant American labor skills to make American labor more competitive, or to enable displaced workers to attain other well-paying jobs. A third approach might be to place an import tax on goods made abroad under unfair labor standards. The companies could avoid the tax by upgrading their foreign labor standards.

Table 19.9 U.S. Factories Abroad

	GOALS	
ALTERNATIVES	**Conservative** Business profits.	**Liberal** Good working conditions.
Conservative No constraints.	+	−
Liberal Prohibits U.S. firms abroad from violating fair labor standards.	−	+
Neutral No free trade agreement without fair labor standards.	0	0
SOS or Win-Win 1. Free trade agreements with guarantees. 2. Import tax on goods made with unfair labor standards.	++	++

That three-part package could be considered as moving in a super-optimum direction in which both business and labor benefit. In the long run, the free movement of goods and factories across international boundaries would raise the national income of all the countries involved, thereby producing a more general super-optimum solution.

The problem of U.S. factories going abroad involves mostly factories moving to developing nations like Mexico or those in Southeast Asia. A partial justification is that doing so helps those developing nations to build their economies so they can become better customers for American products, better suppliers to American producers and consumers, and better outlets for American investment. For example, wages earned by Mexican workers in U.S. factories located in Mexico can be an important part of the ability of Mexico to buy American goods.

International Economic Communities

The relations between each alternative and each goal are shown in Table 19.10 on a relations scale of 1 to 5 or circled score. A 5 means highly conducive to the goal, a 4 means mildly conducive, a 3 means neither conducive nor adverse, a 2 means mildly adverse, and a 1 means highly adverse to the goal.

The conservative goal (C column 1) is given a weight or multiplier of 3 by conservatives (upper left-hand corner) on a scale of 1 to 3 weights, but a weight of 1 by liberals (lower right-hand corner).

The liberal goal (L column 2) is given a weight or multiplier of 1 by conservatives (upper left-hand corner), but a weight of 3 by liberals (lower right-hand corner).

A single cross shows the alternative that wins on the liberal totals (column 4) and the conservative totals (column 5) before considering the SOS alternative.

A double cross shows the alternative that wins after the SOS super-optimum solution is considered. The SOS should score higher

Table 19.10 (Simple) International Economic Communities

	GOALS	
ALTERNATIVES	Conservative 1. Preserve sovereignty and national strength. 2. Satisfy national identity and emotions.	Liberal Promote jobs and consumer goods.
Conservative Nationalism and separatism.	+	−
Liberal One world.	−	+
Neutral Regional government.	0	0
SOS or Win-Win Economic community.	++	++

than both the former conservative winner on the conservative totals (column 5), and simultaneously higher than the former liberal winner on the liberal totals (column 4).

The international economic community scores well on the conservative goal of national identity and stature. No sovereignty is given up. Each member of the community gains some stature by being associated with a larger body, more powerful than itself. The international economic community also promotes quality of life in terms of jobs and consumer goods by allowing a free flow of job applicants across international boundaries, removing tariff barriers to higher consumer standards of living, and providing a better division of labor among the countries, which facilitates more jobs and consumer goods.

Also see Table 2.5 and accompanying text. Both Table 2.5 and Table 19.10 conclude that an international economic community is capable of providing national identity and stature for its members, which should please conservatives. It is also capable of improving quality of life in terms of jobs and consumer goods, which should please liberals. The bipartisan nature of the international economic community is indicated by the support for the North American Free

Trade Agreement from both President Clinton and Senate Minority
Leader Robert Dole.

Trade and Volunteers in Foreign Policy

Trade and Human Rights

This analysis stems largely from the controversy over whether to
withhold trade from China until human rights there are given more
recognition. The issue, however, applies to many countries that would
like increased trade with the United States, but lack certain desirable
domestic institutions.

The conservative position is to permit trade without human-rights
conditions or prerequisites. The liberal position is to use trade to
secure better human-rights conditions, including the possibility of a
pluralistic political system which allows two or more political parties
to compete meaningfully for votes. A neutral position would focus

Table 19.11 Trade and Human Rights

	GOALS	
ALTERNATIVES	**Conservative** Business profits.	**Liberal** Spread democracy.
Conservative Trade without human- rights conditions.	+	−
Liberal Trade with human-rights conditions.	−	+
Neutral Trade with slight condi- tions.	0	0
SOS or Win-Win Promoting trade and rights partly through edu- cation and communication.	++	++

on less substantial human rights, such as visits by Red Cross workers to political prisoners, while condoning political imprisonment.

The conservative position is oriented toward American business profits. The liberal position is oriented toward spreading democracy. Both sides endorse each other's goals, but not with equal weight.

The object of an SOS alternative would be to promote both trade and human rights, partly through education and communication. That means encouraging students from China and other such countries to study in the United States. Doing so means they might return imbued with American values such as democracy. That also means increasing the communication of democracy-related ideas by way of radio, television, newspapers, books, and other media to China and other such countries.

The SOS alternative also recognizes that trade, even without human-rights conditions, can promote human rights by promoting prosperity and education. Democratic institutions can also promote prosperity and trade. There is thus reciprocal causation, even without explicitly linking the two.

Trade, when used to encourage human rights, needs to be presented as a reward or bribe, rather than as a threat or punishment. Trade has worked well to encourage democratic institutions in places such as South Africa. But such use can backfire if trade is withdrawn to the extent that extremists come to power (as in Russia), or it fosters an environment in which the economy suffers long-term damage (as could happen in Haiti).

Trade can also be used as a bargaining chip for other purposes besides human rights, such as tariff reduction and the opening of investment opportunities, which conservatives would endorse, too.

Trade versus Aid in Dealing with Developing Nations

Economic and political gain refers to (1) good customers, (2) good suppliers, and (3) allies in world politics.

Exporting liberalism refers to (1) free elections, (2) free speech, and (3) workers rights.

Table 19.12 Trade versus Aid

ALTERNATIVES	GOALS	
	Conservative Economic and political gain.	**Liberal** Exporting liberalism.
Conservative Trade with preferences.	+	−
Liberal Aid.	−	+
Neutral Trade and aid.	0	0
SOS or Win-Win Skills.	++	++

Volunteerism in Technical Assistance

Hiring expensive, experienced technicians for overseas technical-assistance programs may succeed in producing results desired by liberals, but runs contrary to cost-saving desired by conservatives.

Relying on the initiative of idealistic volunteers such as religious missionaries may not be so effective, but it is cost-saving.

The neutral compromise might place volunteers in the field, with salaried professionals in federal agencies such as the Peace Corps.

Each major alternative can be referred to as Position 1 and Position 2, rather than as conservative or liberal. Position 1 is conservative in form but not in results. Position 2 is liberal in form but not in results.

The SOS alternative might operate through professional associations. For example, engineering associations would actively recruit engineering volunteers. Lawyer associations would recruit lawyer volunteers, and so on. High expertise might be attained through low-cost, idealistic volunteers.

Table 19.13 Volunteerism

	GOALS	
	Conservative Cost saving and efficiency.	**Liberal** Effectiveness.
ALTERNATIVES		
Conservative Buy technical assistance.	+	−
Liberal Rely on "do gooders."	−	+
Neutral Volunteerism agencies, e.g., Peace Corps.	0	0
SOS or Win-Win Work through professional associations.	++	++

Adjusting the Value of the Dollar

A high dollar value means that $1 will buy many units of the currencies of other countries. A low dollar value means that $1 will buy relatively few units of the currencies of other countries.

If the dollar has a relatively high value, then we have difficulty selling to other countries because they have to pay many units of their currencies to buy a dollar's worth of U.S. goods. If the dollar has relatively low value, then Americans have difficulty buying from other countries because they have to pay many dollars to buy foreign products.

If Americans concentrate on improving the quality and prices of their goods, then they can sell more American goods to other countries without lowering the value of the dollar. Selling more to other countries would increase American national income. That would enable Americans a lot more money to buy more goods from other countries without raising the value of the dollar.

Thus improving the quality and price of American goods through upgrading technologies and skills is a good SOS solution because it

Table 19.14 Value of the Dollar

ALTERNATIVES	GOALS	
	Conservative Buy from other countries.	**Liberal** Sell to other countries.
Conservative High dollar value.	+	−
Liberal Low dollar value.	−	+
Neutral Middle dollar value.	0	0
SOS or Win-Win Improve quality and price of U.S. goods.	++	++

can achieve the goals of increased buying and increased selling simultaneously. This contrasts with manipulating the dollar which, increases one goal but decreases the other in a tradeoff pattern.

Chapter 20

Cross-National Development

Economic Developmental Policy

Food Pricing and Developing Nations

Table 20.1 emphasizes the conservative goal of the well-being of people in the farming business and the liberal goal of the well-being of consumers of food products. The 60 and 40 refer to fen which is roughly the China equivalent of a penny. The 60 means 60 fen per kilo of rice.

The SOS alternative is for consumers to pay a relatively low price and the farmers to receive a relatively high price. This is achieved

Table 20.1 Food Pricing

	GOALS	
ALTERNATIVES	**Conservative** Rural well-being.	**Liberal** Urban well-being.
Conservative High price. 60.	+	−
Liberal Low price. 40.	−	+
Neutral Middle price. 50.	0	0
SOS or Win-Win 1. 61 to firms. 2. 49 to workers (with food stamps).	++	++

through vouchers or price supplements given to consumers, which can then be redeemed by farmers. Both the consumer-workers and the farmers could be expected to participate in programs designed to improve their productivity in return for these price supplements.

Business Development

Liberals tend to like small, family businesses. Conservatives tend to like larger, less-personal businesses.

It is possible to emphasize development of small businesses at first since they are easier to help, but to concentrate on those more likely to grow into larger businesses that will employ more people. Such businesses are likely to be manufacturers, rather than retailers. This SOS is an example of sequential compatibility.

Technology Developmental Policy

The conservative Gandhi position is to emphasize handcrafted work. Such work may not be high in productivity, but it provides quality workplaces in terms of safety, dignity, and level of pollution.

The liberalized position is to emphasize assembly-line work associated with industrialized societies. Such work may be high in productivity, but often lacks safety, dignity, and cleanliness.

A compromise is offered by working at home but with machines powered by electricity. Such machines are more productive than handlooms while at the same time not so unsafe, undignified, or unclean as factories.

The SOS alternative might be to use highly automated assembly plants, as in Japan. Such plants do even better on productivity than traditional assembly lines, and generally better on safety, dignity, and cleanliness than electrical machines.

Table 20.2 Business Development

	GOALS	
ALTERNATIVES	**Conservative** Easy feasibility.	**Liberal** Value to economy.
Conservative Large business.	+	–
Liberal Small business.	–	+
Neutral Medium-sized business.	0	0
SOS or Win-Win Small to large (especially manufacturing).	++	++

Table 20.3 Handwork versus Assembly Lines

	GOALS	
ALTERNATIVES	**Conservative** Productivity.	**Liberal** Quality workplace.
Conservative Handcrafted work.	+	–
Liberal Assembly-line work.	–	+
Neutral Cottage industry with small machines.	0	0
SOS or Win-Win Highly automated assem- bly plant.	++	++

Social Developmental Policy

Well-placed subsidies and tax breaks in this context refer to (1) upgrading the skills of workers mainly through on-the-job training, including workers who are displaced by new technologies, and (2)

Table 20.4 Stability and Modernization

ALTERNATIVES	GOALS	
	Conservative Minimize disruption.	**Liberal** Benefits of modernization.
Conservative Stability (stagnation).	+	−
Liberal Modernization fast (disruption).	−	+
Neutral Modernization slow.	0	0
SOS or Win-Win Well-placed subsidies and tax breaks emphasized quality.	++	++

facilitating the adoption of new technologies that create jobs, improve productivity, or increase exports.

Emphasizing quality refers to (1) workplace safety and quality, (2) environmental quality, and (3) quality products.

Political Developmental Policy

New Leadership and Pluralism in Developing Nations

In obtaining independence, many developing nations begin with a one-party system. This occurs not necessarily because opposition parties are prohibited, but rather because the independence party initially is so popular. In time, however, factions or party groups are likely to develop based on different attitudes on such issues as (1) the speed of modernization, (2) economic class divisions, (3) ethnic group divisions, and (4) civil liberties, especially freedom to disagree with government policy.

Many developing nations also tend to begin with a leader who stays on for many years. This is not necessarily because other

Table 20.5 Elderly Founders

	GOALS	
ALTERNATIVES	**Conservative** Stability.	**Liberal** Creativity.
Conservative One party.	+	−
Liberal Opposition.	−	+
Neutral Wait.	0	0
SOS or Win-Win 1. Institutionalized factions to party groups. 2. Provide for alternative jobs.	++	++

candidates are repressed, but rather because of the popularity of the original leader as a founder. In time, however, the increasingly educated segments of the society press for leadership that is younger with newer ideas. It then becomes important to find a graceful way for the original leaders to retire. The alternative is to wait for them to pass away, as has happened in places such as the Soviet Union.

Military versus Civilian Rule

The SOS is to preserve military rule or phase it down gradually, but eventually establish civilian rule:

Guidelines would include: (1)No military person in a policy job while in the military; (2)Police only for crowd control.

Table 20.6 Military versus Civilian Rule

ALTERNATIVES	GOALS	
	Conservative Respect for military.	Liberal Restraint on military.
Conservative Preserve military power as is.	+	−
Liberal Dissolve the military, with Japan, Costa Rica as models.	−	+
Neutral Cut military in half.	0	0
SOS or Win-Win 1. Preserve or phase down gradually. 2. Establish civilian rule.	++	++

Table 20.7 Voting in South Africa

ALTERNATIVES	GOALS	
	Conservative Whites well off.	Liberal Blacks well off.
Conservative Only whites vote.	+	−
Liberal Only blacks vote or majority rule without minority safeguards.	−	+

Neutral
1. Bill of rights: free speech,
   equal treatment, due process.
2. U.S. Constitution: Senate,
   electoral college, special
   majorities to pass, amend.
	0	0

SOS or Win-Win Economic rights: economic growth, upgraded skills com- bined with neutral alternatives.	++	++

Voting Rights in South Africa

Neutral Alternative 1 would provide minority safeguards such as (1) free speech, (2) equal treatment, and (3) due process.

Neutral Alternative 2 includes minority safeguards such as (1) a legislative senate, (2) an electoral college, and (3) special majorities required for important legislative action.

The SOS alternative includes (1) economic growth, (2) upgraded skills combined with Neutral Alternative 1 and some aspects of Neutral Alternative 2.

International Developmental Policy

Table 20.8 is based on the dilemma posed in the book by Katarina Tomasevski, *Development Aid and Human Rights Revisited* (St. Martin's, 1993). The dilemma is whether to provide (1) aid conditional on human-rights improvements that may not occur, or to provide (2) aid anyway in anticipation that it will generate development which in turn will lead to more human rights. Another form of

Table 20.8 Aid and Rights

	GOALS	
ALTERNATIVES	**Conservative** Economic development (prosperity).	**Liberal** Human rights (democracy).
Conservative Aid without pressure.	+	−
Liberal Aid conditional on human rights.	−	+
Neutral Some pressure.	0	0
SOS or Win-Win Aid and trade conditional on human rights and economic development.	++	++

the dilemma is whether to make aid conditional on human-rights improvement in order to help the people, or to provide aid anyway in recognition that the withdrawal of aid will cause the people to suffer.

The conservative position would either provide no aid program at all or allow aid without pressure, especially if a conservative government is involved. The liberal position would make aid conditional on human-rights improvements, as in the case of U.S. aid to the People's Republic of China.

The SOS position, which tends to be broader than either the usual conservative or liberal position, might advocate including trade along with aid. It might also advocate including economic development along with human rights among the conditions for continuing trade and aid. Doing so might achieve more of both those goals than merely manipulating aid policy, and more of them than only concentrating on human rights which may be less important to developing nations.

This SOS example not only illustrates the importance of broadening the alternatives and goals, but also the importance of sequential or delayed SOS. Making trade and aid conditional on improvements in prosperity and democracy might result in a short-run withdrawal of aid and trade. In the long run, however, the developing nation is likely to accept the conditions. Then both conservative business interests and liberal democracy interests will benefit. A good example is to be found in South Africa in the early 1990s.

Legal Developmental Policy

The conservative position in the Northern Ireland conflict is to outlaw and repress the Irish Republican Army. That has not worked over the past twenty years or so.

The liberal or left-wing position in Northern Ireland is to allow Northern Ireland to join the Irish Republic. That is not politically feasible. England does not consider Northern Ireland to be a colony, but a part of the United Kingdom. The Protestants in Northern Ireland have roots that go back hundreds of years.

Giving Northern Ireland more autonomy does not resolve the internal conflict between the Protestants and Catholics in Northern

Table 20.9 Northern Ireland

ALTERNATIVES	GOALS	
	Conservative 1. Remain in United Kingdom. 2. Preserve business profits.	**Liberal** 1. Closeness to Ireland. 2. Worker prosperity.
Conservative Outlaw IRA.	+	−
Liberal Union with Ireland.	−	+
Neutral More autonomy.	0	0
SOS or Win-Win 1. Anti-discrimination legislation. 2. Increasing GNP.	++	++

Ireland. That conflict is more a conflict between the Protestant middle class and the Irish working class than it is a religious conflict, or even a nationalist or ethnic conflict.

A possible SOS alternative is to reduce discrimination against working-class Catholics and increase their job opportunities. What may be needed are well-placed seed money and subsidies for increasing the prosperity in Northern Ireland to the mutual benefit of both sides.

One could generalize to say that if there is actual or perceived ethnic discrimination within a country, there is likely to be disruptive conflict, whether the country is relatively industrialized (like Northern Ireland) or is a developing nation (like Sri Lanka). There is a need to promote mutual prosperity rather than repression, secession, or other such political approaches.

Index

About the Author

Stuart S. Nagel is professor emeritus of political science at the University of Illinois at Urbana-Champaign. He is secretary-treasurer and publications coordinator of the Policy Studies Organization and coordinator of the Dirksen-Stevenson Institute and the MKM Research Center. He holds a Ph.D. in political science and a J.D. in law, both from Northwestern University. His major awards include fellowships and grants from the Ford Foundation, Rockefeller Foundation, National Science Foundation, National Social Science Council, East-West Center, and the Center for Advanced Study in the Behavioral Sciences. His previous positions include being an attorney to the U.S. Senate Judiciary Committee, the National Labor Relations Board, and the Legal Services Corporation. He has been a professor at the University of Arizona and Penn State University.